NEOLIBERAL SELFHOOD

Psychological constructs – such as emotion regulation, creativity, grit, growth mindset, lifelong learning, and whole child – are appealing as aspirations and outcomes. Researchers, policy makers, and educators are likely to endorse and accept them as ways to make sense of students and inform pedagogical decision-making. Few critically interrogate these constructs as they are associated with students' academic achievement, psychological well-being, civic virtue, and career readiness. However, this book shows how these constructs become entangled in a neoliberal vision of selfhood, which is tied to market prescriptions and is thus associated with problematic ethical, psychological, moral, and economic consequences. The chapters draw attention to the ideological entanglement in order to facilitate conversations about selfhood in schooling policy and practices.

Stephen Vassallo is Associate Professor in the School of Education at American University, USA. His previous books have won the Book of the Year award for the series titled *Critical Pedagogy, Critical Constructivism, and Educational Psychology* and the Critics' Choice Book Award from the American Educational Studies Association.

NEOLIBERAL SELFHOOD

STEPHEN VASSALLO
American University

Shaftesbury Road, Cambridge CB2 8EA, United Kingdom

One Liberty Plaza, 20th Floor, New York, NY 10006, USA

477 Williamstown Road, Port Melbourne, VIC 3207, Australia

314–321, 3rd Floor, Plot 3, Splendor Forum, Jasola District Centre, New Delhi – 110025, India

103 Penang Road, #05–06/07, Visioncrest Commercial, Singapore 238467

Cambridge University Press is part of Cambridge University Press & Assessment, a department of the University of Cambridge.

We share the University's mission to contribute to society through the pursuit of education, learning and research at the highest international levels of excellence.

www.cambridge.org
Information on this title: www.cambridge.org/9781108708456

DOI: 10.1017/9781108769402

© Cambridge University Press & Assessment 2021

This publication is in copyright. Subject to statutory exception and to the provisions of relevant collective licensing agreements, no reproduction of any part may take place without the written permission of Cambridge University Press & Assessment.

First published 2021
First paperback edition 2023

A catalogue record for this publication is available from the British Library

ISBN 978-1-108-47723-9 Hardback
ISBN 978-1-108-70845-6 Paperback

Cambridge University Press & Assessment has no responsibility for the persistence or accuracy of URLs for external or third-party internet websites referred to in this publication and does not guarantee that any content on such websites is, or will remain, accurate or appropriate.

Contents

Acknowledgments		*page* vii
1	Introduction: Formation of Selfhood	1
	1.1 Foundational Commitments and Conceptualizations	4
	1.2 Conclusion	16
2	Growth Mindset: Normalization of Perpetual Improvement	17
	2.1 Introduction	17
	2.2 Defining a Mindset	18
	2.3 Growth and Fixed Mindsets	20
	2.4 Critical Analysis	23
	2.5 Conclusion	33
3	Grit: The Technical Management of Passion	35
	3.1 Introduction	35
	3.2 A Narrative of Achievement	38
	3.3 Conceptual Complexity	39
	3.4 Pedagogy, Passion, and Schooling	43
	3.5 Institutional Conformity and Responsibilization	49
	3.6 Ideological Conformity: Passion as an Organizing Trope	54
	3.7 Conclusion	58
4	Emotion Regulation: Strategic Self-Management	60
	4.1 Introduction	60
	4.2 Definition and Conceptualization	62
	4.3 Critical Analysis	71
	4.4 Conclusion	82
5	Lifelong Learning: Sentencing Learners to Life	84
	5.1 Introduction	84
	5.2 From Adults to Children	85
	5.3 Function and Purpose: Market, Democratic, and Humanistic	92
	5.4 A Particular Type of Learner	99
	5.5 Conclusion	104

6	**Creativity: An Organizing Value**	106
	6.1 Introduction	106
	6.2 Definition: Novelty and Use	108
	6.3 Realizing the Creative Student	110
	6.4 Individualism, Politics, and Ideal Citizenry	114
	6.5 Sociocultural Perspectives	121
	6.6 A Constitutive Perspective	124
	6.7 Conclusion	125
7	**Whole Child: Leave No Part Behind**	127
	7.1 Introduction	127
	7.2 Contents of the Whole Child	129
	7.3 No Part Left Uneducated	144
	7.4 Conclusion	147
8	**Conclusion**	149
	8.1 Form of Entanglement	154
	8.2 Contextualizing Values for Selfhood	159

References 160
Index 178

Acknowledgments

I would first like to thank Caitlin Hansen for her invaluable research, editing, organization, and emotional support. Caitlin worked countless hours from the beginning to the very end on this manuscript. She committed to this project because she believes in and embodies a critical spirit. I cannot thank her enough for her selfless commitment to seeing this book to fruition. I was lucky that she agreed to be my research assistant and I look forward to watching her grow in her Ph.D. program.

I would like to thank several other people who helped me reflect on and develop my arguments. I have had conversations with Angel Cabrera, who identifies as a stoic philosopher but whose thoughtfulness, insight, compassion, and knowledge extend far beyond this perspective. Although we had discussions related to various topics, he read and provided specific feedback on emotion regulation, helping me to engage with stoic philosophy principles. Angel provided strong intellectual and emotional support. I would also like to thank Johanna Spath for our many discussions about the ideological implications of contemporary educational policy. Johanna is an amazing educator who is committed to challenging oppressive educational structures and is incredibly thoughtful in imagining and realizing educational possibilities that can mitigate injustice.

I also owe much to my graduate and undergraduate students at American University. I teach educational psychology to teacher candidates and in-service teachers. In my courses, we discuss many of the topics in this book. While working through some arguments, I was able to share my work with them. Their insights and experience in the classroom helped me refine various sections and their support for the work gave me a sense of purpose. There are too many students to name but I want them all to know that they are important to me and my work, and I greatly appreciate them.

I would also like to thank my university. The support they provide made it possible to commit to the book while meeting teaching and service commitments. I wish to thank the dean of the School of Education, Cheryl Holcomb-McCoy, who early in the process expressed excitement about this book. Support from colleagues and my institution was important for sustaining the motivation to write. On that note, I would like to thank Sarah Irvine Belson, Vivian Vasquez, Alida Anderson, Corbin Campbell, Jennifer Steele, and Elizabeth Worden. I would also like to acknowledge efforts of Reuben Jacobs, whose brief discussion on the whole child had a profound impact on my writing of Chapter 7.

I cannot discount the importance of conversations I have had with countless people about topics related to this book. These conversations have helped me to consider possible resistance, limitations, and alternative perspectives, all of which informed the writing. I have had hours of conversation with Jagan Choudhary, who always patiently listened to my ideas and responded with provocative feedback and counternarratives. I would also like to thank Aubrey Ciatto, Subasri Meenakshisundaram, Erin Schmolly, Dan Drayton, Courtney Thomas, Nicole Fisher, and the entire Hardshells crew. I could not ask for a better support system outside of my family.

With that, last but certainly not the least, I wish to thank my family, Frances, Lily, and Anthony. They provided me with the time and space to write the book. Support from my family was instrumental and foundational to this project.

CHAPTER 1

Introduction
Formation of Selfhood

Students are sites of ideological battles; educators, policy makers, and researchers endeavor to form school structures and practices to shape a certain way of *being*. The use of the term *being* is not intended to normalize the notion of self as an inherent category of persons. Aligned with a critical psychological commitment, the notion of self is a culturally, historically, and philosophically specific way of making sense of and making up people (Corcoran, 2016; Hacking, 2002; Martin & McLellan, 2013; Rose, 1999; Sugarman, 2015). From this viewpoint, being can be understood, constructed, and experienced in many different ways. However, through discursive practices, ways of reasoning, categories, context, experience, and tools, certain ways of being take form. Schools are sites where these formations, transformations, and reformations occur. This perspective is not deterministic. Students are confronted with visions of selfhood that operate to normalize and promote possible ways of being that function to ascribe qualities to students, inform pedagogical action, and serve as a compass for students' self-regulation.

This book is about how the application of certain psychological constructs in schooling contribute to the normalization of a contentious brand of selfhood, what is referred to here as *neoliberal self*." This type of self has also been referred to by other names, such as *homo economicus* (Foucault, 2008), *managerial self* (Fitzsimons, 2011), and *entrepreneurial self* (Bröckling, 2015). Despite the different terminology, researchers and theorists generally refer to similar qualities. The neoliberal self consists of an internal, knowable, and calculable set of skills and attributes that can be controlled, managed, and maximized through strategic choice-making. The ideal neoliberal self: (1) makes rational choices to increase value; (2) is responsible for life outcomes; (3) strategically manages choices and adapts, if necessary; (4) calibrates and assigns value to self; (5) perpetually pursues the increase in personal value; and (6) is organized around an ethic of efficiency and productivity. This self initiates iterative and perpetual examination of qualities, actions, goals, and outcomes in order to manage and develop skills and attributes, evaluate the effects of choices, and adjust courses of action, if necessary.

Neoliberal selfhood is a specific way of being that is tied to market prescriptions and is thus a contentious vision associated with problematic ethical, psychological, moral, and economic consequences (Adams et al., 2019; De Lissovoy, 2015; Hogget, 2017; McGuigan, 2016; Richardson, Bishop & Garcia-Joslin, 2018; Rose, 1999; Sugarman, 2015). These consequences include (1) the increase in anxiety, stress, isolation, and selfishness; (2) the orientation of persons to material gain, competition, and economic instrumentalism; (3) disconnectedness from sociohistorical origins and relationships; and (4) the exacerbation of economic inequality. The self is neither inevitable nor natural, although some of the constructs that are associated with this self might suggest otherwise. In fact, the constructs analyzed in this book can serve to naturalize neoliberal selfhood. Lifelong learning (LLL), grit, growth mindset (GM), creativity, whole child (WC), and emotion regulation (ER) may appear to capture natural qualities of persons but instead propagate and normalize neoliberal selfhood.

Herein lies the necessity of this book. Although some researchers, educators, and policy makers may applaud and seek to create policies and practices that normalize neoliberal selfhood, there are many others who want to resist this self. The application of certain psychological constructs in schools ostensibly provides the means and basis for resistance. Some believe that that psychology can support teaching and learning by offering scientifically validated, democratic, and humanistic interpretations of students and classroom practice. However, this position is increasingly questioned by critical psychologists who suggest that applying psychology can contribute to unintended and unforeseen consequences (Corcoran, 2016; Martin & McLellan, 2013; Thrift & Sugarman, 2019; Teo, 2018).

For example, self-esteem tends to be accepted as a natural and normal description of students; something to be observed, measured, and targeted in order to support academic success and well-being. However, Martin and McLellan (2013) argue that this concept and the schooling practices that surround it normalize and promote a sense of self that is detached from context, focused on inner experience, committed to self-mastery, and in need of constant expression. For this reason, the authors link the self-esteem movement to neoliberal values and conceptions of being. Furthermore, as Cruikshank (1999) argues, self-esteem is targeted to generate particular perceptions, attitudes, and emotions so that persons can, in acceptable ways, reflexively participate in economic and political life. The point is that practices around students' self-esteem might seem humanistic and unequivocally beneficial but may have unrecognized consequences related to values for selfhood, normalized states of being, and the rendering of persons amenable to institutional orders.

It might seem odd to link self-esteem and neoliberal selfhood. Likewise, there might be some resistance to situating the constructs discussed in this book in this ideology. There are debates about the ways structures, policies, and practices contribute to the normalization, (re)formation, and transformation of self. Although some researchers and theorists might be inclined to resist neoliberalism, there is not always agreement about what contributes, and in what ways, to the neoliberal self. The narrative told here is that grit, GM, LLL, ER, creativity, and WC instantiate, validate, and normalize neoliberal selfhood. Although these constructs tend to be rationalized as humanistic, democratic, and unequivocally beneficial for students, ideology circulates in and through them to communicate norms and values for a particular brand of self. Rather than opposing or resisting neoliberal selfhood, these constructs can be applied to substantiate and normalize this self.

The constructs analyzed in this book are often included under the rubric of noncognitive skills (NCS). Although this term has limitations (e.g., Duckworth & Yeager, 2015; Lundberg, 2017; Kautz et al., 2014), it is intended to capture a discursive shift away from targeting psychological substance beyond reasoning capabilities. Researchers and policy makers point to the scientific basis for targeting attitudes, perceptions, mindsets, emotions, dispositions, and character as predictors of academic success, preparation for college and careers, democratic engagement, and overall well-being (Bollington, 2015; Darling-Hammond et al., 2018; Duckworth & Yeager, 2015; Dweck, 2006; Garcia, 2016; Humphries & Kosse, 2017; Khine & Areepattamannil, 2016). NCS are associated with humanistic, democratic, and progressive visions of persons and purposes of schooling (e.g., ASCD, 2020; Darling-Hammond et al., 2018; Garcia, 2016; Holbein et al., 2016). Thus, those who champion social justice and humanization in schooling tend to endorse and celebrate this focus. A major challenge with this line of inquiry is that this discourse masquerades as scientific descriptions of students that are natural, humanistic, desirable, and beneficial.

However, a counter-narrative is presented that implicates NCS in a contentious ideology that is associated with market-based prescriptions for being. The purpose of this book is to invite critical conversations about the way ideology runs in and through the NCS discourse. As with self-esteem, some researchers, policy makers, and educators might strive to resist neoliberalism but inadvertently endorse it through the application of certain psychological ideas. Identifying the ideological currents in psychology discourse is not about rejecting certain constructs to be replaced with ones that are neutral and value-free, or to endorse opposing binaries. All of psychology is bound to philosophical, ideological, political, and cultural contexts. The goal of this inquiry is to make the ideological entanglement explicit in order to facilitate ethical conversations about values for and consequences of selfhood in schooling policy and practices. If one assumes that grit, GM, LLL, ER, WC, and creativity are natural descriptors of persons that need to be targeted in schooling, the danger is that neoliberalism can operate freely as a normalizing vision of selfhood with unchecked scientific force to legitimize problematic subject positions.

1.1 Foundational Commitments and Conceptualizations

1.1.1 *Neoliberalism as an Economic Logic*

Neoliberalism is a notion that continues to gain attention as it has arguably proliferated rapidly throughout the globe and in all spheres of life (Davies & Bansel, 2007; McGuigan, 2016; Rose, 1999; Sugarman, 2015). Neoliberalism is defined as an economic and governmental logic that is underpinned by the idea that the best way to achieve prosperity for persons is to transform institutions and relationships to operate like the "free" market. This ideology is typically associated with the normalization, protection, and reproduction of free market structures and relationships. As an economic logic, the foundational commitment is that prosperity is achieved by using state power to remove all obstacles to economic agility and to protect free market operations. Therefore, as Harvey (2007) contends, neoliberal policies center on deregulation, privatization, free trade, and de-unionization. This ideology plays out in efforts to privatize public schooling through vouchers and charter schools, the weakening of the teachers union through a vigorous public campaign to perpetuate the narrative that educational inequality results from "bad" teachers, the reduction of public funding, competition for federal funding, and an increase in school choice. Neoliberalism is more than a commitment that prioritizes free market structures at the economic, institutional, and policy levels. It is an ideology that leads to the construction, reconstruction, and

1.1 Foundational Commitments and Conceptualizations

normalization of specific types of relationships and being (Adams et al., 2019; Apple, 2017; Lipman, 2013; Rose, 1999; Sugarman, 2015)

1.1.2 Neoliberalism as Rationality of Government

Neoliberalism is a form of governance that infiltrates all aspects of interaction, action, and the constitution of selfhood (Fitzsimons, 2011; Peters & Tesar, 2017; Rose, 1999). From this understanding, neoliberalism operates in and through interactions that do not have an immediate economic connection but nonetheless conform to an economic rationalization. Neoliberal governance is about harnessing the self-regulatory capacities of persons so that they can make choices that bring about value to themselves. The underlying commitment is that a citizenry that is self-regulated, enterprising, entrepreneurial, adaptable, and flexible supports individual interest, which is tied to economic vitality. Sugarman (2015) captures this way of thinking: "This relation [well-being of the state and of individuals] consists in the premises that the economy is optimized through the entrepreneurial activity of autonomous individuals and that human wellbeing is furthered if individuals are free to direct their lives as entrepreneurs" (p. 104).

For neoliberal governance, persons do not necessarily have to make choices that secure the most material wealth but must treat life as a project to be developed and managed regardless of the economic return. In this regard, neoliberal selfhood can be instantiated in efforts to maximize happiness, democratic engagement, and physical well-being.

In order to manage, develop, and optimize value, Sugarman (2015) notes that persons are required to make choices and are thus, consequently, rendered responsible for the outcomes of those choices. Davies and Bansel (2007) call this the *responsibilization* of subjectivity. Freedom, liberation, and empowerment are exercised and realized through choices. The belief in meritocracy is foundational to this rationality. Persons must believe that through their choices, they can achieve whatever goals they set. Therefore, pedagogical interventions are directed at helping students make those choices, which involves self-examination, the identification and articulation of goals, the development of the instruments (e.g., skills and dispositions) to achieve goals, and reflections on the consequences of thoughts and actions.

Herein lies a paradox with neoliberal governance. Although rhetorically based on the commitment to autonomy and freedom, there are cognitive, behavioral, and noncognitive prescriptions and obligations (Rose, 1999;

Vassallo, 2012). One must make choices, practice autonomy, pursue fulfillment, pursue self-actualization, and obtain self-mastery to be recognized as a valuable contributor to modern structures, whether familial, democratic, economic, medical, or educational. As Rose (1999) puts it, neoliberal governance obliges persons to be free, which is not metaphysical freedom but a way of being that counts as such in relation to an ideal. Making choices and pursuing the maximization of value count as freedom, autonomy, and independence. Yet, such practices are restrictive visions of selfhood. Neoliberalism governance is about disciplining persons to be compliant to market-consistent behaviors, as well as justifying interventions for those who fail to comply. In education, interventions often look like well-intentioned practices to make people better, healthier, productive, and efficient. These interventions are designed to shape dispositions, character, and other mental faculties so that persons can develop the attitudes, perceptions, behaviors, and desires to be enterprising persons.

Although seemingly humanistic and natural, the pedagogical target of NCS reflects institutional efforts to produce persons who can perform market-consistent behaviors. This set of skills is not inevitable, inherent, neutral, or value-free but rather is entangled in ways to normalize and validate neoliberal selfhood. A feature of neoliberal governance is not that it suppresses but rather creates possible fields of action. NCS provide a framework for making sense of students, acting on them, and helping students to reflexively act on themselves. The NCS discussed in this book serve as a framework to make up students in ways that rely on a neoliberal vision for ideal selfhood.

1.1.3 Neoliberal Selfhood

In order for neoliberalism governance to work, persons must embody neoliberal selfhood, or at least view this being as an aspirational and normalized subject position (Apple, 2006). If students do not embody neoliberal selfhood, the goal is to promote that ideal as a reference to evaluate and calibrate selfhood and to serve as a compass to evaluate and make sense of themselves. In the free market, ideal persons are consumers who make choices that are strategically organized around bringing value to oneself so as to be competitive, marketable, and useful. Neoliberal selfhood is organized around the idea that one has a set of skills and attributes that need to be managed, maintained, and developed (Sugarman, 2015). The self is constructed as a knowable, calculable, and internal set of qualities that must be centered in decision-making about personal investment. That

1.1 Foundational Commitments and Conceptualizations 7

is, one constructs and calibrates selfhood in terms of strengths, weaknesses, interests, goals, and a myriad of dispositions in order to inform decisions that are intended to optimize personal value.

Consequently, as Sugarman (2015) notes, the neoliberal self is organized around management and performance vocabularies, which include satisfaction, productivity, effectiveness, goal attainment, risk, and worth. The concepts of enterprise and entrepreneurialism are key features of this self as the expectation is normalized that persons autonomously and creatively consume knowledge and experiences that add value to their being. Choices and their consequences must be evaluated to judge the degree and achievement of value.

These principles of selfhood are normalized and validated in various ways in PreK-12 policy and practice. Researchers and theorists point out that psychology has long contributed to the production and normalization of this type of self (Adams et al. 2019; Martin & McLellan, 2013; Sugarman, 2015). For example, as Adams et al., (2019) assert, dominant psychological narratives tend to comprise visions for being that include (1) the sense that one is free to choose and radically abstract from context; (2) the idea that selfhood is a project of ongoing development that needs to be managed; (3) a commitment to growth and personal fulfillment to achieve well-being; and (4) the need for affect regulation. Although the authors contend that dominant psychological narratives tend to be informed by these commitments, they implicate neoliberal ideology in the acceleration and naturalization of these values. In education, emphasis on and the naturalization of GM, ER, grit, creativity, LLL, and the WC contribute to this acceleration.

1.1.4 Merging Neoliberalism with Noncognitive Skills

Implicating NCS in representations and the normalization of neoliberal selfhood might seem counterintuitive. Typically, neoliberalism is associated with economic instrumentalism, which involves centering curriculum and assessment on skills and attributes that are associated with ideal workers. There is certainly this element in the NCS discourse. Researchers and policy makers often justify the importance of cultivating NCS for competition and functionality in the economic market, and are thus the key for mitigating economic inequality (e.g., see the 2015 report by the bipartisan working group that included the American Enterprise Institute and Brookings Institute). The twenty-first century economic environment tends to be conceptualized as in flux, rapidly changing, unpredictable, and global – conditions that require schooling to center character traits and dispositions that support adaptability, flexibility, self-regulation, LLL, optimism, and creativity. NCS provide a framework to target those qualities associated with economic participation.

Rhetorically, the value of NCS extends beyond economic instrumentalism to include a range of ethical, social, and personal benefits. Researchers and policy makers contend that targeting and developing students' NCS can support their relationship building, democratic engagement, happiness, and well-being (e.g., Darling-Hammond et al., 2018; Schön, 1983; Garcia, 2016; Holbein, 2016; Jarvis, 2008; Kalin, 2016). Regardless of the ostensible broad benefit, NCS are entangled in a neoliberal rationality of government and function to produce a type of being who is well matched for a neoliberal agenda. The concepts analyzed in this book are not uniquely neoliberal, nor are they part of a coherent and organized agenda to endorse and protect market-based prescriptions for selfhood. The constructs in this book have been part of psychological discourse prior to the dominance of neoliberalism. However, in a neoliberal ethos, NCS function in a specific way and are take form in ways that align with neoliberal values for selfhood. NCS normalize a particular brand of self that is well suited for a neoliberal agenda because these skills are entangled in the performance language of maximization, optimization, and management. In addition, these skills invoke a sense of selfhood and valued qualities that align with neoliberal ideology. As Sugarman (2015) points out, there is not a centralized body orchestrating and organizing psychological discourse to endorse neoliberal selfhood. Rather, a neoliberal-informed narrative about ideal being is implicated in the acceptance of, value for, and, at times, the conceptualization and treatment of NCS.

1.1.4.1 Growth Mindset: Normalization of Perpetual Improvement

The analyses begin with a critical interrogation of GM, which is defined as the perception that hard work and effort are responsible for the development of intelligence, talent, and ability (Dweck, 2006). This mindset is contrasted with a fixed one, which is defined by the perception that intelligence, talent, and ability are fixed entities. Few are likely to argue that schools should endorse, validate, and value a fixed mindset. The presence of an unappealing binary can operate to conceal the dangers with the alternative construct. Although seemingly innocuous, the values for being and engagement in the GM discourse align with foundational

1.1 Foundational Commitments and Conceptualizations

features of neoliberal selfhood. Like ideal neoliberal selfhood, one with GM is bound to projections into the future in pursuit of perpetual improvement and growth, which must be strategically managed. This commitment requires assessments of personal incompleteness, which provide the motivation to continuously pursue, yet never reach, fruition, goal attainment, and mastery. GM is driven by fear of complacent, content, and complete persons, as these opposing subject positions misalign with values of productivity, consumption, and the attainment of normative standards of success. The use of GM to make sense of students normalizes a neoliberal life ethic, engenders potentially dangerous psychological consequences, and invalidates various subject positions.

1.1.4.2 Grit: Technical Management of Passion

Another construct that is featured in the discourse of NCS is grit, which is often coupled with GM as important requirements for academic success (e.g., Duckworth & Yeager, 2015; Goodwin & Miller, 2013; Jiang et al., 2019; Shechtman et al., 2013). Researchers assert that the perception alone about the controllability of talent, intelligence, and ability is not enough; persons must tenaciously pursue growth, development, and improvement. That is, they must display grit. A common definition of grit is a tendency to persist in overcoming challenges to achieve long-term goals in the face of obstacles or distractions (Duckworth et al., 2007; Shechtman et al., 2013; Tough, 2013). Grit encompasses the individual character traits of goal-directedness, motivation, self-control, and positive mindset.

The use of grit in schools has been more contentious than the NCS featured in this book. Theorists implicate this so-called skill in neoliberal values (Golden, 2017; Saltman, 2014; Stokas, 2015). One point of alignment relates to the rendering of persons responsible for their life outcomes and endorsement of a meritocratic view of economic structures. As with GM, persons have control over their outcomes and can attain normative versions of success through their own effort, which is made possible in contexts that present equal opportunities for everybody. There is another way that grit is entangled in neoliberalism, one that can be rationalized as humanistic and natural. The notion of passion is included in some conceptualizations and is treated as necessary to long-term goal pursuit. Although typically thought about as quintessentially human, the requirement for passion makes the emotional connection to goals a pedagogical target and means for management.

If grit is a pedagogical target and passion is required, then it is imperative for students to identify, articulate, and pursue a passion as a measure of their value. Pedagogical interventions must be shaped and analyzed in terms of the opportunities for students to find and pursue passion. Metaphors circulate about passion as something to be discovered, ignited, or cultivated. Passion is a category used to evaluate students, rationalize interventions, and normalize a particular type of engagement. Grit can be disentangled from ideological commitments by rationalizing that long-term goal pursuit originated from persons and ultimately supports the realization of an innate purpose or calling. However, the targeting of passion in schooling may seem appealing because it aligns with an emerging economic trope of the passionate worker. There are values for the entrepreneurial, purposeful, innovative, and dedicated worker who commits to greatness, expertise, mastery, and specialization.

1.1.4.3 Emotion Regulation: Strategic Self-Management
Students' emotion responses and expressions are implicated in their engagement and performance. Despite the fact that emotions are conceptually and methodologically ambiguous, this relationship tends to be accepted. Certain emotions are associated with academic achievement. Part of the problem is that the pursuit and embodiment of NCS can invite counterproductive emotional responses. Proponents recognize that grit and GM are not without psychological consequences. A life ethic of perpetual growth that must be strategically orchestrated can generate stress. Personal assessments of incompleteness can create anxiety, especially if efforts toward completeness are not detected or quick enough (Sugarman & Thrift, 2017). Efforts to improve and achieve mastery are likely to involve setbacks and failures, as paths to improvement are seldom linear and consistently positive. The passionate pursuit of a long-term goal is seldom without suffering. With values for grit, GM, and creativity, students are expected to take risks, which increase possibilities for failing. GM and grit have the potential to invite debilitating fear and pessimism, all of which are counterproductive for academic learning. All these potential consequences can invite fear and flight responses, which can lead to disengagement, quitting, withdrawal, and anxiety.

There are important debates about what counts as an emotion and the role of emotions in performance. There is allusion to these debates but the focus is on how ER, while itself aligned with neoliberal selfhood, is increasingly necessary because of the normalization and validation of this brand of self. The discourse on ER is informed by the idea that emotions affect learning in adaptive and maladaptive ways. Students can be taught to strategically manage their emotions in order to support their adaptability to schooling contexts. The process of regulating emotions itself is entangled in neoliberal values. What was once thought to be an unmanageable and private human experience has been placed under the scientist's microscope and dissected for the purpose of a type of self-management. Furthermore, valued emotional displays are aligned with neoliberalism values. Regardless of conditions and contexts, students must remain optimistic, calm, and happy and should feel safe. Students are expected to identify and strategically express certain emotions in order to count as regulated. In other words, there are emotion rules that align with neoliberal values for selfhood and function to make neoliberal relationships tolerable.

1.1.4.4 *Lifelong Learning: Sentencing Learners to Life*
LLL fits into a neoliberal narrative by promoting a life sentence of self-management, ER, assessments of incompleteness, and pursuit of mastery. This concept is defined as the self-directed, intentional, and strategic pursuit of the acquisition of knowledge, skills, and dispositions that enable one to pursue goals throughout the lifespan (Field, 2000; Jarvis, 2008). The ideal lifelong learner analyzes action and calibrates one's qualities to ensure that the consumption of experience renders one flexible, adaptable, and useful – making it possible to be responsive to structural conditions and demands. This type of learning is contrasted with that which might be conceived as whimsical, capricious, and undirected. The value for LLL is that strategic, intentional, and flexible adaptations to environmental conditions support efforts to be productive, efficient, economically prosperous, happy, healthy, and democratically engaged.

The notion of LLL can break down barriers and expectations about age-related categories, such as child and adult, that designate when learning happens. Breaking down these barriers can open possibilities for understanding oneself and for engaging in and contributing to a democracy and economy. The concern with LLL, however, is that it functions to render persons amenable and adaptable to contextual demands, making them governable. LLL is not just about learning through the lifespan, which persons arguably automatically do. This is about rendering persons effective, efficient, and productive in relation to technological, economic, and democratic changes. Persons must develop the disposition, aspirations, and competencies to respond to changing contexts. They must be flexible, adaptable, and responsible in order for their consumption of knowledge and experiences to be relevant and useful. LLL extends institutional power beyond formal K-12 experience to a person's lifespan in order to make them governable through their responsiveness to structures and conditions.

1.1.4.5 Creativity: An Organizing Value

Creativity can be defined as an idea or product that is novel and useful (e.g., Robinson, 2015). The dual criteria can relate to identity, personal work, and everyday living, as well as broadly applied to community, institutions, or structures. Taking up the aim to foster creativity in school appeals to researchers and theorists from a variety of academic and ideological camps. Although several conceptual, methodological, and pedagogical complexities persist, the objective of this chapter is to highlight ways that creativity is targeted for instrumental purposes, which is connected to human capital accumulation. Creativity is conceptualized as a skill that needs to be developed and harnessed so that persons can maximize their value for modern contexts. The changed acronym from STEM (Science, Technology, Engineering, and Math) to STEAM (Science, Technology, Engineering, Arts, and Math) is driven by the value that creativity has for global competition, technological innovation, entrepreneurialism, community vitality, and worker competence. The so-called creative fields are associated with economic development and growth wherein students must learn to participate in those fields in order to support that growth. The economic benefit of a creative workforce invites the integration of practices to calibrate, measure, and cultivate creativity.

1.1.4.6 Whole Child: Leave No Part Behind

The aforementioned topics often appear in the discourse on the WC, which is often contrasted with practices of fragmentation (Darling-Hammond et al., 2018; Garcia & Weiss, 2016; Noddings, 2015). Researchers and policy makers argue that including emotions, perceptions, creativity, and passion into pedagogical practices is essential for teaching the WC. The appeal of this claim results from discontent with the overemphasis on cognitive reasoning as measured by standardized test scores. The common phrase to describe the pedagogical emphasis was "teaching to the test." In relation to this commitment, the notion of the whole has broad appeal, especially given that character, attitudes, perceptions, and beliefs have come to be associated with academic and life success.

Ostensibly, targeting cognitive reasoning failed to support achievement, as well as led to the fragmentation of students. WC schooling promises to support achievement in a humanistic way.

In this chapter, the purpose is not to endorse fragmentation or a return to cognitive testing. Rather, the purpose is to examine what counts as wholeness. The idea of the WC is abstract but rendered concrete by compartmentalizing children in terms of parts, which typically include social, emotional, cognitive, psychological, and physical. Shaping pedagogy to include, account for, and develop all these parts is the goal. If done well, outcomes include students who are self-regulated, collaborative, emotionally regulated, passionate, creative, democratically engaged, and adaptable. A major concern is that the promises of WC schooling are well aligned with neoliberal values for selfhood. The approximation to an ideal representation of self governs evaluations and efficacy of this focus. In this regard, WC schooling is not about bringing all the contents of students into the context but shaping environments in order to realize a vision for the ideal person, one who shares many qualities of the ideal neoliberal self. Not conforming to standards for what counts as creative expression, passion, adaptability, and collaboration signals incompleteness and fragmentation – which some policy makers and researchers connect to neurological deficiencies.

Even if students can be wholly known and environments carefully crafted in accordance with that wholeness, there is an issue related to efforts to leave no part of students unaffected by institutional influence. WC schooling is driven by the purpose to shape students' attitudes, perceptions, desires, beliefs, and body in specific ways. Neoliberal governance is about targeting a broad educational substance so that students can conduct themselves in particular ways. The WC provides a commitment to broaden educational substance by providing a profile for educational targets. From this profile, norms and values can be comprehensively propagated to infiltrate all aspects of being.

1.1.5 The Crisis of Character

All the constructs discussed earlier have unappealing opposing subject positions. Fixed mindset stands in contrast to GM. One with a fixed mindset is deterred by failure, likely to avoid challenges, and not governed by an imperative of growth. GM can mitigate stagnation, anxiety, and task avoidance. Grit is supposed to counter the complacent and lazy quitter who does not passionately pursue mastery of a normative goal. LLL is a position to remedy the stubborn, inflexible, and unwilling learner. The emotionally regulated student contrasts with the uncontrollable, impulsive, anxious, and detached student. The idea of the creative student stands in opposition to the one who is uncommitted to the consumption of knowledge and experience to generate something novel and useful. The WC is not only in contrast to a fragmented one, but evidence of wholeness is in opposition to the unregulated, disconnected, and maladaptive child.

Existing in these binaries, it might make sense to adopt the commitments to normalize, endorse, and value the constructs discussed in this book. However, a critical commitment is that students do not have to be conceptualized, measured, and acted on in terms of these two positions. If considered natural categories that delineate a limited set of subject positions, then it makes sense to choose some categories over others. However, if recognized as bound to culture, history, politics, and ideology, then the possibility opens up to denaturalize those positions and rethink students beyond them. Moving beyond these binaries might be difficult because they provide neatly codified subject positions that align with modern aspirational character values.

The discourse on NCS is about character education. There are norms and values that inform ideal representations of students' behaviors, perceptions, desires, and attitudes. The emphasis on NCS is not simply about delineating students but constructing an ideal selfhood toward which to work. As stated earlier, schools are sites where selfhood forms, transforms, and reforms. There are explicit efforts to produce particular effects on being. Selfhood is a site of ideological battles. Implicit and explicit, a driving force for targeting selfhood results from negative assessments of students' character and fear that their character will develop in a certain way. Often accompanying defense of NCS in schooling are representations of students' poor character. There is a governing image about the ideal person who is suitable for modern contexts, along with concern that students might not be exposed to the right experiences to realize that image.

There is a seeming crisis in character and threats to right character development. These assumptions underpin the thinking from persons across a variety of ideological camps. For example, consider the distinction between democratic and neoliberal selfhood. Critical theorists tend to see these brands of being as incompatible. Critics raise concern that neoliberal selfhood orients persons to self-interest, material gain, competition, and economic docility at the expense of the common good, life quality,

1.1 *Foundational Commitments and Conceptualizations* 15

solidarity, and empowerment (Adams et al., 2019; Apple, 2017; De Lissovoy, 2015; Martin, 2004; Sugarman, 2015). However, democratic selfhood is associated with a commitment to mitigate injustice through the negotiation and restructuring of policies and practices. Those who endorse democratic selfhood are concerned that neoliberal selfhood increases anxiety, stress, isolation, and selfishness – ultimately competing with civic virtue. Those who endorse neoliberal selfhood might argue that students need to develop the character that has exchange value in the marketplace. Failure to develop in those market-valued ways will lead to persons who are complacent, useless, lazy, maladaptive, and resistant. Researchers and theorists in both camps are concerned about possible crises and threats to the kinds of persons who can realize a particular vision for being.

Although neoliberal and democratic selfhood are incompatible in some ways, both rely on a neoliberal practice of generating and leveraging crisis. Neoliberal ideology is implicated in both manufacturing and capitalizing on crises (e.g., see Klein, 2007). Typically, these crises relate to public structuring and organization of public institutions. However, as Atasay (2014) contends, crisis thinking is also applied to personhood. In contemporary discourse, the character narrative is that students must learn how to think, create, innovate, take risks, adapt, embrace failure, learn from failure, collaborate, be passionate, persist with problems and solutions, and strategically learn. These characteristics are included in frameworks for twenty-first century competencies (e.g., see Partnership for 21st Century Skills, 2009), which are representations of dispositions and skills that align with neoliberal selfhood (Vassallo, 2014).

Neoliberal values circulate through these frameworks and function to generate and justify crises or threats to selfhood. The seeming crisis in character is a consequence of these values for being, not an inherent problem with students. However, accepting twenty-first century conditions as described and also accepting that NCS can produce the right character for success in the modern world, it becomes possible to justify the existence of a crisis in character for those who fail to demonstrate ideal competence via systems of assessment and measurement of NCS. The idea is that neoliberal values support ideal representations of being that provide a basis for concerns about a crisis in character. To avert this crisis, neoliberal forms of selfhood must be achieved. The formal integration of NCS in schools is an example in which neoliberal solutions are offered to address problems created or manufactured by neoliberal relations.

1.2 Conclusion

School discourse contributes to the making of students' selves. At times, this function can remain implicit and ignored. In addition, there might be different values for selfhood and interpretations of the ways that structures, policies, and practices contribute to a particular kind of self. The aim of this book is to link the discourse of GM, grit, ER, LLL, creativity, and WC to neoliberal ideology by suggesting these constructs can be implicated in the normalization, validation, and propagation of neoliberal selfhood. Even if rhetorically bound to humanistic and democratic rationalizations, these constructs tend to be mobilized, understood, and applied in ways that align with neoliberalism. Regardless of the endpoint, the NCS discussed in this book are entangled in values for an ideal being who has the right attitudes, beliefs, dispositions, and skills to manage life by making strategic choices to bring value to oneself.

CHAPTER 2

Growth Mindset
Normalization of Perpetual Improvement

2.1 Introduction

GM is defined as the belief that persons can improve their intelligence, talent, and ability if they exert effort and work hard (Dweck, 2006). This mindset contrasts with a fixed one, which is characterized by the opposite belief that intelligence, ability, and talent are fixed entities and beyond personal control. Researchers associate GM with academic success and a fixed mindset with impediments to achievement (Claro et al., 2016; Dweck, 2006; Hochanadel & Finamore, 2015; Yeager et al., 2016). For this reason, there is increasing interest in formally integrating instruction to foster GM in students. Such an effort arguably subverts deficit-based thinking and supports an egalitarian view of achievement (Claiborne, 2014). GM encapsulates the belief that all persons through their own efforts can develop and improve their intelligence, abilities, and capabilities – thus impacting their outcomes.

Formally and explicitly teaching students to adopt a GM seems like a commonsense and appealing goal. Communicating that intelligence, ability, and talent are malleable and under personal control is a positive message when considered in relation to a fixed mindset. However, educators do not have to be locked into choosing one position within this binary. Problems with a fixed mindset should not immediately and necessarily invite the acceptance and propagation of GM. Critically analyzing GM does not mean advocating for a fixed one, nor does it suggest that a third or fourth mindset categorization is necessarily needed to mitigate the limitations of only two subject positions. Mindset, in general, is not a "natural" category of persons that teachers need to use in order to define, calibrate, make sense of, and sort their students. Specifically, GM is a description of students that is historical, cultural, philosophical, political, and ideological (Claiborne, 2014; French, 2016). The focus of this critical analysis is on the ways that GM aligns with neoliberal visions of the ideal person. The parts of the discourse that align with neoliberal values include: the need to continuously project oneself into the future, the commitment to perpetual improvement, and the requirement for self-assessments of personal lack. Integrating GM in the classroom can be a subtle way to validate, normalize, and propagate neoliberal selfhood.

2.2 Defining a Mindset

Fixed mindset and GM are beliefs about oneself and the nature of intelligence, ability, and talent. Some foundational questions are: (1) What is a mindset? (2) Why are such beliefs called *mindset*? (3) What are the consequences of applying this term to those beliefs? Although often accepted as a psychological descriptor, the notion of mindset is not without ambiguity. As French (2016) points out, the term *mindset* appears in academic literature and public discussions often without a definition or allusion to its theoretical origins. In an effort to illuminate this context, French contends that this notion is rooted in cognitive psychology and has been defined as the sum of total activated cognitive procedures in response to a task. French describes a four-phase process associated with these procedures: predecisional, preactional, actional, and postactional. The predecisional phase has to do with assessing the desirability of completing a task. In this phase, one is attuned to information that supports the deliberation over the pursuit of the task. During the preactional phase, one contemplates plans for completing the task. The actional phase is the carrying out of the plan, and the postactional phase is the evaluation of the action plan for achieving a task goal. As French explains, each part of the proess involves an appraisal of information that is directed at achieving a particular goal.

Mindset from its origination existed in relation to a particular task. That is, a mindset was not a set of beliefs, although belief can play a role in the four phases and is not independent of a task. Thus, the concept was situated and relational. The activation of cognition is characterized as signifying a particular mindset when persons were interpreted as having a tendency to perform cognitive or behavioral activity in relation to similar tasks. French (2016) states: "Fundamental to the original ... theory of mindset is the tethering of a specific task and a particular grouping of cognitive processes. Mindset theory and characterization therefore attempted to identify both a task and the cognitive mechanisms that were activated to successfully perform said task" (p. 674). In this conceptualization, mindset is likened to a cognitive disposition. From this perspective, similarities across contexts can invite task evaluations, plans, procedures, and reflections that bear resemblances. The sum total of cognitive and behavioral schema as observed in relation to tasks across events signifies a mindset. French notes that each phase can involve distinct cognitive tendencies, but all together reflects a particular mindset, which he points out was not classified into different types.

There is a clear departure from how mindset is deployed in the positive psychology literature of Carol Dweck and others (French, 2016). Those operating from within this field use this notion to capture a set of personal beliefs about the nature and malleability of abilities, intelligence, and talents. From this perspective, mindset captures beliefs that guide the interpretation of oneself, goals, action, and persistence across different tasks. In the positive psychology discourse, belief is something that organizes the world and gives meaning to experience (Dweck, 2006). In this conceptualization, the relationship to context is severed and belief is the mindset, which is treated as causally related to action and success. Furthermore, in the positive psychology discourse, mindset is categorized into two types, growth and fixed, leaving only two possible subject positions.

A concept does not need to resemble its theoretical origins in order to be valid, useful, and acceptable. However, there are a number of philosophical, conceptual, and pedagogical concerns with the use of the term mindset in positive psychology. For one, the grouping of persons into two categories is a problematic binary. If one believed that mindset was a natural feature of students that can objectively describe their psychology, are there only two possible subject positions? It is possible that some students have neither. It is possible that some students have both. In any given situation, students could shift between feeling confident about the development of their abilities and feeling stagnant. Or, some students may not even reflect at all on their beliefs about the malleability of their intelligence. However, the GM discourse orients persons to an ethic of improvement and a causal factor for that improvement. It is possible that we cannot know their mindset as behaviors and verbal utterances are not reliable sources for representing beliefs. Yet, there are two categories in which we place students that reflect stable and organizing belief systems that are implicated in their engagement and outcomes.

Even if teachers could unequivocally know what students believe and that belief was justifiably an organizing source for engagement, there is still an issue of dividing students into two categories. In the mindset discourse, expanding categories of mindsets may do little to address issues with binary thinking and mitigate the ideological currents that run through the mindset discourse. For example, consider the expansion of intelligence from a single organizing entity to multiple possible intelligences (Gardner, 1983). The theory of multiple intelligences is less exclusionary than a theory of general intelligence. However, the expanded framework is still based on the problematic concept of intelligence and, thus, as Klein (1997) contends, serves merely to multiply problems. Expanding frameworks may seem humanistic because a range of persons may find their experience reflected in the framework. However, concerns with foundational assumptions underpinning categories may go unaddressed. In the case of mindset, moving beyond the binary does little to address the foundational assumption that students have a coherent and knowable set of beliefs that is causally related to their aspirations, motivation, behaviors, and outcomes. Furthermore, an expanded framework might do little to invite the critical interrogation of the neoliberal currents that run through the mindset discourse.

2.3 Growth and Fixed Mindsets

2.3.1 Malleability of Intelligence

The foundational feature of the mindset discourse has to do with beliefs about intelligence. In the early to mid 1900s, the assumption that intelligence was a single, fixed entity dominated education discourse. This idea is dangerous if students and teachers assume that success in schools results from intelligence and that developing intelligence is stable and beyond control. GM subverts these assumptions and is implicated in supporting students' engagement and success. As Dweck (2006) argues, the permanence of self-evaluations and negative assessments of intellectual abilities can cause students to withdraw, give up, avoid trying, disrupt class, and cheat. For this reason, Claiborne (2014), who is a pioneer in critical educational psychology, lauds the GM discourse. The idea that intelligence is malleable and impermanent can have broad appeal to educators and researchers across the political and ideological spectrums.

Critical theorists might be inclined to endorse GM because it reflects a commitment to resist institutional measurements and provides tools to define one's intelligence and capability (e.g., Claiborne, 2014). Critical theorists often start with the position that there is an imbalance of power in schools (e.g., Freire, 1968/2000; Giroux, 2001; McLaren, 2007).

Assessments, measurements, and performance outcomes can be a way this imbalance is validated and reproduced. Thus, resisting tools and practices that are supposed to represent students' cognitive capabilities can be an important part of critical action. GM, thus, has the potential to equip students with the critical disposition to resist the power of assessments and performance to fix their being, to limit the perception of their opportunity, and to mitigate beliefs about personal deficits.

However, according to Dweck (2006), having a GM does not mean invalidating and questioning school performance and assessments altogether. Rather, performance is validated as a marker of one's place on a trajectory of improvement not the permanence of potential. Students with a GM are supposed to treat performance outcomes and assessments as formative. In this regard, authority is assigned to performance and assessments as indicators of being, just not in a permanent way. Assessments, measurements, and performance outcomes are held up as valid representations of students and are supposed to serve as a compass for making choices, improving oneself, and directing behavior. Thus, GM validates assessments, measurements, and performance outcomes as markers and calibrators of students as long as they are used as information to direct processes of improvement.

2.3.2 Response to Failure

GM is associated with certain perceptions, attitudes, and behaviors, particularly in relation to the notion of *failure*. The perception of and response to failure is a key distinction between growth and fixed mindsets. For example, Dweck (2006) argues that those with a GM see failure as information for pursuing self-improvement. Measures of failures are given validity and treated as information for those pursuits. Those with a GM actively seek out challenges and potential for failure, so as to have information for which activities to pursue and what abilities to develop. They are willing to take risks, seek challenges, fail, and admit mistakes because they do not believe that they are powerless to improve. In fact, Dweck argues that those with a GM feel smart when they struggle. According to Dweck, in order to improve and realize potential, students must (1) be taught to embrace failure as opportunity for growth, (2) acknowledge failure openly and honestly, and (3) self-regulate in order to remedy deficiencies.

On the other hand, those with a fixed mindset (1) respond to failure with a helpless response, (2) believe that self-assessments are valid and permanent, (3) treat performance outcomes as indicators of capabilities and potential, and (4) view failure as sources of knowledge for what tasks and subjects to avoid. Such students are less likely to take risks because of the fear of failure. Dweck (2006) argues that these students are ashamed and afraid this possibility, which is believed to reflect inherent intellectual shortcomings. For this reason, students may be less likely to seek challenges and take intellectual risks. For those with a fixed mindset, not performing in valued ways in relation to tasks is a signal of enduring qualities, capabilities, and abilities. As a self-preservation strategy, the threat of under performing provides information for which tasks to avoid. As an example, Dweck cites the case of Enron. She argues that the chief executive officer had a fixed mindset and refused to acknowledge and learn from his failures. From this perspective, leaders can capitalize on failure if they humble themselves enough to acknowledge it, learn from it, and use that knowledge to support corporate growth. However, as Dweck phrased it, "As at Enron, those with the fixed mindset did not [*profit*] from their mistakes" (p. 111). The GM response to failure, however, would have purportedly led to different outcomes.

2.3.3 *Being versus Becoming*

The growth and fixed mindset discourse centers on the perception of time. Dweck (2006) argues that those with a fixed mindset are committed to what she calls the *now*. For example, students who are committed to the *now* are concerned primarily with performance, outcomes, and products such as grades. Dweck adds that students who have this commitment are likely to become frustrated, disengaged, and anxious when they fail at a task. A product orientation is about grade attainment, group comparisons, and well-defined end points. Those with fixed mindsets tend to seek out competition in order to judge themselves in relation to their peers or they might avoid competition altogether because of the fear of losing, as such an outcome might be treated as signaling static weakness or deficit in abilities and capabilities. Dweck contends that these students who are oriented to the *now* are not intrinsically motivated and experience challenges with delay of gratification and impulse control. These students view failure not as a source of learning and a step in a process but an indictment of their capabilities. Dweck treats an orientation to the *now* as a roadblock to academic success.

On the other hand, Dweck (2006) contends that those with a GM are committed to the *not yet*. She uses this phrase to suggest an orientation to growth and becoming, rather than being. A commitment to *not yet* is a projection into the future, one that she argues is instrumental for fostering children who dream and believe that they can do anything. This commitment requires a belief that one is incomplete and perpetually in process. If persons believe that they have come to fruition, the logic is that they might not have a need to exert effort to improve. If, for example, persons view themselves as reaching maximum or a satisfactory level of intelligence, however measured and determined, the logic is that there is no impetus for improvement. Those who are oriented to the *not yet* see all experiences, knowledge, failures, and learning as parts of the process of becoming, which is a perpetual state. For this reason, those with a GM do not stigmatize being behind their peers, nor do they see themselves as in competition with others. Rather, in theory those with a GM value personal growth and improvement over the performance against others.

2.4 Critical Analysis

The distinction between growth and fixed certainly makes the former appear to be a worthwhile pedagogical goal. Advocating for setting goals, persisting in the face of failure, valuing process, and treating intelligence as mutable and under personal control are appealing. GM appears to be a better option than the opposing mindset. With that said, this critical interrogation is not about rejecting one mindset in favor of the other. Instead of operating within and preserving a binary, the critical analysis is intended to invite a rethinking of the notion of mindset and possibly change the way it is understood and used in school settings. In particular, the purpose is to invite researchers, educators, and policy makers to recognize the ideological underpinnings of the mindset discourse and reflect on the possible consequences of adopting and validating the discourse in the classroom. The illumination of these critical considerations can invite possibilities for thinking about students beyond fixed and growth, and use ethically informed decision-making related to pedagogical pressures associated with GM.

The critical analysis begins with highlighting complexities with some of the claims and assumptions that underpin the GM discourse. These include the claims that GM (1) supports a shift from deficit-based thinking, (2) orients persons to process and not product, and (3) can explain differences in academic performance. There are contradictions and complexities with the mindset discourse that warrant attention. In addition, the notion of GM is entangled in neoliberal ideology. The ways of relating to and making sense of the self resemble features of the ideal neoliberal self. In particular, the parts of the GM discourse that align with neoliberal values include the need to continuously project oneself into the future, the commitment to perpetual improvement, and the requirement for assessments of personal lack. This connection helps to highlight the values that underpin GM and the dangers of using this notion to inscribe and constitute students' being. Even if researchers resolve conceptual, pedagogical, and methodological controversies and legitimize mindset as a psychological construct, there is still concern with the ideological alignment with neoliberalism.

2.4.1 *Claims and Assumptions*

2.4.1.1 *Deficit-Based Thinking*

Viewing intelligence as incremental and within personal control helps to move education discourse away from static and fixed deficit-based models of achievement. Although GM can support this movement, deficits are still a foundational and necessary component of GM, just not in the way that implies permanence and fixedness. There is potential for temporarily constructing students as deficient in two ways. The first relates to the requirement for students to perceive themselves as lacking, incomplete, and inadequate. Those with GM must construct themselves as lacking in some way and in need of improvement. This construction requires a reliance on intelligence, performance, and social feedback, which are used to constitute oneself as lacking, incomplete, and deficient. These types of evaluations are essential but can be counterproductive if persons do not have the desire to mitigate them nor the belief that they could through their own means.

Herein lies the second way deficit-based thinking informs GM discourse. Students who do not have the beliefs and perceptions that constitute GM are subject to having their reasoned deliberations about themselves and their realities pathologized and delegitimized. Regardless of accuracy and motivational consequence of belief, if students believe that they cannot improve a talent or circumnavigate a structural condition, promoting a GM invalidates those deliberations and assessments. The purpose of invalidating deliberations is to avoid complacency and encourage improvement toward an institutionally sanctioned goal. The perception that one has realized potential, maxed out on ability, and does not need improvement is feared to invite complacency and lack of motivation, which in GM is valued insofar as it is directed toward a normative vision of success. The complacent person might be unlikely to calibrate and calculate strengths and weaknesses because there is no indication that such evaluations are needed.

Neoliberal selfhood and GM counter complacency by continually projecting persons into a future that is never fully realized. A student with a GM is projected into the future and oriented toward the continuous setting and achievement of goals. If students are not oriented toward improvement and making strategic actions that are coherently part of an improvement trajectory, then they might be regarded as complacent, lazy, unmotivated, and without direction. However, a point that will be elaborated later, the GM discourse is prescriptive, legislative, and ideological – entangling GM in an ethic of compliance and docility.

2.4.1.2 *Process and Product*
The distinction between the notions of *now* and *not yet* correlates with the notions of product and process, respectively. In the GM discourse, there is value for an orientation to the *not yet*, to see performance and outcomes as part of a process. Yet, the product seems to be foundational to GM. Although Dweck characterizes those with GM as oriented toward process, her goal is for students to be successful in school, which is measured by fixed end points such as grades, access to high-level classes, college admittance, and winning competitions. Although growth is ideally measured by self-comparisons, these measures of success indelibly lock students in a system of group comparisons. Dweck (2006) raises concern about competition with others but at the same time touts the value of GM for winning, as well as validates the characterizations of performance as signifying losing and failing, which are always in relation to others or a normative standard.

The endorsement of normalized views of success and the subservience of process to product are clear in the association of GM with successful students and business owners. Those who endorse GM often do so within a specific set of products, or markers and standards for success. GM interventions are about shaping students' psychology in ways that keep them motivated to achieve those products. The danger is that in environments that stress the attainment of certain markers of success, levels of performance, and products, students must have certain beliefs and perceptions so that they can mitigate potential barriers to product attainment. GM is supposed to help students cope with the challenges and demands of school by keeping them motivated to work despite failures. Pedagogical strategies to cultivate and reward GM are intended to mitigate students' anxiety and support their success by getting them comfortable with failure, which is only experienced in pursuit of a product and measured by specific ideas about what success looks like. The temporary experience of failure is acceptable as long as students make progress toward and eventually achieve success. The commitment to product still is the primary objective, and the orientation to process functions to render students amenable to artificial structures of success.

2.4.1.3 Targeting Beliefs and Fixing Environments

In the GM discourse, belief is causally related to action and outcomes. However, the underlying causes of behavior have been contested and debated by scientists, theologians, and philosophers for centuries. However, theorists who endorse a positive psychology view of mindset rest comfortable on the idea that belief is an internal psychological quality that can be known and that causes behavior. The corollary conclusion is that if students have the right types of beliefs, they can perform the right types of behaviors and progress toward success. Herein lies one of the ways that GM discourse aligns with neoliberal selfhood. Concluding that beliefs cause behaviors and outcomes and the right beliefs are needed for academic success has long informed a meritocratic view of society. This view is informed by the idea that opportunity is equally available to all. Those who succeed within the opportunity structure do so because of their hard work.

As Dweck (2006) suggests, a roadblock to hard work is the belief in the immutability of potential, ability, and talent. The logic follows that if teachers can shape students' beliefs to reflect GM, then the opportunity structure is such that all students can succeed and compete on a level playing field. Although this view of school and society is romantic and likely considered an ideal toward which to strive, there are many critics who doubt that schools operate as a meritocracy (e.g., Frank, 2016; Kohn, 2015; McLaren, 2007). However, the assumption that belief is associated with particular academic outcomes silences those doubts and accentuates the responsibility of individuals for their own predicaments. Kohn (2015) contends that such a message has the consequence of fixing and defending structures, silencing critique, and targeting perceptions, belief, and attitudes to render persons adaptable to those structures.

2.4.2 Neoliberal Values

As explored earlier, there are contradictions and complexities in the mindset discourse that warrant attention. Even if resolved, there is concern with the ideological implications of GM, which aligns with and endorses neoliberal values. Although attribution of success and failure are contestable and complicated individual responsibility is emphasized. Consequently, support for academic achievement involves targeting students' beliefs, attitudes, behaviors, and choices. Those with a GM make choices and enact behaviors that are geared toward realizing potential and maximizing value by pursuing perpetual improvement. They project themselves into the future, while pathologizing orientations to the past and present. GM requires persons to attribute deficits and lack to themselves and believe that through hard work they can improve. In order to respond to failure by improving the self, there must be an understanding that the source of failure and lack is personal. This conception of being aligns with neoliberal values for selfhood.

2.4.2.1 *Perpetual Improvement*

In the GM discourse and in depictions of neoliberal selfhood, the ideal person perpetually pursues improvement by projecting oneself into the future. As noted, in the mindset discourse, there is a temporal dichotomy between the *now* and the *not yet*. Orienting oneself to *not yet* is associated with GM, whereas an orientation to *now* is associated with a fixed mindset. A commitment to the former involves constructing identity, selfhood, intelligence, ability, and talent as in process and improvable with strategic efforts. From this view, persons do not see themselves as completed beings but perpetually in process. Goal achievement and improvement must not signify an end but a point of reflection on what more needs to be done. With each goal attainment or improvement, new goals must be set to perpetuate a continuous cycle of improvement. This feature of GM resembles a key feature of neoliberal selfhood, which Atasay (2014) calls the "infinite futurity for continual improvement" (p. 290).

As with the characterization of those with GM, the ideal neoliberal self continually makes and remakes itself for the purpose of pursuing a better self than what has previously been determined to exist. This remaking requires projections into the future by calibrating what one is, what one needs to do in order to improve, and what one is supposed to attain. The making and remaking of oneself is not supposed to seize but must be part of a perpetual cycle of improvement. In neoliberal discourse, this cycle must be strategically managed whereby individuals make choices that are rationally and coherently organized around an improvement trajectory. The infinite futurity for perpetual improvement is a foundational feature of neoliberal selfhood.

Although organizing action around perpetual and cyclical improvement seems like an appealing life ethic, there are philosophical and practical concerns. One concern relates to issues with what counts as growth and improvement. In the neoliberal and GM discourse, improvement is understood as changes to one's being that are centered on the increase of value. This way of understanding improvement can commodify students and reduce them to their human capital accumulations. Another concern is with the reliance on psychological categories that are used to make claims about value, as well as the legitimacy given to performance as branding one's being. In order to justify growth as improvement, persons must calibrate themselves using psychological categories and performance evaluations to temporarily suspend their being in time and place. Without these evaluations, claims about growth and improvement, as well as projecting into the future, cannot be justified. A particularly notable consequence of projecting into the future on a trajectory of improvement is the requirement to render one as always lacking, deficient, and incomplete. Improvement can be celebrated as moving toward completeness and adequacy but this evaluation must be followed by an assessment of lack and a commitment to further improvements.

2.4.2.2 Standards of Improvement

The idea of perpetual growth and improvement may not be considered an inherent problem. One might argue that persons perpetually grow and improve even without the intentional orchestration of activity to facilitate that growth. One might also argue that growth and improvement are natural realities of the human condition. On the other hand changes in one's life might actually signify devolution or a worse state than what has been previously determined to exist. For example, some might see the progression toward the ideal neoliberal self as improvement and growth, whereas others might see it as a devolving sense of communal selfhood and social responsibility. Both claims involve operating with a predetermined outcome and are underpinned by specific ideas about what persons should be and move toward. Herein lies an issue with the infinite futurity for improvement. Any claim about growth and improvement is grounded in cultural, ideological, political, and philosophical narratives and trajectories. Even the so-called self-comparisons are not independent of a normative standard.

Although students might be improving at different rates and moving toward different points on a trajectory, GM normalizes the notion of value in trajectories. Regardless of the outcome and rate of improvement, actions and experiences are calculated in terms of value for moving toward an ever-elusive endpoint. Atasay (2014) writes, "the neoliberal subject is transformed into unfinished project with the potential for imminent failure or lack and thus adapt to an ever-increasing economic value ... " (p. 299). The commitment to value serves as a compass for making and evaluating choices. Such a life ethic commodifies persons in economic terms and reduces them to the sum total of their human capital accumulations. Such commodification can render students susceptible to economic exploitation. Persons have to be attuned and subservient to environmental demands and expectations so that they can make the right choices to optimize their value and make economically better selves. Although better is supposed to be an individual assessment, Dweck couches these assessments in normalized visions for success. In the GM discourse, the purpose of pursuing measures of value to oneself is to be competitive, marketable, productive, and efficient. The emphasis on value and improvement orients persons to the products of learning, although rhetorically supposed to be oriented to the process.

2.4.2.3 Suspension of Being

The ideal neoliberal self evaluates personal qualities, rationalizes choices, and acts in ways that are organized around growth and improvement, which is strategically and intentionally managed. To achieve control and intentionality over improvements, persons must evaluate their psychological qualities and ensure that they are making choices and enacting behaviors that add value to themselves. In order to make claims about the added value persons must calibrate and measure their psychology. They must use psychological concepts, frameworks, instruments, and models to observe, measure, and assess themselves to ensure their actions are organized around achieving a particular goal, albeit temporarily. Without a baseline as a referent, claims about improvements and betterment are difficult. Thus, the projection into the future to pursue improvement requires a declaration of one's psychological characteristics. In particular, persons are expected to constitute themselves in terms of intelligence, ability, talent, strengths, and weaknesses. Once students have calibrated themselves, they must believe that they are not realized, and they must have a sense of an ideal endpoint toward which to strive. Each achievement that brings one closer to this ideal endpoint is simply a place marker for a point on a trajectory, which requires students to create a gap between what they supposedly are and what they need to become.

This gap between what persons are and what they need to become only exists because of the temporary static rendering of one's being. Such rendering of being is made possible by certain psychological terminology and validity of performance indicators as signifying being. Persons must trust that psychological descriptors and performance on certain tasks validly represent them. For example, students are expected to use concepts, such as intelligence, and measure themselves in relation to what is accepted and valued as signifying intelligence. Improvement must be judged using a particular yardstick so that students can know if their choices and actions yielded improvements. The projection into the future can render persons submissive to psychological categories and tools for personal evaluations. The relationship to standards, assessments, and tasks not only provide sources of information about the self but also serve as the justification for value-added activity.

2.4.2.4   Lacking and Incompleteness

One of the consequences of pursuing perpetual improvement, suspending being, and committing to action to increase value is the continuous attribution of lack and deficiency. The pursuit of improvement starts with and requires the assessment of lacking; otherwise, there is no need to pursue improvement. Persons must try to maximize their value by continuously assessing their qualities, which must always be assumed to be incomplete, in process, inadequate, and lacking. These types of evaluations must lead one to exert effort, make choices, and consume knowledge and experiences to mitigate that lack, only to reassess one as still lacking. Thus, as Atasay (2014) argues, a key feature of neoliberal selfhood is *homo aegrotus*, which means a sick person. *Homo aegrotus* lacks and is inadequate, disastrous, and in danger of being complacent. Like the ideal neoliberal self, GM requires *homo aegrotus*.

Improvement, maximization, and added value are made possible if one is calibrated as sick, lacking, and failed. If persons were not lacking, they might be described as having their potential realized or they might be conceptualized as completed beings, which in both GM and neoliberal discourses is a problem. The fear is that there is no need for persons to pursue improvement unless they have concluded that they are not in process. Thus, as Atasay (2014) writes the projection into the future for perpetual improvement is compelled by the articulation of a disastrous past. He explains:

> The optimized-self becomes the sole object of desire that the individual perpetually strive[sic] to achieve. However, this desire for a pleasurable

futurity is instantiated by the simultaneous discovery of a disastrous past versus a present that is never fully captured but trivialized by a future. The neoliberal subject ... is caught in a whirlpool of continual quest for optimization and destruction and the continual reoccurrence of sickness and failure shapes its subjectivity. (pp. 289–290)

The pursuit of the optimized self is accompanied by and is made possible by a lacking subject who is always in process of becoming. This process is assisted through schooling, interventions, and training.

GM requires assessments of personal lack and inadequacy, and must construe certain performance outcomes as instances of failure – albeit temporary, mutable, and under personal control. If one does not perform as expected on a task, that performance must be understood as failure and an indictment and representation of a personal shortcoming. Although attributed to personal inadequacy, those with GM believe that they can improve. GM is about students articulating weaknesses and getting them to believe that they can improve them with hard work. Those with GM operate with a discrepancy between actual and potential, whereby the present is flawed and the future is never fully realized. Lack and failure in GM are protected as inevitable. According to Dweck, students must be taught that there is always work to be done and that they exist in a state of perpetual deficiency, lack, unfulfilled potential, and incompleteness. According to Dweck, it is harmful to let children believe that they are enough. Although it may seem counterintuitive, Dweck (2006) reasons that communicating lack is necessary to protect students' self-esteem and keep them motivated, but works only if teachers convince students that they can improve those inadequacies with effort. Thus, educators must praise students' effort to improve and keep them invested in personal evaluations of lack.

2.4.3 Energizing the Cycle of Lack

The teaching imperative from both GM and neoliberal discourse is to energize the cycle of assessments of lack and improvement. A key achievement of this pedagogy is instilling the desire to fill the lack that has been validly determined to exist using available language and tools. It is the assessment of lack and the desire to improve that render persons vulnerable to the processes of subordination. As Atasay (2014) argues, neoliberal discourses "create and sustain the gap between desire and lack in order to exploit individual conduct and processes of subjectification .... It is that lack and failure which psychology is constantly asked to remedy, explaining the failure to appropriately consume as pathology" (p. 289). Atasay contends that lack and desire may require teachers and students to submit to value-added assessments. If students lack and are committed to perpetual improvement, then it would make sense to be governed by value-added discourse. One must make strategic choices and continually measure the outcome of those choices in order to show that there is growth as signified by some assessment. The assessment of lack and expression of desire render persons docile not only to a life ethic of improvement but also to the norms, standards, and tools that signify value.

Like the ideal neoliberal self, those with GM engage in a perpetual cycle of lack, desire to address lack, action to mitigate lack, and evaluations of flaws in those actions. One sets a goal to improve, achieves that goal, and then sets a different goal to improve further. There must be a perpetual commitment to inscribe and "cure" a lacking self, which should never be assumed as adequate and complete. The cycle is powered by desire. Atasay (2014) explains, "In a neoliberal society . . . workers and students need to desire continual improvement and optimizations; teachers should submit to policies of control (for example, Value-Added Assessment) over their conduct – and there needs to be a set of standards identified by a fabricated lack, which we learn to desire" (p. 292).

Atasay uses the word *fabricate* to describe the inscription of lack. Interaction with historically available language, ways of reasoning, assessments, tasks, interpretation of performance on assessments, and norms for engagement give form to and validate a lack subject. Lack is made possible only because of the assessments and standards that are used to assess students and show improvements. Persons do not have inherent lack but are made to be lacking subjects given the validity and legitimacy of norms and standards. In the GM discourse, however, researchers assume that students have inherent qualities of intelligence and ability that are rendered knowable via specific tasks.

Students need to desire improvement and consequently affirm personal lack. Atasay suggests that this desire comes from convincing students that they are incomplete, in process, and lacking something. If students are convinced that they have failed and are not good enough, but could be, they will display the desire to improve. Therefore, to convince students of personal inadequacy, there needs to be the creation, propagation, and validation of certain standards and assessments that serve as sources of information for personal qualities. For this reason, the production of the cycle of lack and desire renders teachers and students docile to a number to institutional practices, norms, and values.

As Atasay (2014) argues, "*Homo aegrotus* represents the optimal docile life-long learner and consumer, who desires, foresees and demands what is offered as cure and relief by the neoliberal market" (p. 291). This docility is reflected not only in the appropriation of concepts and measurements to represent personal characteristics but also to others who are charged with supporting students' efforts to manage their improvements. One must rely on others, assessments, and measurements to both ascribe lack and affirm improvements. One must be directed by others in the pursuit of improvement, as not all forms of improvement are valued and validated. This type of docility is not passive, as persons are expected to seek out resources, self-analyze, strategize, and assess. If students are not engaging in these behaviors and thought processes, they must be conditioned to do so. If they are engaging in those behaviors and thought processes, there must be assessments to ensure they are directed at valued endpoints. If students fail to improve in ways that are documentable and sanctioned, then they must be directed in the right way.

2.5 Conclusion

GM is a specific way of constructing selfhood and ways of thinking about and relating to the self. Persons do not inherently have growth or fixed mindset but are rationalized, understood, and constituted using these terms. Using the mindset discourse evokes and endorses a specific ideological context. The point of this chapter is to show the alignment between the ideal neoliberal self and GM. In this exploration, GM validates and aligns with the neoliberal imperative to grow, improve by projecting one self into the future, and pursuing the increase of personal value. This imperative fosters consumption and an ethic of self-management. *Being* is treated as a problematic life ethic that needs to be remedied via pedagogical interventions. Consequently, issues with pursuing perpetual improvement are ignored and the value of being is delegitimized. Naturalizing an ethic of improvement can lead to the pathologization of those who do not organize their lives around an explicit improvement trajectory.

It is a mistake to disregard the value of *being* and conclude that resisting the strategic pursuit of self-improvement is complacency. An orientation to *being*, which is a problem in the GM discourse, can manifest as a sense of comfort for students. Rather than attempting to calibrate, measure, and assign value to oneself in order to pursue improvements, one can be focused on that moment, suspending all types of personal evaluations that are employed to rationalize the value of a task. *Being* connotes a sense of stasis, a consciousness of the moment that is not caught in the throes of forces (fear and desire) that entail deficiency, and the need to change or improve. An orientation to the *now* can serve as a source of resistance to the instrumentalism of *being* and action, as well as resistance to the pressure to consume experiences and products to increase values.

CHAPTER 3

Grit
The Technical Management of Passion

3.1 Introduction

Researchers and policy makers tend to feature grit in the profile of those NCS that support and predict academic and lifelong success (American Enterprise Institute & Brookings Institute, 2015; Credé et al., 2017; Duckworth & Yeager, 2015; Hoeschler, Balestra, & Backes-Gellner, 2018; Tough, 2012; Usher et al., 2019). Consequently, there is growing discourse on defining, measuring, and formally teaching grit in K-12 schooling (e.g., Clark & Malecki, 2019; Duckworth & Yeager, 2015). One of the motivations for such efforts is the assumption that grit predicts academic success, while trumping intelligence, talent, and economic conditions as determining factors. A common definition of grit is a tendency to persist in overcoming challenges to achieve long-term goals in the face of obstacles or distractions (Duckworth et al., 2007; Goodwin & Miller, 2013; Shechtman et al., 2013; Tough, 2012). Grit encompasses the individual character traits of goal-directedness, motivation, self-control, and positive mindset.

The concept of grit as a desirable character trait to formally develop in students appears in academic writings and educational conversations in the past two decades, with growing attention over the past ten years. The narrative is characterized by the belief that all students can experience academic success – regardless of what might be construed as inherited, immutable, and uncontrollable conditions – if they work hard and long enough. One of the appeals is the belief that academic success is possible for all students. In this narrative, grit tends to be construed as something that students control and that can be developed in schools. Thus, the more effective the grit pedagogy, the better schooling can serve to mitigate academic and economic inequalities.

Despite the promises, the grit narrative is rife with critical concerns. The conclusion that all students can succeed is not in itself one of those problems, although the notion of success certainly requires critical interrogation. While more appealing than deterministic attributions of success and failure, the grit narrative does not necessarily have to be accepted as the only other explanation and solution to educational disparities. Optimistic beliefs about students' potential for academic achievement do not have to be realized through the imperative to teach grit or construct students as more or less gritty. On the contrary, critics provide compelling analyses that formally endorsing grit in schools competes with students' academic success, efforts to recognize their humanity, and the potential to mitigate economic injustice (Kohn, 2014; Ravitch, 2014; Saltman, 2014; Stokas, 2015). Furthermore, the grit narrative is ideological, supporting a neoliberal vision for persons and societies.

It may not seem far-fetched to situate grit in neoliberal ideology and visions for personhood. The story of grit is a rehashing of a long-standing narrative that effort, motivation, and personal choice explain economic conditions and predicaments (Adams et al, 2019; Apple, 2006; Saltman, 2014; Stokas, 2015). In this line of thinking, inequalities are addressed by shaping the dispositions and motivation of persons in order to help them make the right choices that optimize their personal value. As Stokas (2015) contends, such thinking is part of an American narrative that hard work, good choices, and persistence are key to success. In a public radio report, Smith (2014) presents segments of a commentary with Duckworth, who acknowledges this cultural specificity by stating: "It's [grit] a very, I think – an American idea in some ways – really pursuing something against all odds." Such a narrative, Stokas suggests, has been propagated through tropes of the cowboy and boxer. She contends that these images function as "cultural propaganda that convinces the individual that success is the result of hard, relentless work regardless of systemic privilege" (p. 515). She adds that "These cultural imaginings reinforced the belief that social hardships, such as poverty and inequality, are overcome through heroic individual effort rather than through an ecosystem of supportive environments and policies" (p. 515). A key achievement of neoliberal ideology is the responsibilization of persons for their academic and life outcomes. Neoliberalism benefits from the propagation and normalization of those cultural tropes that demonstrate the power of determination and hard work for achieving a normative measure of prosperity.

The grit narrative is not without its critics, and there are various reasons to be concerned. Existing critiques are not endorsements of deterministic explanations of achievement and success. Critics are not likely to conclude that effort does not matter; nor are they likely to endorse the idea that social, cultural, personal, and economic conditions are determining. Both suggestions are oversimplifications and are underpinned by specific ideological and philosophical readings of the world. One does not have to be locked into the binary of determinism and individual human agency. To illustrate such a commitment, Stokas (2015) aims to examine the social and historical conditions that contribute to the conceptualization and use of grit to explain inequalities and disparities. She argues not for the necessity of grit, nor for its validity as a descriptor of students. Critique can be about exploring the function and consequences of the grit narrative, as well as situating the expansion of grit discourse within contemporary economic conditions. The purpose of this critical analysis is to implicate neoliberal ideology in a certain understanding of grit and to demonstrate how that understanding normalizes subject positions that instantiate neoliberal selfhood. A foundational premise is that grit is not a natural description or category of personal qualities but an ideologically specific way to make sense of and act on students.

The analysis is focused on the notion of passion, which appears in conceptualizations of grit and is broadly considered as an important twenty-first century pedagogical target (e.g., see Davidson, 2020). In the grit discourse, passion is typically thought about as a strong emotional connection to a goal that makes it possible to sustain engagement, pursue mastery, and feel a sense of fulfillment (Duckworth, 2016). As a requirement for grit, passion becomes a pedagogical goal, a measure of character, and a necessary state for economic participation. Although focusing on students' passion has humanistic appeal, the normalization of emotional connections to long-term pursuits, the association with high-performance language, and the value for economic contribution entangles passion in neoliberal management discourse. There is a normalized state of feeling that becomes the target for pedagogical deliberations, rationalizations, and evaluations.

The motivation for this target is associated with the representation of the ideal twenty-first century worker who is specialized, dedicated, and satisfied in economic activity, whether in corporate settings or entrepreneurial endeavors (e.g., Davidson, 2020; McRobbie, 2015; Sandoval, 2018). However, as a feature of modern work and workers, the grit discourse is concerning because not all students have the opportunities to develop and explore passions. The grit curriculum for students from low-income backgrounds, a demographic often targeted for such interventions, is geared toward behavioral compliance and docility to authority. If necessary for economic participation, then it is possible to implicate the grit curriculum in contributing to the social reproduction of inequality by denying some students the opportunity for passionate pursuit, while simultaneously producing the message of personal responsibility.

3.2 A Narrative of Achievement

Grit is appealing because it promotes optimism that academic achievement is possible for all who simply focus on and relentlessly pursue long-term goals, regardless of obstacles, setbacks, distractions, and failures. If effort is responsible for success in school and students can control their effort, then it makes sense from an economic justice perspective to organize schooling around the development of grit. Tough (2012) characterizes NCS broadly and grit specifically as an antipoverty tool for disadvantaged young people. Likewise, in their United States Department of Education's published report titled *Promoting Grit, Tenacity, and Perseverance: Critical Factors for Success in the Twenty-First Century*, Schechtman et al. (2013) assert: "Regardless of socioeconomic conditions, all students can encounter difficult challenges and setbacks throughout their schooling as they learn conceptually complex material, deal with distractions, persist through academic assignments that are important but not necessarily intrinsically interesting, manage competing demands, and prepare themselves for the complex and rapidly changing 21st-century workplace" (p. 93). It is not uncommon for researchers and policy makers to endorse grit to mitigate educational and economic disparities.

Given the perceived importance, research tends to be about figuring out how to measure and teach grit. In March 2015, the Brookings Institute hosted a panel titled Ready to be Counted: Incorporating Non-Cognitive Skills Educational Policy. The panelists supported making the teaching of grit an explicit curricular goal, one that teachers are held accountable for achieving. They endorsed the construction of a how-to guide for educators and policy makers to teach and measure grit. Gabrieli et al. (2015) published a working paper outlining these commitments. Sparks (2015) reports that the National Assessment of Educational Progress plans to start formally assessing grit at the instructional efficacy level and students' embodiment. Policy makers continue to push for the formal integration of grit in schooling.

3.3 Conceptual Complexity

Despite the growing acceptance, there is ambiguity around the conceptualization of grit. Although understood as the tendency to persist in overcoming challenges to achieve long-term goals, it is not clear if one can be gritty toward multiple goals and how long commitment must endure. Although unclear, the singularity, difficulty, sustainability, and commitment to a goal become evaluative tools of students. In the grit discourse, valued goal behaviors are associated with certain performance standards and language, including mastery, greatness, and specialization. Shifting goals too often or too quickly might not be construed as grit but rather as quitting, caprice, and lack of focus, all of which signal deficiencies in character and are counterproductive to mastery, greatness, and specialization – important values of neoliberal selfhood. Norms for the number, length, and duration of goal pursuits can inform pedagogical decisions to shape in a specific way. In this regard, the grit discourse functions to normalize the evaluation of students based on assumptions about ways that the qualities of goal pursuit lead to a high level of performance. Although persons may have different perspectives on the acceptable duration of goal pursuit and measures of greatness, the qualities of goal pursuits stand as references to make sense of students and inform interventions. The qualities of goal pursuit act as indicators of character and can inform interventions to produce particular behaviors and thoughts in relation to goals.

In addition to the consideration of duration and outcomes, passion is another evaluative concept for goal pursuit. Although featured in the discourse, the notion of passion is a source of ambiguity. In addition to challenges in definition and measurement, it is not clear what strength of emotional ties is necessary to support grit. The differences in language use around this concept help to illustrate this ambiguity. At times, Duckworth (2016) contends that long-term goal pursuit requires passion. However, in early iterations of her grit scale, the word *interest* is used and there is no mention of passion (see https://angeladuckworth.com/grit-scale/). The inclusion of *passion* and *interest* qualifies grit as something that requires at least some type of emotional connection, excluding the possibility that grit can be displayed for things about which one cares little. With that said, the types of connection that these words imply are significantly different. *Mildly interested* is a common expression, but one is unlikely to use *mildly passionate*. *Passionately in love* is a common expression, but *interestingly in love* means a totally different thing. If one thinks of passion and interest as being on a spectrum, extremely interested can overlap with *passion* and *passionate* is more extreme than just *interested* or *very interested*. Generally, passion implies a stronger, more sustainable emotional connection than interest.

Definitions evolve and researchers may use different words across situations. A concern, however, is that certain words invoke different interpretations – ones that have ideological implications. What might seem like a clearly definable and measurable character trait is conceptually complex and unclear. Without clarity and consistency on the definition, educators, researchers, and policy makers might think they agree on the grit narrative when in fact they may not. The complexity in definition can allow persons to project and presume their own ideas in the grit discourse. Consequently, neoliberal ideology is implicated in normalizing grit as a subject position, as well as in shaping the understanding, acceptance, and application of this notion. The neoliberal emphasis on the responsibilization of being is clear. Less clear is the way the integration of passionate pursuit of long-term goals endorses neoliberal values of selfhood.

3.3.1 Passion, Persistence, and Goals

Although not always explicit, passion is typically included in the conceptualization of grit. In fact, Jachimowicz et al. (2018) argue that without it, grit does not correlate with achievement. They conduct a meta-analysis that shows *weak* or *insignificant* relationships between grit (absent passion) and various indicators of success (p. 9980). The authors point to empirical evidence that the link between grit and academic success is tenuous. They explain these empirical results as a consequence of grit scales accounting for only perseverance and interest while ignoring passion, which they define as "a strong feeling toward a personally important value/preference that motivates intentions and behaviors to express that value/preference" (p. 9980). These researchers conclude that perseverance coupled with passion toward a goal predicts academic success.

Duckworth (2016) does not discount the importance of passion. She contends that grit is not possible without passion. In an often-cited quotation from an article in *The New Yorker*, Dahl (2016) reports Duckworth stating:

> I think the misunderstanding – or, at least, one of them – is that it's only the perseverance part that matters. But I think that the passion piece is at least as important. I mean, if you are really, really tenacious and dogged about a goal

that's not meaningful to you, and not interesting to you – then that's just drudgery. It's not just determination – it's having a direction that you care about.

In this quotation, Duckworth suggests that persons can be gritty without passion but such engagement is unpleasant. Notwithstanding, in an interview with Smith (2014), Duckworth goes as far as contending that grit counts as such only with passion. She states, "I don't think people can become truly gritty and great at things they don't love." Here she suggests that passion and love are necessary for the sustainability of long-term goal pursuit and that greatness is not achievable without it. This sentiment speaks to the old adage "if persons love what they do, they never work a day in their lives." A similar way of thinking is captured in a well-known quote by author and motivational speaker Simon Sinek: "Working hard for something we don't care about is called stress; working hard for something we love is called passion" (https://simonsinek.com/).

From this way of thinking, perseverance and effort are possible without passion, but, as these authors suggest, the proposed psychological consequences might threaten well-being, enjoyment, the sustainability of effort, and meaningfulness. Although both love and passion are used, which arguably signify different emotional connections, the idea is that there must be a strong emotional connection to a long-term goal to count as grit. Effort and persistence directed at something one loves is grit. Perseverance without emotional connection is not grit and cannot lead to "greatness." As Jachimowicz et al. (2018) contend, without passion grit is weakly correlated with and predictive of academic achievement.

Researchers bring love and passion into the grit narrative. At times, Duckworth (2007) and other researchers use words that arguably capture a much less strong emotion than passion (Jachimowicz et al., 2018). It is not clear how strong the emotional commitment needs to be toward the goal in order to count as grit, as well as how one knows that love or passion is the source of grit. One behavioral indicator is the persistence in the pursuit of a goal despite setbacks, hardships, and consequences. Another indicator might be performance based. The achievement of greatness and mastery might be explained as made possible because of passion. In these cases, the attribution of passion is *post hoc*. One might assume the commitment toward long-term challenging goals is underpinned by passion because of the obstacles, challenges, and suffering associated with pursuing greatness. Perhaps, without passion persons might be inclined to give up on goals and not achieve levels of mastery that are recognizable and valuable.

The inclusion of passion presents a number of methodological, conceptual, and pedagogical complexities. Defining and measuring passion are difficult. Organizing instructions to teach, ignite, harness, or discover it is a challenging pedagogical task. Notwithstanding, passion serves as an organizing concept to make sense of students and act on them in order to realize the vision of the gritty student. The integration of this concept is informed by representations of successful people and has become entangled in the trope of the committed worker or entrepreneur who has a steadfast work ethic that is sustainable, ongoing, and impactful.

3.3.2 Passionate People and Success

Proponents of grit often reference "successful" people as instantiating the power of passion, persistence, and long-term goal pursuit. For example, in her book, Duckworth (2016) references the following: Jeff Bezos, the founder of Amazon; Will Shortz, the *Times* crossword-puzzle editor; Jamie Dimon, of JPMorgan Chase; Francesca Martinez, the British woman with cerebral palsy who became a famous stand-up comic; and the women's soccer team at the University of North Carolina. Duckworth's initial research was on participants in a spelling bee, cadets at West Point, and students at an Ivy League university. All these participants have had success in their respective endeavors. Persons who *emerge* from poverty are held up as paragons of grit (Tough, 2012). The assumption is that those who move up the social ladder do so because of sheer persistence and will. In addition to economic and competitive contexts, grit is associated with driving democratic and social change. Stokas (2015) mentions that persons such as Fidel Castro and Martin Luther King Jr. are often construed as displaying passionate pursuit of long-term challenging goals.

There is a mix of groups and figures included in this list who have various backgrounds. A unifying factor is that those referenced as displaying grit have achieved some type of recognized form of success, including economic structural change, winning a competition, and valued forms of participation in the economy. Another unifying factor is the assumption of passion as the cause for that success. As Duckworth (2016) defends, to be *great* one must remain committed and loyal to a particular goal, regardless of distractions, obstacles, failures, and setbacks. Longevity for goal pursuit ostensibly requires an unwavering direction of passion toward that goal. This type of focus is made possible by being optimistic, having a GM, and embracing and learning from failure. Grit is not just having passion and resilience in the face of failure but also having an enduring commitment over many years. It means choosing to pursue a particular goal, not quitting that pursuit, giving up other pursuits, and ignoring goal trajectories that are without passion. Informing this version of grit is the romantic image of the undeterred, undistracted person who is excited to pursue and endure the challenges and frustrations associated with pursuing greatness.

3.3.3 Suffering for Passion

Although grit with out passion might be construed as drudgery or unpleasant, grit with passion is not without psychological and emotional consequences. The grit narrative normalizes and valorizes suffering in pursuit of mastery and greatness (Stokas, 2015). The connotation of unpleasantness is built in the narrative as well as common vernacular. As a character trait, to count as gritty one must embrace, learn from, endure, and remain undeterred from the types of unpleasantness that are associated with greatness. In an interview with Del Giudice (2014), Duckworth speaks to this feature of the narrative when she quotes Martha Graham, a well-known dancer from the early to mid-twentieth century. Duckworth references Graham's description of the physical toll that dancing had on her body: "There is a fatigue so great that the body cries, even in its sleep. There are times of complete frustration; there are daily small deaths." Despite the frustration, crying body, and daily deaths, Duckworth highlights Graham's persistence with her craft and holds her up as embodying grit, and, in so doing, normalizes and valorizes a tormented pursuit of greatness.

There are emotional, physical, psychological, and social consequences to performing the type of grit that researchers hold up as exemplary. Grit discourse is entangled in efforts to normalize, validate, and value engagement that is directed at attaining a measure of success and greatness regardless of the potential consequences. Suffering is built into this narrative, but endurable if the endpoint is driven by passion. Those who are impactful are haunted by an idea and pursue that idea until greatness is attained in relation to it.

3.4 Pedagogy, Passion, and Schooling

If responsible for academic success, then it makes sense to operate with the assumption that grit can be cultivated and that schools should formally take up this aim. Treating passion as the source of grit and the target of pedagogical interventions has the potential to increase the appeal. If straightforward, then of course measuring students in terms of grit and igniting passion and formally structuring schooling to support its development make sense. However, the association between grit, passionate pursuit, and attainment of greatness invites several questions: (1) How is passion measured? (2) How long must a student remain committed? (3) What is the time frame to articulate a passion? (4) Must passion be cultivated, ignited, discovered, unleashed, or harnessed? (5) Should schooling be responsible for the experience of passion? (6) Is academic success possible without passion? (7) What types of environments are ideal for the expression of passion? There is little consensus on the answers to these questions. In general, Ruiz-Alfonso and León (2016) contend that there is little theoretical and empirical coherence around the notion and the role of passion in schooling.

Rather than explore the nuances of the empirical incoherence, the goal of this critical analysis is to explore the ideological forces that contribute to the acceptance of passion in grit and the normalization of the passionate person. Like with other concepts discussed in this book, proponents of neoliberalism obviously did not invent the notion of passion to be strategically integrated into a vision of being. However, the passionate worker is a normalized trope in modern discourse, contributing to both the conceptualization and the acceptance of grit. Success in the modern economy is represented as requiring maximum output, avoiding distraction, innovating, working diligently to produce something of value, and aligning a sense of purpose with an organizational goal. Grit, broadly, and passion, in particular, are key features of this trope and consequently have become part of a rationality of management to make up students into a certain type of being.

3.4.1 *The Quest for Passion*

Without passion, there are questions if persons can be gritty, great, focused, and of good character. Thus, there is an imperative for students to articulate and develop a passion to drive their perseverance in the pursuit of goals. The expectation is for students to identify passion as early as possible and demonstrate an unwavering commitment to it. The longer students operate without passion, the more time they lose pursuing mastery and greatness. Given that mastery requires 10,000 hours of practice (Gladwell, 2008), the earlier students start on that commitment, the more likely they will be able to achieve mastery and avoid wasteful indulgence. It is not surprising that parenting guides and early childhood education discourse have taken up interest in structuring experiences to support children's discovery and articulation of passion (e.g., Gray, 2013). An underlying assumption in this discourse is that passion is natural and that all persons, given the right contexts and experiences, have the potential to recognize, discover, or ignite it.

Exploration and experimentation are important pedagogical commitments for this way of thinking. The pedagogical task is to expose students to as many experiences as possible so they can figure what makes them feel alive, enthusiastic, and happy. These feelings must be accompanied by the commitment to engross oneself in that area. Once discovered, passion must be nurtured and guided in order to support the trajectory toward acceptable measures of success and greatness. The assumption is, however, if one has passion, they will, without prodding or coercing, engross themselves in that domain and desire to achieve acceptable standards of *greatness*. Researchers suggest that exploration to discover or ignite passion must happen with as little external determination as possible, otherwise passion may not function to generate satisfaction and support for long-term challenging goals (Vallerand et al., 2003).

3.4.2 The Right-Kind Passion

To make this point, Vallerand et al. (2003) distinguish between two types of passion: harmonious and obsessive. The former is regarded as adaptive and supportive of well-being. Harmonious passion is engaging in activity that is aligned with values perceived as autonomously originated and personally driven. The alignment between identity, personal values, and activity is evidence of this type of passion. Bonneville-Roussy et al. (2013) contend that this type of passion is more likely to be developed and expressed in classrooms wherein students believe that teachers support autonomy. As Ruiz-Alfonso and León (2016) point out, this type of passion requires explicit efforts in the construction of identity. They describe passionate pursuit as the desire to achieve something that is relevant for a sense of self. Passionate pursuit, as opposed to intrinsic motivation, is a strong inclination toward something associated with identity (Alfonso & León, 2016). Thus, to have a passion, one must have a sense of self, accompanied by a commitment to pursue a goal that has direct relevance for that self.

Conversely, Vallerand et al. (2003) use the term *obsessive passion* to describe a strong inclination to do something because of social pressure or to feel some type of esteem and social acceptance. For this type of passion, external influence plays a strong role in influencing the commitment to a goal. Bonneville-Roussy et al. (2013) contend that obsessive passion is more likely to occur in contexts where students perceive their teachers as controlling. Researchers suggest that harmonious passion leads to adaptive behaviors, well-being, and positive emotions, whereas obsessive passion creates internal conflicts and negative emotions. Although not using this distinction, grit researchers rhetorically favor and endorse harmonious passion. Harmonious passion is associated with positive affect, meaningfulness of goal pursuit, and self-actualization of identity. If the goal toward which one strives is considered socially determined and driven by external sources, then there is less likely to be the persistent pursuit of a goal that brings one fulfillment and happiness. If administrators and educators commit to a grit curriculum, it seems that there should be a commitment to harmonious passion.

3.4.3 *Growing Grit*

To appear as though not externally determined, Duckworth (2016) frames pedagogy as *growing* grit, which denotes a natural disposition that is internal to, inherent in, and originated from within persons. Framed as growing, pedagogical efforts are inoculated from claims that the institutionalizing grit is oppressive and dehumanizing. The assumption is that pedagogical environments are not imposing the experience of passion nor controlling the objects of desire but setting up contexts to support the emotional connection to a goal. Thought about this way, finding and pursuing harmonious passion can be viewed as humanizing because it involves the formation of selfhood, identification of self with unique desires, opportunities to explore and indulge those desires, and autonomy and choice in goal pursuit – all of which from a particular ontological perspective are inherent features and motivations of persons.

Despite the fact that proponents of grit are likely to endorse efforts to grow harmonious passion, there is a question about its adaptability to schooling. Coleman and Guo (2013) allude to this possibility when they describe passion for learning as a long-term focused interest in a particular domain that involves disinterest in activities that are interesting to others. If students are deeply committed to a particular domain, one that they "autonomously" discovered, so much that their thoughts are consumed by that domain, they might not be adaptable to the demands and structures of schooling that require shifting focus and interest in many domains. If passionate about something outside of the schooling curriculum, then attention to and strong inclinations toward schooling might be absent. If only passionate about a particular schooling domain, then displaying grit in other subjects might be unsustainable drudgery. Unless students are passionate about schooling in a broad sense, gritty students with harmonious passion can make teaching difficult. Although treated as a necessary emotional connection to display grit, igniting and cultivating passion might compete with institutional structures and aims.

As a broad example, consider zealotry, which is a fanatical and uncompromising pursuit of religious, political, or other ideals. A zealot is likely to be ranked high on the grit scale. Zealots are individuals who are completely undeterred by the cost of reaching their goals. There is not a single item on the grit scale that does not correlate with zealotry. Zealots are likely to rank high on any passion scale. A zealot is typically understood as undistracted and undeterred, not derailed by setbacks, committed to finishing what they started, and maintaining interest over time. Pointing to the adaptability of students and the ethics of certain social groups reveals the way passion is entangled in issues of control and value. Passion in persons is desirable if it leads to conformity and adaptability to structures and values. The imperative is not just to grow grit by igniting, discovering, and supporting passionate pursuit but also to ensure that the pursuit conforms to a value system. This requirement is clear in the application of grit in Knowledge Is Power Program (KIPP) schools.

3.4.4 *Values for Obsessive Passion*

Although harmonious passion is valued in the grit discourse, Duckworth's partnership with the KIPP charter school network, which typically serves students from low-income backgrounds, suggests a mixed message. Across the network of KIPP schools, there is an explicit and rhetorical integration of a grit curriculum, as well as emphasis on cultivating optimism, zeal, gratitude, curiosity, and self-control. Framed as a focus on character, the expectation for this curriculum is that students display these traits in all domains of schooling. An issue is that KIPP schools are known for their emphasis on behavioral compliance, zero-tolerance disciplinary models, reliance on external rewards, high suspension rates for trivial offenses, and behavioral uniformity (e.g., students sitting with hands on desk and walking in straight lines in the hallway). In some schools, students have to earn their desks and uniforms. KIPP schools are known less for supporting autonomy and more for regimented and scripted engagement. Herein lies a potential concern. KIPP environments do not seem to support and endorse harmonious passion and do not appear to be informed by efforts to ignite, discover, and harness students' passion, unless one believes that passion ignites from following rules. The application of grit in KIPP schools supports the assumption that children from low-income backgrounds need character development in highly structured contexts.

3.4.5 Neurophysical Deficiencies

At times Duckworth (2016) seems like a strong advocate of centering love, meaningfulness, selfhood, and happiness, yet she partners with a schooling network that can be accused of ignoring passion altogether or valuing the obsessive type. This potential contradiction speaks of differences in assumptions about students from different identity groups. For example, it is not uncommon for researchers and policy makers to claim that students from low-income backgrounds have neurophysical deficiencies that result from economic conditions. Proponents of formalizing grit in schooling reference deficits in students' prefrontal cortices that result from poor attachments, stress related to poverty, and lack of stimulating environments (Center on the Developing Child at Harvard University, 2011; Johnson et al., 2016; Wang et al., 2017). With thinner prefrontal cortices than their affluent counterparts, children from low-income backgrounds, as the reasoning goes, may struggle with impulse control, attention, self-control, and delay of gratification – many capacities that make grit possible. Furthermore, as Tough (2012) contends, poverty can affect neural structures in ways to produce a highly sensitive stress-response system. As a consequence, he reasons that persons are likely to be overly sensitive to threats or may perceive something as a threat that others might not. Tough adds that these responses produce self-defeating behaviors, such as fighting, talking back, acting up in class, disconnectedness to peers, and resistance to outreach from teachers and other adults.

The characterization of the neurophysical structures of students from low-income backgrounds suggests that they lack the cognitive and behavioral dispositions to pursue harmonious passion, even if it was to be ignited. Thus, one might reason that the highly structured, regimented, and disciplinary nature of KIPP is necessary for reconditioning neural structures to support the eventual experience of and capacity to manage harmonious passion. An explicit grit curriculum that is focused on obedience, compliance, and uniformity, as well as enduring potential drudgery (given the absence of harmonious passion), it seems, can counteract the neurophysical effects of low-income settings.

Not all researchers share this optimism, however. For example, Denby (2016) reports that Jack Shonkoff, the director of Harvard's Center on the Developing Child, opposes grit because of these neurophysical consequences of poverty. The reasoning is that if children have not developed the right neurological structures early in life, then the lack of grit in later grades is not something necessarily in willful control. Thus, Shonkoff argues that students are unfairly held responsible for their environments through low values for their character scores. For that reason, Shonkoff suggests that if not targeted early in children's lives, then a grit curriculum is irrelevant and abrasive. In this line of reasoning, the existence of neurophysical deficiencies is not challenged or problematized but rather the expectation for certain cognitive capacities and functions from persons from low-income backgrounds. Shonkoff contends that expecting grit from those who do not have the necessary brain structures can create frustrating learning environments that set up students to fail. From this line of reasoning, it makes sense to strongly advocate for formalized early childhood experiences that focus on cultivating capacities for self-control, impulse control, and delay of gratification. Perhaps helping children to form neural structures during the so-called critical periods when brains tend to be more plastic than later in life is a key to developing the character traits to mitigate poverty.

3.5 Institutional Conformity and Responsibilization

There are several concerns with grit, in general, and the inclusion of passion, in particular. The focus here is on the neoliberalization of passion, which manifests in different ways. In the example with KIPP schools, schooling practice does not support harmonious passion but rather complicity and conformity, which aligns with obsessive passion. It is reasonable to challenge that the type of engagement in KIPP schools is underlined by any form of passion. However, one of the consequences of neoliberal ideology is the interpretation and explanation of behavior and engagement in terms of passion. There are several ways to explain forces of behavior. Likewise, there are vastly different ways to conceptualize passion and its place in being and engagement. However, a typical consequence of neoliberal ideology is the attribution of behavior and being to individual and internal components. Thus, passion functions to explain differences in behavior, outcomes, and character, consequently becoming a pedagogical target and feature to manage. Deliberations and rationalizations center on this feature of persons because of the ostensible value for twenty-first century environments. In this regard, passion is treated as a form of human capital whereby technical means are created to support its development. Regardless of the type or its absence, in a neoliberal ethos, passion functions as a measure of character and learning environments.

As represented in models of the ideal citizen, worker, and student, passion should be harmonious. If one cannot be "truly" gritty without passion and grit is essential for academic and economic success, then to serve as a great equalizer schooling must be successful as helping students discover, ignite, or develop harmonious passion. Committing to economic justice requires pedagogical environments that support strong emotional connections to goals through discovery, autonomy, and connection to a sense of self. However, in some environments that are centered on grit, this commitment is absent. If harmonious passion supports grit, as well as aligns with the trope of the twenty-first century economic participant, then the grit curriculum in KIPP schools endorses ways of being that are not valued and rewarded by being exchangeable in the modern economy, and can thus be implicated in the social reproduction of inequality.

Herein lies a concern with the application of grit. Norms and values for grit function differently across student populations. Although researchers contend that all students can benefit from efforts to grow grit, there is particular emphasis on the value for students from low-income backgrounds. However, there tends to be an absence of a commitment to harmonious passion in curriculum and practices for students from this demographic. The absence may not seem all that surprising. Researchers continually illustrate the subtle and explicit ways that schooling targets different dispositions, knowledge, and skills to reproduce class position (Ainsworth, 2018; Bourdieu et al., 1977; Bowles & Gintis, 1976; Reichelt et al., 2019; Sullivan et al., 2018). If harmonious passion is required for persons to participate in the economy, and do so with satisfaction, meaning, and fulfillment, then the grit curriculum in KIPP schools seems counterproductive to support certain types of economic participation. One might defend KIPP disciplinary measures as necessary to create the psychological and neurophysical foundation to make the pursuit of harmonious passion possible.

This reasoning makes sense against problematic characterizations and pedagogical needs of students from low-income backgrounds.

3.5 Institutional Conformity and Responsibilization

Assumptions circulating in the discourse are that students from this demographic (1) have neurophysical structures that inhibit their ability to self-control, focus, be amenable, optimistic, and safe; (2) lack the character traits to be gritty and academically successful; (3) need highly regulated contexts to recondition character traits; (4) should be grateful for reconditioning efforts; (5) should be receptive to adult outreach and support; and (6) can be academically and economically successful if they conform to institutional expectations. Although this way of thinking appears to reflect an optimistic appraisal of opportunities for academic success that run counter to socioeconomic determinism, the assumptions are rife with problems.

This way of thinking is centered on deficit-based assumptions that operate as objective realities buttressed by neuroscientific claim that students from low-income backgrounds have thinner prefrontal cortices that make it difficult for them exercise self-control, impulse control, and attention, which are all capacities necessary to sustain a long-term commitment to a goal. Although one can applaud proponents of grit as being optimistic about the potential for fixing brain structures, and thus fixing character and cognitive capacities, the grit narrative is based on deficit thinking, class-based pathologization, and the disciplining of students from low-income backgrounds. The application of grit in the KIPP contexts is about cultivating certain capacities, attitudes, perceptions, behaviors, and relationships so that children are amenable to schooling lessons, regardless of the schooling structure, background, and curriculum.

Any application of a grit curriculum, even one based on discovery and autonomy, can be justifiably considered obedience and compliance. However, the institutional compliance in KIPP schools is different in its explicitness, apparent necessity, and form. In the KIPP context, the optimism for academic success is based on the following idea: students can be academically successful if they embody an agreeable and docile character who is thankful for the opportunity to address cognitive, neurological, and character deficiencies so that they can escape the context that created those deficiencies. Given this message, Saltman (2014) describes grit in the following way:

> 'Grit' is a pedagogy of control that is predicated upon a promise made to poor children that if they learn the tools of self-control and learn to endure drudgery, they can compete with rich children for scarce economic resources. Proponents of teaching 'grit' contend that the poor are biologically and psychologically traumatized by poverty. The trauma of poverty,

> they argue, can be overcome through learned self-control and submission to authority within the school. (Saltman, 2014, p. 42)

Although the message may look different in other contexts, Saltman captures the grit message as it applies to KIPP and other schools that adopt a grit curriculum to support academic success for students from low-income backgrounds. The emphasis is on self-control, which can actually be counter to the experience and indulgence of passion. If students are continuously expected to suppress any type of impulse or action toward a goal that is incompatible with schooling, then it might be challenging to explore, discern, and create strong emotional connections to a domain that has not been shaped by others. Students are expected to follow the grit program under the guidance of school personnel or endure the consequences.

Although one might reason that students from low-income backgrounds need biological and neurophysical reconditioning in highly scripted contexts to counter the trauma created from poverty, this pedagogical commitment reflects what Freire (1968/2000) calls *false generosity*, which he implicates in the reproduction of inequality and dehumanization. The idea is that character and cognitive improvements are gifts bestowed onto persons so that they can participate in and adapt to existing structures. False generosity is based on a hierarchy of power in which persons in advantaged positions believe that they can form and reform persons in disadvantaged positions by imparting knowledge, dispositions, and character. A contradiction, however, is that the gift is not one centered on realizing harmonious passion, which is the type that signifies grit and has value in twenty-first century economic contexts. In the KIPP context, grit cannot even be associated with the commitment to inculcate the culture of power as a means to address inequalities.

The gift of harmonious passion, however, does not make such generosity any less false. The point here is to not suggest that integrating explicit commitments to harmonious passion frees one from the entanglement of neoliberalism. Neoliberal ideology directs attention to the technical development of psychological qualities that have value for economic participation. Harmonious passion is one of those qualities that underpin grit and reflects the trope of the ideal twenty-first century participant. If harmonious passion is a valued characteristic for economic participation, then students in KIPP schools who are conditioned to be obedient, compliant, and uniform are not encouraged to develop the character that has value for modern economic conditions.

3.5 Institutional Conformity and Responsibilization

The application of grit in KIPP schools functions as an explicit disciplinary tool, whereby obedience and compliance are rewarded. In this application, the message is about personal responsibility and rugged individualism. In the KIPP context, the grit curriculum functions to cultivate and validate a "no excuse" mentality, which accompanies a specific interpretation of the opportunity structure. For the grit narrative to be valid, one must believe that opportunity is equally available to all and that effort and persistence determine outcomes. Regardless of existing disparities, relentless work serves as an equalizer. The narrative of grit is about individual control over inequalities, rather than socioeconomic conditions, disparity in privilege, and immutable talent and intelligence. Although some researchers suggest that grit is not possible given certain brain structures, there is general optimism that brain structures can be changed and that persons can grow their grit if they submit to institutional demands.

Although the application of the grit curriculum can invite a highly structured context that is seemingly responsible for shaping students' character, the message communicated to students is that if they submit to teacher authority, school structures, and perform the "right" character, they can be academically successful and can compete with their affluent counterparts for positions in the economic structure. The irony is that although a disciplinary educational structure is responsible for reconditioning students, the message from the grit curriculum in general is that success is achieved by having certain internal states, dispositions, and traits.

As such, inequality and disparities are a consequence of personal factors and, to some extent, individual choices. Adams et al. (2019) assert that "prevalent constructions of economic growth emphasize characteristics of self-interested individuals capable of acting independently from their material and societal context. From this perspective, economic scarcity is the result of poor choices and deficient attributes, such as insufficient motivation or grit" (p. 203).

From this model, addressing inequalities happens at the level of the individual person, which means targeting character, reconditioning neural structures, shaping behaviors, and conditioning perspectives and attitudes. This attribution is essential for the legitimization and exacerbation of inequality as they validate economic hierarchy by convincing others that they are responsible for their outcomes and can overcome whatever limitations that result from socioeconomic disparities, discrimination, and economic policies. If persons think they are responsible for success and failure, they may accept or miss entirely problematic structural conditions that can be implicated in social reproduction of inequality. Stokas (2015) makes this point: "I posit that without understanding that grit has been used as a cultural trope to legitimate individual success while ignoring the systemic reasons for its need, we risk continuing to entrench the systemic inequality that educational researchers ... have identified as at the root of underachievement in schools" (515). This point is not to endorse a deterministic view of achievement but to suggest that the logic in the grit narrative spotlights personal responsibility as the source and explanation of achievement influences narratives about students and their behaviors.

One of the more concerning features of the grit narrative is that any resistance to schooling might be conceived as neurophysical deficiencies and poor character. The grit discourse is not typically associated with dismantling existing structures or resisting a competitive ethos. Cultivating optimism and gratitude about what is possible, students can be disarmed with critical interrogative methods about structures and policies. The expectation is for students to trust schools, schooling, teachers, and peers and to be amenable to the lessons from those sources. Any resistance is a reflection of poor character and neural deficiencies.

3.6 Ideological Conformity: Passion as an Organizing Trope

The notion of passion is obviously not a neoliberal concept but one that has been present throughout history to explain and describe human composition and behavior. However, in this historical moment, passion is used in ways to reflect norms for neoliberal selfhood. What counts as passion, values for it, and its place in institutional discourse have changed throughout history (Tröhler, 2008). In contemporary discourse, passion is a target of pedagogical interventions, normalizing the presence and articulation of a strong emotional connection in the pursuit of a long-term goal. Although there might appear to be opportunities for discovery, diverse experiences, autonomy, and choice, passion is centered as an eventuality and normal state of being. As a subjective description of an invisible force, evidence of passion is a long-term commitment to immerse oneself in an area with the goal of attaining a high measure of performance. Like grit in general, passion is tied into performance language such as greatness, mastery, enhancement, and goal attainment. In this regard, passion is entangled in neoliberal values for selfhood. In addition to performance

3.6 Ideological Conformity: Passion as an Organizing Trope 55

language, the trope of the passionate worker informs visions for ideal economic participants who operate with purpose and satisfaction.

3.6.1 Working on the Self

Passion is not an inherent feature of neoliberal selfhood but can be understood and applied to align with neoliberal values. In addition to being tied to performance language, passion as a normalized state for persons is something to be managed and supported through technical means. Regardless of the debates about the ontology of passion, this notion governs the way students are understood, success is constructed, and pedagogical environments are shaped. Underlying such framing is the assumption that students have the potential for passionate pursuit and may intrinsically desire its manifestation but may need an igniting experience. Thus, failing to articulate a passion or show an unwavering commitment are an unacceptable form of being and engagement. Passion serves as an organizing tool to rationalize pedagogical decisions and to evaluate the motivation for students' goal pursuits.

As an organizing tool, passion justifies prescriptions for learning that exclude other possible subject positions and ways of being. Although seemingly through choice, autonomy, and exploration, there are strategic decisions for technically supporting the articulation of passion. Students without passion must be worked on and students with passion need support for their engagement. Passion renders schooling instrumental, both in terms of reducing learning to the discovery of passion and supporting efforts to immerse oneself in that passion. Learning without passion might be treated as wasteful exploration or indulgence, unless that learning eventually leads to the emergence and discovery of a strong desire for something. Broad experience is valued to the extent that it functions as a precursor to the articulation of a singular, enthusiastic focus.

In the grit discourse, passion is an eventuality of experience, a normalized state, that requires work on the self. The requirements include developing a certain sense of selfhood, uniqueness, commitment to self-development, and desire to achieve mastery and greatness. If a student has a sense of self but no interest in pursuing a goal that has meaning for that self, the pedagogical task is about conditioning desire for self-enhancement and indulgence. If students do not have a sense of self to anchor meaning and goal pursuit, then the pedagogical task is to create that self, which can occur through exposure to diverse situations and contexts. From these experiences, emotional states and performance outcomes become markers for the contents of selfhood and worthiness of goal pursuit. Passion requires an articulation of self that informs the meaningfulness and coherence of a goal pursuit. Such reasoning is informed by the assumption that students have selves that serve as the foundation for meaningful making and the evaluations of goals.

Thought about in this way, passionate pursuit is made possible via commitments to what Martin (2007) refers to as expressive selfhood. This form of selfhood, which is prominently featured in educational psychology, is centered on inner experience, uniqueness, expression, and actualization. The governing idea is that persons have a unique, essential, and inner core that needs to be explored, developed, and expressed. As Martin and McLellan (2013) contend, terms such as self-actualization, self-concept, and self-esteem provide the structure to make sense of and validate this version of selfhood. One of the lines of the passion narrative is informed by this commitment to selfhood. As Martin (2007) suggests, expressive selfhood aligns with neoliberal visions for being as persons are extracted from sociohistorical context and conceptualized as unique beings who must celebrate, indulge, and develop that uniqueness. Part of the push for this type of self is associated with values for specialization, consumption, and choice-making. The passionate person will make choices about what knowledge and experience to consume in order to pursue high levels of performance in the area that brings them fulfillment.

3.6.2 Problems with Character

The justification for passion is entangled in narratives about problems with students' character, as well as images about what students need to be. Researchers and policy makers worry that students are afraid to take risks, give up on problems, have a sense of entitlement, look for easy solutions, and quit when confronted with challenges (Bialostok & Kamberelis, 2012; Duckworth, 2016; Dweck, 2006). Thus, schooling should support students' comfort with risk, uncertainty, setbacks, failures, and complex problems. As a result, there are intentional efforts to structure classrooms to produce complexities, obstacles, and opportunities for risk (e.g., Mills & Kim, 2017; Williams, 2018). Some researchers suggest that educators should strategically orchestrate challenging and difficult situations for students in order to expose them to setbacks and frustrations. The goal is to challenge students in ill-defined domains while providing them support to be comfortable with these domains. With that comfort, the expectation is that students remain humble, persistent, gracious, and optimistic.

3.6 Ideological Conformity: Passion as an Organizing Trope

Connecting this type of engagement with passion ostensibly supports this pedagogical target.

Students are expected to embrace challenges and problems, persist in solving them, be comfortable with uncertainty in the exploration of solutions, remain undeterred by setbacks, and treat setbacks as sources of knowledge. All the while, they must remain optimistic about the learning, themselves, and efforts to solve the problems. And of course, they should be thankful for the opportunity to have their character built from this learning opportunity. If students are passionate about problems, the work will not be experienced as drudgery and can support creative expression, innovation, and fulfillment. In an article by Davis (2015) written in Edutopia, the title is "5 Ways of Bringing Student Passions to Student Learning." The subtitle is "Learning and learning outcomes are more meaningful to students when teachers engage their passions, unleash their creativity, and give them time and tools for innovation." To unleash passion, Davis suggests the use of *genius time*. Although the frequency and amount of time can change based on several factors, the so-called genius time is carving out a space in the curriculum for students to become *experts* in anything they choose. The idea is that passion, personalized learning, self-regulation, ingenuity, and creativity can be practiced and developed in contexts in which students have autonomy and choice.

3.6.3 The Passionate Worker

The grit narrative uses passion to validate innovative, creative persons who enthusiastically pursue greatness, expertise, and specialization. The gritty person may not always pursue material gain but is governed by the push to achieve what is recognized as *greatness* and *mastery*. This narrative is normalized in the modern workplace. Like for genius time, Pink (2011) explores ways companies create situations to support high-quality software innovation. He contends that rewards and punishments are counterproductive for sufficiently motivating workers to create and innovate in quality ways. Instead, he defends the position that autonomy and purpose are driving forces for the production of new and useful products. Pink reports that Atlassian gives their developers one afternoon per month to work on any product that they want. He makes the argument that in this limited time, persons had opportunities to pursue their passions, leading them to develop innovative and high-quality products. In this context, the passion functions as a human management tool to support product development.

McRobbie (2015) contends that, what she calls, "passionate work" has become an essential requirement for neoliberal economic arrangements. By this term, she means the tying of emotional fulfillment and purpose to justify the commitment to an economic goal. She contends that passionate work is connected to human capital accumulation but makes it more powerful by tying it to meaningfulness, fulfillment, and spiritual rewards. To be great, one cannot quit or change interests too often. The grit narrative values the person who directs energy to develop expertise and specialization. Denby (2016) contends that the passion imperative is an effort that entangles a person's desires and aspirations to institutional and corporate goals. If such an alignment is achieved, one is likely to direct creative and innovative power toward a corporate objective. Success in the modern economy is constructed as requiring a focus on maximum output, avoiding distraction, and working diligently to produce something valuable. One who performs this identity is judged as having good character, regardless of the consequences and implications of actions.

Even if not serving a corporate agenda, the justification for passionate pursuit can be connected to the value for entrepreneurialism. As Sugarman (2015) argues, the neoliberal self is responsible for creating economic activity. For this reason, risk-taking, optimism, persistence, and passion are necessary. Creating economic activity can be difficult, rife with obstacles and setbacks. Passion can serve as the emotional force to continue with the personal investment in oneself and the enterprise. In their literature review exploring the relationship between passion and entrepreneurship, Chen et al. (2015) argue that research shows both negative and positive effects on enterprise. When economic activity is associated with identity, passion is linked to productivity, innovation, and viability. The authors, however, also note that too much passion can inhibit creative problem solving by generating an inflexible and unwavering commitment to a particular goal. As Chen et al. illustrate, the literature on entrepreneurship is fairly new, growing, and in need of more empirical work; the point is that the passion is conceptualized as an influence on economic activity, productivity, and innovation and has thus come under the scrutiny of the scientific gaze in order to cultivate, manage, harness, and unleash passion for economic purposes.

3.7 Conclusion

The grit discourse in general is about cultivating a particular type of character, while communicating messages about economic structures,

3.7 Conclusion

opportunities, and norms for being. However, framing pedagogy as growing grit can naturalize and normalize these messages, concealing the ideological implications of the conceptualizations and practices around grit. The inclusion of passion for grit further legitimizes assumptions about naturalness. Consequently, institutional efforts to target grit can be perceived as humanistic, neutral, and value-free. Yet, the institutionalization of grit makes the child's character the target of pedagogical interventions, a commitment connected to neoliberalism. Neoliberal values for personhood run through and validate the grit narrative, which is based on the premise that perseverance and passion toward singular long-term goals are the key to academic and life success. Highlighting the ideological currents is not a pessimistic appraisal of academic possibilities, nor is it an endorsement of deterministic views of achievement. Rather, the purpose is to show that grit functions to normalize, validate, and endorse a neoliberal view of persons, schooling, and the economy.

There was a time when grit and passion were not used as a way to make sense of students, engagement, success, and teaching. These notions are now a normalized part of a framework for thinking about visions of school and personhood. There are reasons why the grit narrative has traction in education conversations. It is not because researchers discovered a new character trait and a set of pedagogical techniques for developing that trait. Rather, the traction results from the alignment with neoliberal values for personal responsibility, individualism, specialization, management, performance, and instrumentalism. To center passion for grit and success is about targeting students in ways to support the reflexive pursuit of predetermined standards with excitement, enthusiasm, and sustainable commitment.

CHAPTER 4

Emotion Regulation
Strategic Self-Management

4.1 Introduction

The role that emotion plays in learning has been well explored over the last three decades. Researchers have been interested in the ways that certain emotions support or hinder learning. A prevailing belief is that certain types, intensities, and behavioral manifestations of emotions are key to student success. However, not all emotions have the same impact on learning; some emotions improve learning in certain contexts, while those same emotions might hinder it in others. The reason for this difference is that emotional expressions, values, for emotions, and consequences are negotiated among persons within contexts (Boddice, 2017; Scherer et al., 2001; Zembylas, 2005; Zembylas & Fendler, 2007). With that said, there are some general agreements about which emotions support and curtail learning. The former includes happiness, calmness, optimism, and zeal, whereas the latter might include stress, fear, and anger. Notwithstanding debates about which emotions best support learning, there is general consensus that emotions are essential determinants of learning and must be taken into account by teachers, especially if they had a humanistic commitment to teach the WC.

Although there is a push for teachers to evoke emotions from students that support learning, it is difficult to predict and homogenize emotional responses to instruction. Not all students will have the same response during a teaching event. Thus, there are calls for teachers to implement instructions for students to regulate their own emotions in order to support optimal performance. This pedagogical commitment is associated with a number of related terms, such as emotional intelligence, social-emotional learning, emotion literacy, and emotion regulation (ER). Despite the fact that these terms have slightly different nuances, there is a common assumption and theme that runs throughout the discourse of emotion in school. This theme is informed by the ideas that emotions affect learning in adaptive and maladaptive ways, emotions can be strategically self-managed, and it is the teachers' responsibility to teach that self-management (Elias et al., 1997; Newberry et al., 2013). This chapter is about that theme and is anchored particularly in the ER literature because of the widespread use of this term. Furthermore, the aforementioned terms listed all have a regulatory component to them.

ER is defined as a process that involves influence over the existence, experience, and expression of emotions (Gross, 1998). It is about ensuring that the right emotions are experienced, or, if maladaptive ones are experienced, students exercise control over its behavioral manifestation ER is treated as an adaptive process that supports academic success, the development of positive relationships, hard work, and positive attitudes. Done well, this regulatory ability is associated with academic success across all school levels and argued to predict success beyond K-12 contexts (Graziano et al., 2007; Gross & John, 2003; Gumora & Arsenio, 2002; Ivcevic & Brackett, 2014). Researchers suggest that control over emotions is the means to improve everyday life and to help persons become creative, entrepreneurial, loving, responsible, caring, fair, and respectful (e.g., see Cooper & Sawaf, 1997; Lopes et al., 2012; Zembylas, 2006). Consequently, ER is associated with valued qualities of twenty-first-century workers (Garcia, 2016; Grandey et al., 2013; Heckman & Kautz, 2013; Pinos et al., 2013; Scorza et al., 2016). For this reason, ER is generally considered a skill to be developed, mastered, and employed in order to manage life and succeed with tasks in and outside of school. Given the purported value, there is no shortage of research on the processes, development, and pedagogy of ER. Researchers tend to commit to the idea that the better emotions and regulatory mechanisms are understood, the better teachers can facilitate students' control over their emotions.

Boler (1999) argues that teachers and researchers might applaud this focus in schooling because of the decades-long privileging of rationality and the ostensible compartmentalization of students that resulted from ignoring emotions. Explicitly integrating emotion in curriculum and pedagogy appears to align with a humanistic commitment to teach the WC and to develop the character traits that can support adaptation to schooling and work environments. Although ER is generally represented quite favorably in the discourse and can be used as a humanistic pedagogical tool, there are several causes for concern.

Although Explicitly integrating ER in schools may seem humanistic, democratic, and unequivocally beneficial for students, the analysis will reveal that ER is also entangled in a neoliberal rationality of government and in representations of ideal persons. Although, for centuries, researchers and philosophers have emphasized the importance of understanding and mastering emotions (e.g., see "Epictetus: A Stoic and Socratic Guide to Life," by Long, 2002), throughout history the tools and purposes of such control have changed. In contemporary discourse, researchers treat ER as a skill that can be developed for the purpose of being successful in and out of school. This understanding is driven by the use of science to inform regulation frameworks and instruments to render emotions knowable, measurable, and controllable (Boler, 1999: Braunstein et al., 2017; Ogata, 2013; Zembylas & Fendler, 2007). What was once thought to be an unmanageable and private human experience, as Boler (1999) argues, has been placed under the scientist's microscope and dissected for the purpose to realize willful and masterful control over oneself. Contemporary discourse is distinct in the use of science for the purpose of strategic self-management. This management by itself is aligned with neoliberal ideology, a connection that is deepened by the treatment of ER as a skill and twenty-first century competence. In addition to aligning with a neoliberal rationality of government, there are particular emotion rules that govern what counts as adaptive ER. These rules can be connected to neoliberalism and the emphasis on optimism, zeal, gratitude, grit, and GM.

4.2 Definition and Conceptualization

4.2.1 What Is Being Regulated?

Any conceptualization of ER requires an understanding of emotion which must extend beyond instantiations such as anger, sadness, gratitude, and fear. Defining emotion beyond examples has been a challenge to scientists, social scientists, and philosophers. These challenges in part have to do with: (1) the unreliability of subjective experience for making objective claims about emotions, and (2) the tangible parts of emotion, such as behavior and biophysical responses, are not always good sources for defining and discerning emotions. If relying on self-reported information, researchers are restricted by persons' perceptions, memory, interpretation, and language. On the other side, relying on behavior and biophysical responses are generally considered only parts of emotional experience. With that being said, there has been no shortage of work on defining and conceptualizing emotion. Although taken up by classical Western philosophers several centuries ago, the conceptualization of emotion will

4.2 Definition and Conceptualization

begin here with William James, who is considered the father of American psychology. Working in the late nineteenth century, James is a key figure in bringing the study of emotion into scientific space.

In 1884, James published an article titled *What is an emotion?* In this text, he defined emotion as a biophysical response, or what he called "biological disturbance," to an environmental trigger (p. 189). This view is not unlike the one that might be endorsed by a behaviorist. However, James adds that there must be a cognitive component. The first operation of the cognitive component is the perception of an environmental trigger. There must be a percept of something in the environment, which has the effect of producing a biophysical response. From James' view this perception is cognitive but not necessarily under willful control. The second cognitive operation is the "feeling" of that biophysical response. One must be aware of and then interpret the meaning of the biological disturbance. James states, "the bodily changes follow directly the perception of the exciting fact [environmental trigger], and that our feeling of the same changes as they occur is the emotion" (pp. 189–90). For James, the defining feature of emotion is the feeling of the biological disturbance that resulted from an environmental provocation or trigger. Although essential, feeling does not occur without the environmental and biophysical components.

James' (1884) conceptualization informs much contemporary theorizing on emotion. Typically there is a perceiving person, an environmental provocation, a biophysical response, and an interpretation of that response. Behavior is also important to James' viewpoint not as a manifestation of an emotion, but an antecedent. He argues that emotion follows this sequence: a percept, an environmental trigger, a biophysical response, a behavior, and then the feeling of the biophysical and behavioral responses. James uses an example of a confrontation with a bear to explain. He states that if one saw a bear, that person would run. According to James, one doesn't run because they are afraid, but rather they are afraid because they run. It is the interpretation of the biophysical response associated with a behavior that is the emotion. A foundational assumption in James' conceptualization is the relationship between behaviors and environmental triggers. He describes the nervous system as "a bundle of predispositions" that reacts (behaviorally and biophysically) in specific ways to particular environmental conditions (p. 136). These reactions are automatic and are accompanied by specific biophysical reactions.

Although James' (1884) theory of emotion informs modern theorizing, there are some departures. First, it is not common today to conclude that persons behave and then experience an emotion. This way of thinking makes it a challenge to control the emotion and its behavioral manifestation. In our contemporary culture, there is optimism in the ability to exercise control over all aspects of human functioning. Second, missing in James' theorizing is the presence and role of belief, which informs much contemporary discourse. Some theorists treat belief as influential, foundational, and even synonymous with emotion (Calhoun & Solomon, 1984). Cognitive-behavioral theorists tend to argue that environmental events do not cause emotions and that persons do not have a bundle of predisposed responses to environmental triggers, but rather the belief about an event sets a particular internal sequence in motion. For example, beliefs about bears will influence whether persons have a biophysical response and run at the sight of them. In this conceptualization, beliefs are antecedent to emotions and can determine which ones are experienced. Cognitive behavioral theorists argue that there is an environmental provocation but no set responses to it, and that such provocations can be interpreted differently, thus leading to different emotions (Campos et al., 2004). In this account, belief mediates environmental triggers. Thought about this way, persons are not passive in the reception of environmental stimuli but rather can shape the capacity for a trigger to elicit an emotion by shaping beliefs. Of course then, there is debate about whether belief is controllable and adequate to exercise control over a biophysical response to an environmental trigger.

The ancient stoics are optimistic that emotions can be controlled through choices related to beliefs. Rather than the use of the term *beliefs*, in the translation of *Enchiridion* by Long (2004), Epictetus uses the word *judgment* and contends that control over emotions results from judgments of external conditions and triggers. Like earlier stoics, Epictetus rejects the idea that such emotions are imposed on people. Rather, he concludes that they emerge as a consequence of the judgment of value related to a stimulus or trigger. Early stoic philosophy is based on the idea that control over emotions is made possible via the manipulation of other psychological phenomena, such as judgments, perceptions, and beliefs. Although stoics were not trying to suppress emotions altogether, there are clear values for certain emotions and their behavioral manifestation. Those emotions that need to be suppressed include grief, fear, envy, desire, and every form of anxiety. According to this philosophy, these emotions emerge as a result of incorrect judgments and perceptions about the controllability of situations. As long as one knows what is and is not controllable and acts on that which is controllable, that person should not experience the aforementioned emotions. To foster the right emotions, one merely needs correct judgment.

4.2.2 The Need for Emotion Regulation

As mentioned earlier, control over emotions has been a concern for philosophers and theologians for centuries. The reason for the necessity of ER varies across time and philosophical perspectives. Consider that the ancient stoics treated ER as an exercise of self-mastery and the realization of a virtuous life. Stoics did not suppress all emotional life, nor did they deny that emotions were a quintessential feature of humanness. However, the ancient Stoics distinguished reason from emotion, privileging the latter as the mechanism for deciding if an emotional experience aligned with Stoic principles, if that emotional experience was good, and how one should act following an emotional experience. For the Stoics, emotions were responses to situations and did not always lead to control and disciplined responses, which are key for a virtuous life. Thus, for a good life and one in which persons master themselves, reason was necessary. Early Stoics were speaking to themes that run throughout science, philosophy, religion, and everyday thinking about emotions. Emotions tend to be treated as potentially problematic, difficult to control, and distinct from reasoned judgment.

In the modern context, the overarching justification for the need to regulate emotions is for adaptability and character development – both of which are implicated in an ethic of self-management. Contemporary researchers argue that regulating emotions is essential for adaptation, which can be defined as successfully responding to change, novelty, and uncertainty in a situation (Burns & Martin, 2014). The assumption is that a change can produce debilitating anxiety and fear, which can negatively affect motivation and performance. Thus, if persons learn to regulate emotions by suppressing fear and anxiety, the thinking is that they are likely to take on and persist with any emerging challenge. ER and adaptability are also tied to calls for developing certain character traits in young people. The contemporary narrative that circulates about young people today is that they are experiencing a crisis in character. This narrative is informed by claims that young people are too easily offended, are afraid to take risks, cannot handle failure, and are too self-centered, impetuous, and anxious. To address these problems of character, researchers and policy makers argue that children need to learn grit, develop a GM, learn to delay gratification, take risks, and embrace creativity and entrepreneurialism. For example, frustration with *failure* can arguably hinder students' motivation. Students may disengage and avoid tasks because of the fear of failure and the desire to avoid the confrontation with failure. To mitigate this response, researchers suggest that students can develop certain beliefs, such as a GM, to modulate the frustration, anxiety, and depression that might follow an experience of *failure*. The need for ER in the modern context is to support students' display of character in ways that support their successful adaptation to schooling contexts.

It is important to note that, in this narrative, adaptability is not only about suppressing maladaptive emotions but also about harnessing adaptive ones. Contemporary researchers argue that emotions can be an important source for motivation, volition, and persistence in the pursuit of goals (Eccles & Wigfield, 2002; Pekrun & Stephens, 2009; Turner et al., 2002). Certain emotions should not always be suppressed but activated and embraced. Emotions still need to be regulated, just in strategic ways that can support goal attainment. For example, the absence of happiness and passion in the pursuit of learning goals might produce students who are indifferent toward learning. Thus, one must learn to harness passion to sustain interest and goal attainment, as well as suppress emotions that are deemed unproductive (Hall & Goetz, 2013). In the modern context, ER is foundational to an ethic of self-management.

Regardless of the time and place, there are similar assumptions about emotions that warrant explicit efforts to control them. Persons need to regulate their emotions when (1) there is a discrepancy between the interpretation of what one is feeling and what one wants to feel whether it be pleasant or unpleasant (hedonic component); (2) there is a discrepancy between the interpretation of what one is feeling and what one understands that they ought to feel (moral component); (3) there is a discrepancy between the behavioral consequence of an emotion and what is deemed acceptable behavior in a particular context; (4) emotions are unwanted intruders, a consequence of something outside of one's control; and (5) emotions can be harnessed to achieve particular goals. With an exception of the last of these reasons, emotions are treated as pernicious and the source of conflicts. This view of emotions pervades contemporary discourse, as failures of ER are treated as the source of various problems (Fried, 2010; Gross, 2002). As reflected in the fifth reason, ER is also about activating and harnessing productive emotions. Regardless of whether emotions are sources of conflict or an energizing force, the ER literature identifies emotions as a key source of behavior, outcomes, and, therefore, in need of control.

4.2.3 The Points of Emotion Regulation

The understanding of an emotion will influence the conceptualization of how to control it. Researchers and philosophers contemplate the points at which emotions can be regulated, parties involved, and mechanisms responsible for regulation. The regulation of an emotion can happen in relationships between teacher and students, parents and children, students and students, and, arguably, as a self-regulatory process (Fried, 2011). Much of the ER discourse is committed to cultivating the self-regulatory kind, as this may seem less oppressive, transferrable, and adaptable than being regulated by others. The idea is that students need to be "empowered" to regulate themselves across all contexts in order to display adaptive behaviors. Given the diversity of types of emotions, levels of intensity, and behavioral manifestations, researchers argue that it is more efficient and effective for teachers to get students to regulate their own emotions (Macklem, 2007). In addition, ER is considered an adaptable skill that must be transferred to other contexts (Gross, 2002). So the questions guiding research and pedagogy are: (1) What are the points at which emotions can be regulated? (2) How can students learn to regulate their emotions in ways that are adaptable and effective for achieving learning goals?

The conceptualization of emotion and ER shapes the points at which control can be exercised. For example, let us consider James' (1884) conceptualization of emotion. According to James, an emotion can be viewed as a passive biophysical response that results from some sort of trigger; persons are predisposed to react to environmental triggers. Perhaps persons can be reconditioned to react differently to those triggers, but assuming these reactions are programmed into humans, exercising control at this point is difficult. However, if one knows the triggers that elicit certain emotional responses, then control can be exercised by avoiding or seeking these types of triggers. Thus, one point of regulating emotions is to control exposure to triggers so that certain emotions are experienced or their intensity is modulated. For example, if a student tends to respond with anxiety to math class, a regulatory strategy can be to avoid math. Of course, this regulatory strategy would likely be branded as maladaptive. Students are expected to be gritty; they are pathologized for not persevering in the face of challenges and struggles that schooling creates. One complexity here is that there is an expectation that students modulate debilitating emotions, such as academic performance anxiety, not by mitigating exposure to triggers but by changing their perceptions and reactions so that the triggers do not create the emotional effect.

Gross (2002) identifies five points at which emotions can be regulated. Four of them are what he calls "antecedent conditions." Like in James' model, Gross emphasizes the relationship between an environmental trigger, a perception, a biophysical response, and a behavior. In his theory, persons can exercise control by selecting the situation that is likely to evoke a targeted emotion. Or persons can exercise control over the features of a situation in order to evoke a targeted response. If one is in a situation from which it is difficult to be removed, such as in school, the exercise of control might involve an attempt to alter features of the situation. The relationship between an environmental trigger and emotions is preserved in this model, but if one knows the ways situations evoke particular responses, they can select or modify those situations to control their emotions. This strategy for regulation, however, is challenging as school contexts are not easy to change. Another point of regulation in Gross' model involves the attention to features of a situation. Rather than modifying, avoiding, or seeking certain situations, persons select what they pay attention to. Like in James' theory, there must be a perception, whether conscious or not, of an environmental trigger for an emotional response to occur: control of attention is the point of control over emotions.

Another point of control is at the point of an appraisal of a situation. Persons can interpret the meaning of a situation in order to control the emotional response. The idea is that emotions start with a response to a trigger, but the response is dependent on the meaning of that trigger. For example, if a test is perceived as high stakes and one's self-efficacy is low, anxiety might debilitate performance by decreasing motivation and eliciting a flight response. Change the perception of the test or oneself, a different emotion and set of behaviors might be elicited. If one changed the perception of the test to render it low stakes or increased self-efficacy for performing well on the exam, the idea is that one is less likely to experience debilitating anxiety. At this point, one's values and judgments are believed to serve as the source for an emotional experience. Control can be exercised by changing values and judgments. This type of control can also be exercised in the form of a reappraisal of the trigger, the emotion, or the response.

Another point of control over emotions is over the response. Some researchers describe this point of control as "reactive" (Graziano et al., 2010; Gross, 2011). Gross' theory is called *antecedent* because the regulatory process is directed at ensuring certain emotions are experienced rather than trying to reactively suppress or harness a particular emotion. At the behavioral phase of the ER process, control is exercised following an emotional experience in order to bring the body back to some form of stasis or to, at the very least, shape the behavioral manifestation of the emotion. Control may involve responses such as meditation, deep breathing, and journaling. Control may also involve a reflective process in which one recognizes an emotional experience and tries to shape the consequent behaviors. Some researchers contend that the emotional experience is not necessarily the problem for learning, but rather the behavioral manifestation (Campos et al., 2004). In this line of thinking, part of the problem is that students are not aware that their behaviors are a consequence of emotions. Thus, the goal is for students to recognize this relationship and that at one has a choice for a consequent behavior.

Success at emotional regulation via control of antecedent conditions can be challenging in schools given the limited opportunities to choose, change, and attend to situations. Emotionally regulating by controlling antecedents is impacted by compulsory schooling, the existence of school structures, and efforts by school personnel to protect and reinforce those structures. Students cannot change any situation in any way that they wish in order to produce a targeted emotion. The expectation is that students work on their emotions so that they can display adaptive behavior to existing contexts. The points of ER that seem most suitable for classroom learning are (re)appraisal and response modulation. For (re)appraisal, ER can be carried out by shaping students' perceptions to see situations in a particular way so that the right types of emotions can be experienced, or if an emotion is experienced that can lead to maladaptive behaviors, then students can exercise control by modulating the behavioral manifestation of the emotion.

4.2.4 Emotion Regulation in Schooling

Although historically absent from explicit schooling curricula and arguably not implemented enough today, initiatives and programs to support the development of students' ER are growing. Emotions and academic performance have a complex relationship. Certain emotions and their intensity and duration are implicated in curtailing or supporting academic performance. Whether an emotion has this effect depends on students and the context of their learning. For example, researchers have shown that negative emotions can overload working memory, making it difficult to process information and perform certain functions (Linnenbrink & Pintrich, 2000). A classic example relates to test anxiety. Some students may have mastered content but still perform poorly on exams because of anxiety. The theory is that anxiety overwhelms and consumes cognitive processing capabilities, making it difficult to remember information that one might otherwise remember in a low-stress state. Weare (2004) explains that when a student is under stress, the majority of the brain shuts down and reverts to defensiveness, self-preservation, fight, flight, and attention-seeking, which may not be conducive to learning in formal schooling contexts. Generally, certain levels of stress and anxiety are considered impediments to academic learning.

There is a widespread agreement that students can benefit from regulating their emotions and that such regulation is important for supporting adaptability in schools. Teachers are tasked with teaching students to regulate their own emotions to support optimal learning and achievement given contextual demands. The expectation is that teachers help students read contexts in ways to determine which emotions are facilitative and debilitative. ER programs are designed to get students to treat emotions as foundation to behavior and outcomes, evaluate which emotions are associated with which behaviors and outcomes, and harness or suppress emotions or behaviors in ways that enable them to achieve their learning goals.

ER is not just about enhancing performance via the control of emotions but reasoning about performance in terms of emotions. Not doing well in school might be interpreted as an emotional problem. Behaviors such as fighting, avoiding tasks, maladaptive risk-taking, and withdrawal from academic activities might be interpreted as being underpinned by problems with ER. The pedagogical strategy to address academic problems is to explicitly teach ER. One approach involves direct instruction of emotion strategies. Another might be to change students' perceptions, beliefs, and judgments. For example, fear and the experience of failure can produce debilitating stress and evoke maladaptive classroom behaviors (Isen, 2001; Sylwester, 1994; Zeidner, 1998). To address this problem, researchers suggest that students should adopt a GM. The assumption here is that if students treat intelligence as changeable and within their control, they are less likely to perceive performance as a static indication of their abilities. In this literature, the static rendering of abilities is the source of stress. Thus, the assumption is that a certain mindset can mitigate the fear of failure and encourage the pursuit of challenging tasks.

Another approach to teaching ER might involve teaching students coping mechanisms to mitigate the maladaptive behaviors that result from an emotional experience. In the case of stress, for example, the regulatory focus is on changing the coping mechanisms related to the experience of stress. One source of stress for students relates to the degree to which home and school culture align (Macklem, 2007). As Macklem (2007) argues, a mismatch between family culture and school culture can place considerable stress on children and the school. To address these challenges, the author suggests that teachers include strategies for stress reduction, provide emotion coaching, model ER, and directly teach coping strategies. The big idea here is that certain emotions can negatively impact learning and these negative impacts can be mitigated by changing students in some way, whether by providing coping strategies, changing perceptions, adopting a GM, or increasing self-efficacy, to name a few.

Although the dangers of emotional responses for school performance have been well researched, there is also research on ways emotions support the construction and remembering of experiences, which is beneficial in some learning contexts (Ludmer et al., 2011; Slywester, 1994; Tyng et al., 2017). Activities that draw out emotions via simulations, role playing, and cooperation may help with the recall of information processed during those activities. In addition, emotions can help increase attention and encoding of information (Tyng et al., 2017). Psychologists use the terms hot and cold cognition to describe the role of emotion in cognitive processing (Ferree & Merrill, 2000). Hot cognition refers to the biophysical arousal surrounding a cognitive event, whereas cold cognition refers to the cognitive processing that occurs independent of an emotional experience. In some situations, hot cognition supports recall. However, the strong presence of emotions is also implicated in competing with critical thinking (Ochsner & Gross, 2005). Herein lies the goal of teaching ER in schools: cultivating practices, skills, and thought processes that enable students to identify the emotional underpinnings of performance and to strategically manage that performance by controlling the emotion.

4.3 Critical Analysis

There are compelling reasons to value and endorse an explicit curricular and pedagogical focus on students' ER. As Boler (1999) commented, it seems reasonable to celebrate the integration of emotion in schooling because it had seldom been an explicit consideration and was often treated as less important than the kinds of cognitive processing valued for academic tasks. As Fried (2011) argues, it was not until emotions were treated as enhancing cognitive processing that they became integrated into conversations about schooling. Attention, memory, decision-making, motivation, and relatedness were seen as inextricably tied to emotions, which if managed well could improve performance. It was this discursive shift that Fried argues made emotions of interest to researchers and practitioners. This shift might be welcomed by those who have humanistic commitments to teach the WC by avoiding the isolation of only certain parts as objects of pedagogy. Rather than strictly trying to cultivate certain kinds of reasoning processes and rote engagement, the pedagogical focus is on teaching students to suppress or evoke emotions that can support their adaptation to schooling contexts. The hesitation that Boler expresses about embracing the integration of emotion in schooling has to do with the function and purpose of ER.

Bringing emotion to the forefront of the pedagogical task is to recognize students' humanness for the purpose of targeting what can be thought of as a private experience in order to achieve institutional goals. That is, emotions are part of the curriculum now because they are tied to the adaptation to school, as well as considered a necessary skill for modern work environments. Displaying certain types, intensities, and durations of emotions are associated with good character, adaptive functioning, efficiency, and productivity. ER tends to be treated as necessary for the development of certain types of students with particulars skills and traits.

The integration of emotions in schooling for these instrumental purposes aligns with the neoliberal logic of governance. As Boler (1999) points out, what was once thought to be a private experience was subject to the gaze of authorities who are charged with making an explicit effort to help students use emotions in order to make themselves adaptable to schooling contexts. Persons are supposed to learn to manage themselves in ways to optimize and maximize their learning by controlling their emotions. This type of management might seem like an exercise of freedom and empowerment by providing persons with the knowledge and tools to exercise control over their "bodily disturbances." Persons are not treated as passive responders to environmental triggers, nor are their behaviors a direct and uncontrolled consequence of a physical state. Rather the assumption in the ER literature is that persons can learn to use particular strategies to affect their perceptions, beliefs, and behaviors – all of which have implications for an emotional experience and the consequent behavior. The harnessing of students' emotional regulatory capacity to respond to institutional demands and achieve learning goals is a defining feature of neoliberal governance.

Neoliberal governance is about targeting persons' desires, choices, aspirations, and thoughts for the purpose of generating particular behaviors (Lorenzini, 2018; Ria et al., 2003; Rose & Abi-Rached, 1999). According to Lorenzini (2018), neoliberal governance functions by cultivating and harnessing the self-regulatory capabilities of persons so that they can strategically respond to conditions of and changes to the environment. The author points to adaptability as a key feature of the ideal neoliberal subject. Adaptability can be considered a natural and automatic, and possibly unintentional, human response to evolving and negotiating social, ecological, and psychological contexts (Piaget, 1976). Broadly, this concept can capture small changes in ecologies and species over long periods of time. However, adaptability is also considered a cognitive, emotional, and behavioral skill that can be developed and controlled to affect what one becomes, does, and feels in changing conditions (Fendler, 2001; Griffin & Hesketh, 2003; Gross, 1998; Trilling & Fadel, 2009). Researchers tend to use the notions of adaptive and maladaptive to describe students' success or dysfunction at ER, respectively. If students display the right type, intensity, and duration of an emotion that enables them to achieve learning goals, they are likely considered adaptive.

4.3.1 Adaptability

Adaptability is treated as a key twenty-first century competence that can be developed via formal schooling (Greenberg et al., 2003; Levin, 2015). A consistent message about the twenty-first century is that it is fast changing, evolving, and unpredictable. Such conditions can generate a number of problematic emotions such as anxiety and stress which can be connected to withdrawal, resistance, and a lack of productivity. However, researchers reason that if persons were adaptable, they can moderate anxiety associated with change and commit with a positive attitude to meeting any challenges associated with change (Bradberry, 2020; Durlak et al., 2011; Waters & Sroufe, 1983). Waters and Sroufe (1983) describe emotionally competent people as those who have the abilities "to generate and coordinate flexible, adaptive responses to demands and to generate and capitalize on opportunities in the environment" (p. 80). Writing for the World Economic Forum, Bradberry (2020) asserts that adaptability is made possible with skillful ER, which is associated with communication, collaboration, curiosity, creativity, persistence, and even critical thinking – all competencies and character traits that are repeated in representations of ideal twenty-first century workers. The idea is that economic conditions change rapidly and are arguably unpredictable. The ideal person needs to understand and respond to those conditions with a positive attitude, calm deliberations, and eager persistence.

Adaptability is generally regarded as an essential noncognitive skill that is associated with success in schools and beyond. It is generally considered as something that persons can develop, control, perfect, and strategically employ in contexts to mitigate maladaptive emotions, promote adaptive emotions, and, therefore, persist with and achieve goals. In this narrative, ER supports adaptability and can limit the experience of emotions, and their consequent behaviors, that are maladaptive. ER is about supporting students' intentional and orchestrated adaptations to environmental conditions. The ER literature is explicitly committed to achieving this type of adaptive self-management. The hope is that regardless of the situation and whatever changes occur, persons will work toward ensuring that certain emotional experiences do not lead to maladaptive emotions and behaviors.

4.3.1.1 *A Paradox of Autonomy and Control*

Managing adaptations to change environmental conditions might be interpreted as an act of self-control and autonomy. The idea is that the environment does not determine what persons feel and do, but rather they rely on choice-making to decide what they feel and do. In this line of reasoning, the problematic distinction between rationality and emotion is preserved. As part of this distinction, rationality is treated as the mechanism for willful control, whereas emotions are treated as *untamed* and *wild* responses resulting from the body. Although this distinction is worth lengthy critical consideration, the paradox that is discussed here pertains to notions of control, autonomy, and personal responsibility. The so-called rational, calm deliberations that are supposed to signify freedom from environmental and biological determinants are also what render persons docile.

The strategic, intentional, and self-managed adaptations that signify autonomy and control also signify docility to a particular management logic. Consider that to make personal adjustments that are deemed adaptive, one must be attuned to environmental conditions. They must correctly assess the demands of the environment and exercise strategies to evoke those emotions that can support one's success at meeting, or even exceeding, those demands. This type of relationship to the environment is one of the ways in which neoliberal governance works (Fendler, 2001; Lorenzini, 2018). The attunement to environmental conditions and the strategic management of responses to those conditions are what render persons governable. The neoliberal self is governable from a distance, responding to changes introduced into the environment. Lorenzini (2018) states, "the neoliberal art of government heavily intervenes on the social field in order to shape the conduct of individuals, inciting them to act in a specific way and modifying their environment so as to alter their behavior" (p. 156). For this type of governance to work, Lorenzini argues that persons must act on themselves in accordance with environmental demands. Docility can be understood first as the disposition to assess environmental conditions and the commitment to validate that assessment and coordinate emotions and behavior accordingly.

4.3.1.2 Reading Context and Doing It Correctly: Emotion Rules and Culture

The good, productive, and emotionally regulated person disciplines attention in order to calculate the needs and demands of a context. There are particular values and norms that inform the interpretation of demands and needs of a situation. In order to contribute to adaptive ER, persons must have a particular reading and judgment of those demands to ensure that their emotions and behaviors conform to them. This starting point of ER orients persons to the evaluation of contexts to figure out which emotions are valued and permissible. If students read a context and conclude that anger is needed to challenge the asymmetrical operation of power in classrooms and schools, they will likely be pathologized and considered maladaptive. In schools there are what researchers call "emotional rules" or "emotional culture" (e.g., Boler, 1999; Zembylas, 2006). Students' reading of context must be informed by and aligned with these rules and culture.

Emotional culture refers "to the collective attitudes, meanings, and beliefs that a group of people (e.g., teachers) maintains toward emotions and their expressions and includes ways in which institutions reflect and encourage or discourage these attitudes" (Zembylas, 2006, p. 202). The adaptiveness or maladaptiveness of ER is determined by conformity to emotional rules or a culture of emotions. These rules can evolve, transform, and be negotiated, but still reflect an organizing framework to judge and evaluate students' adaptability. Culture, ideology, and politics have a direct impact on the shaping of emotions through these rules that inform appropriate emotional experience and expression (Boddice, 2017; Boler, 1999; Gerhards, 1989; Zemblyas, 2006). Zembylas (2006) contends that emotion rules are "held together by a network of socialization practices that are influenced by political, economic, social, and other educational factors" (p. 203). The point here is that emotion norms and culture serve particular interests and students must not question those interests, but rather regulate their emotions in accordance with them. ER is about ensuring that persons can conform to emotional rules, which that serve political and ideological purposes.

Emotional rules reflect techniques for the discipline of emotional expression and communication. These rules provide a basis for judging deviant and normal emotional expressions. Students' ability to conform to and manage their emotions in accordance with these rules determines adaptability. Ford and Mauss (2015) state, "emotion regulation may be adaptive when it is consistent with its cultural context, and maladaptive when it is inconsistent" (p. 2). The effectiveness of ER comes down to the degree to which students can adapt to the culture norms and rules of schooling context, which requires a reading and interpretation of what emotional expression is needed and required. Aside from being governed by the reading of context, this commitment makes persons easily governable. If one develops that commitment to assess and respond to the environment, one only has to introduce changes in the context in order to generate self-managed responses.

4.3.1.3 Performing and Enacting Regulatory Scripts
The distinction between adaptive and maladaptive ER suggests that students may not assess or respond correctly to environmental demands. They must not only learn to assess contextual demands but also figure out how to respond accordingly. In the context of ER, students must be attuned to what emotions are acceptable to be felt and expressed in any given context. They must aspire to have emotional congruity with the norms and culture of the context. Moreso, they must have the strategies for evoking and suppressing those emotions that are and are not in alignment with the norms and cultures of schooling. This process begins with being attuned to the environment and reading it so as to inform oneself of what they need to do in order to function and be adaptive in that context. This type of governing from a distance works only if persons have strategies for responding adaptively to environmental conditions. If students do not have ER scripts and strategies already, they must learn them. In schools,

teachers are in positions to judge and evaluate which emotions and ER efforts are adaptive or maladaptive. Such evaluations can provide information on which students might need interventions. Not all types of ER are valued and validated in schooling contexts. Those who are deemed to exhibit maladaptive ER must learn strategies for controlling their emotions in the right way.

A paradox of adaptive ER is that autonomous self-management requires acceptance of environmental conditions and the expertise of others for developing and evaluating ER. Adaptability involves accepting the environmental condition and conducting oneself in accordance with that condition in ways that conform to the rules of the context. A feature of the ideal representation of the neoliberal self is an attunement to an awareness of environmental conditions, coupled with the adjustments of thoughts, behaviors, aspirations, and desires in accordance with those conditions. Often, these responses must be coached, modeled, and explicitly taught. Personal control is recognized as effectiveness at responding to and conducting oneself in accordance with environmental demands and conditions. The paradox is that although these adaptations might be considered an act of autonomy, they are dependent on the reading and conditions of a context, which can be artificially changed and structured to produce a particular behavior.

The argument is that managing adaptive emotional responses requires students to be attuned to environmental demands and to develop the scripts to ensure that their emotions enable them to adapt to those demands. The idea is that students must learn to detect and embrace change with a positive attitude, calm deliberations, and eager persistence. Such adaptations need to be explicitly and systematically managed, which is made possible through explicit curricular efforts to cultivate ER. Persons must see environmental conditions in a particular way, adapt themselves to those conditions, and be subject to evaluations about their adaptive or maladaptive emotions and behaviors. There is an understanding that this process is intentional and strategically orchestrated to make learning in schools efficient, effective, and self-regulated. Working on students' emotional lives in order to promote self-management is a key feature of neoliberal governance. In this regard, studying and controlling emotions to adapt to school reflects autonomy within a particular management logic. Thus, ER is not an unrestricted instance of autonomy and control. Instances of ER are arguably evidence of the effective operation of neoliberal governance.

4.3.1.4 Habit and Intentionality

There is a potentially dangerous by-product of a neoliberal narrative of control and freedom. In a neoliberal context, students are made to be over-responsibilized, which means that they are treated as rational choice-makers who with the right information can manage their lives in ways to increase their value and stay on a continuous path of growth. Any issues with self-management via choice-making have to do with information, not the underlying neoliberal logic of personal responsibility. The attribution of personal responsibility is particularly a problem in the ER discourse. A neoliberal ethos lends itself well to the assumption that if students are adaptive, rather than maladaptive, then they necessarily exercised ER. So students who persist with challenges, take risks, and have a positive attitude are regulating their emotions. If students display valued types of curiosity and pursue creative solutions to problems in a calm, deliberate way, one might conclude that they are regulating emotions. If students conform to school demands and perform accepted behaviors, they might be regarded as emotionally regulated and competent.

Herein lies a particular danger with neoliberal thinking: it invites a way of reasoning about adaptation and maladaptation that may overstate personal responsibility, intentionality, and control over actions and performance. Neoliberal thinking invites a way to calibrate persons and use those calibrations to explain performance. It is commonplace now to evaluate persons in terms of their emotional competence and use those evaluations to reason about the forces, mechanisms, and processes responsible for performance. It is common to describe emotionality as a competence or skill that is not only responsible for performance but also that can be developed and strategically used to adapt to schooling contexts. This rationalization about engagement and outcomes ignores habit, instinct, and automaticity.

A consequence of this line of thinking is that failing to adapt to school becomes a disease or pathology, one that is explainable in terms of failure at ER. Students who are maladaptive have emotional problems and executive functioning deficiencies. The corollary conclusion is that these students had parents who did not provide the right types of experiences to support optimal ER. Too often, emotions are overstated as the source of academic outcomes; not performing in particular ways can be regarded as emotional problems. This way of thinking is captured in the following statement, "many students lack social-emotional competencies and become less connected to school as they progress from elementary to middle to high school, and this lack of connection negatively affects their academic performance, behavior, and health" (Durlak et al., p. 405).

4.3 Critical Analysis

The authors reason that a lack of connection to schooling results from a lack of social-emotional competence. This lack of connection has nothing to do with cultural incongruence with schools or resistance to hegemonic discourse. Schooling is normalized as a neutral, value-free context to which students must be connected and adapt; otherwise, they have emotional problems, lack emotional competence, and fail at ER. This way of reasoning contributes to the responsibilization of personhood for outcomes and normalization of particular social and political orders in schooling. A common critique of neoliberal thinking is that so-called pathology for maladaptations is a result of poor self-management and not the context to which students are expected to adapt.

This attribution can make it difficult to recognize that some contexts may affect students in different ways, requiring varying degrees of ER. Students have to regulate emotions if there is a discrepancy between that emotion and its expression with what is permissible in a particular context. If there were no discrepancies, then there would be no need for regulation. If there was a discrepancy, the burden is on the child to modulate the emotion and its behavioral manifestation. Not performing acceptable emotions and behaviors in order to be adaptive can be treated as psychological and behavioral pathology. This line of thought can conceal the operation of power and limit the usefulness of emotions as sources of knowledge for unjust social orders. Consider that researchers make the case that when students' home culture misaligns with school, they may have maladaptive emotional responses that need to be regulated (Ford & Mauss, 2015; Macklem, 2007). Macklem (2007) states, "When a child's family culture does not match the predominant culture of the school, considerable stress can be placed on the child, the family, and the school. Issues around culture, gender, and various student-handicapping conditions make helping children develop emotion regulation a considerable challenge" (p. xxi). Some students might have different experiences in school that require different amounts of ER and some may not have to do it much at all because of cultural congruence. If some students are successful within a schooling context, it is dangerous to assume that they were strategically adapting by regulating their emotions. It is also dangerous to assume that students who are branded as maladaptive experience regulatory dysfunctions or have the same regulatory burden as others. Although adaptability is regarded as a positive quality, a concern is that some contexts can be dehumanizing, oppressive, unjust, and unequal. What might be branded as "maladaptive" emotions and their associated behaviors can be sources of knowledge about the emotional rules and educational structures. However, efforts to develop ER can be ways to support amenability and conformity to those contexts. Neoliberal thinking involves pathologizing students for their maladaptive emotional responses. Furthermore, failing to adapt to contexts is failure at ER and remedied through interventions to make ER explicit, strategic, adaptive, and effective.

4.3.1.5   The Character of Neoliberalism
Although emotional rules can be negotiated within classrooms and schools, the current discourse in education certainly communicates a value for particular emotion rules. Some of these rules relate to particular character traits. The demands of neoliberal marketing forces require a particular type of emotional life, mandating that students and teachers adopt a prescribed set of emotions such as positive attitudes toward change (cf. Ria et al., 2003). Not only are persons supposed to be attuned to change and have a positive attitude toward it, but they must also display particular character traits in relation to that change. In particular, there are values for perpetual improvement, mastery, creativity, and risk-taking that can generate counterproductive emotional responses. For example, a key feature of GM involves embracing and learning from "failure," which can create debilitating anxiety and invite task-avoidance. GM involves accepting and responding to criticism and consequences in positive ways. Persons are not supposed to allow defensive emotional responses, which can be maladaptive by curtailing ability to use criticism and consequences as information for improvement. Failure and criticism can invite emotional responses that hinder academic engagement, volition, and performance. ER is supposed to help students suppress those responses and possible behaviors that limit the usefulness of failure and criticism. Being able to suppress defensive emotional responses and use "failure" to learn is key for entrepreneurialism and managing the consequences of taking risks (Dweck, 2006; Fang He et al., 2018). The idea is that students treat criticism as a source of knowledge to help them improve. They must pursue that improvement and be grateful for having the opportunity to obtain information to help them improve. Students must be optimistic and have positive attitudes toward criticism and consequences.

Exercising ER to suppress anger, frustration, and fear in response to criticism makes good sense. Students can recognize that schools are ideological places with particular values and norms. Therefore, criticism about the effectiveness of conforming to those rules does not have to indicate static qualities, which is associated with negative emotional responses.

Students can disassociate their sense of competence and being from schooling performance. The power of schooling to define selfhood can be limited and mediated. However, in the discourse on character and NCS, mitigating maladaptive emotional responses to criticism is not about challenging the authority of schooling to define persons. Indeed, authority is preserved. ER is about preserving that authority and rendering students docile to it so that they can receive criticism calmly and deliberately to inform their strategies of self-improvement. When researchers talk about developing the right types of character so that "failure" and criticism are used to improve, the message is that (1) the evaluation of performance of failure is valid; (2) students should accept and even welcome this evaluation; and (3) students should change to improve performance. This message can also be read in the following way: ER can help to ensure that students are self-regulating their docile response to systems of measurement and institutional authorities.

4.3.2 Skill and Commodification

Persons are supposed to control emotions in order to mitigate stress and frustration from failure and to assuage fear from taking risks and being wrong while problem-solving. They must mitigate emotional responses that might result from peer ridicule in the face of academic challenges. What we can glean from these expectations is that neoliberal values underpin specific ideas about what it means to be a good, productive student. There are explicit efforts to cultivate character traits and management techniques in alignment with this ideal student. Curriculum and pedagogy are set up to cultivate particular character traits. The demands of the neoliberal market require students to be a particular way and ensure that they govern themselves via ER to achieve that way of being. Treated this way, ER is a skill that can be developed in order to bring value to oneself so that one may achieve a particular way of being that is deemed necessary for the modern world. As Zembylas (2007) noted, treating ER in this manner is a way to conceptualize emotions in terms of capital. He references the work of Gendron (2004) when he describes emotional capital:

> Gendron (2004) refers particularly to the importance of emotional capital as a set of resources (emotional competencies) that are useful for an individual's cognitive, personal, social and economic development. He argues that emotional capital is crucial in knowledge and self-management for companies, schools and organisations in the increasingly complex and competitive global workplace .... The emphasis is on how individuals can 'use'

emotional capital, i.e. how it can be valuable in facilitating certain actions .... Therefore, an important component of emotional capital, according to Gendron, is its successful management through learning the appropriate emotional competencies – that is, controlling undesirable emotions and acquiring the desirable ones. (Zembylas, 2007, p.456)

For this way of thinking, regulating emotions is rendered a skill to manage the self in contexts that can bring optimal value to oneself. This type of management is self-policing in ways that enable a person to conform to particular rules. The rules for emotional expression and suppression are aligned with neoliberal values for ideal personhood. By rendering ER as a skill, Zembylas (2007) argues that ER is "stripped of its social and political context, and cultural differences or social hierarchies are not accounted for in the manifestation of emotional practices" (p. 456).

One of the more glaring neoliberal underpinnings of ER discourse is the commodification of ER as a skill. Representations of the ideal twenty-first-century worker include ER. In the modern economic context, which shapes values communicated in schools, there are calls to make persons entrepreneurial, risk-takers, adaptable, and collaborative. In a neoliberal context, schools serve economic purposes. One way this manifests is through support for the cultivation of human capital, which is the knowledge, skills, and dispositions that can enable persons to efficiently and effectively perform specific functions within the economy (Chernyshenko et al., 2018; Schleicher, 2018).

4.4 Conclusion

The words used in relation to emotions are not assumed to be simply names for emotion entities, describing preexisting things or coherent self-characteristics. Rather, these words are seen as actions or ideological practices serving specific purposes as part of the process of creating and negotiating reality. Emotions and their regulation are not neutral, value-free products of an advancing science. Rather ER appeals to historically situated sensitivities, styles of reasoning, rules for conduct, ways of ordering persons, and specific norms and values. This explanation brackets debates about the conceptualization, mechanisms, measurement, and teaching of ER. Instead, the function, value, and ideological underpinning are highlighted. Thought about this way, the question – why has the imperative to value, reward, validate, and cultivate students' ER become important in schooling? – can be answered by examining social, cultural, historical, philosophical, and political contexts.

4.4 Conclusion

The growth of ER coincides with the spread of neoliberal ideology. Neoliberalism emerged in the 1970s and started to reshape schooling policy and practice in the 1980s (Davies & Bansel, 2007). The coincidence between the growth of ER and neoliberalism is not arbitrary. Neoliberal governance is characterized by an intense examination of being in order to manage life to achieve a particular goal. ER discourse is a tool for examining, interpreting, and managing the self. ER is often referred to as a skill – a key feature of human capital for the twenty-first century. Conceptualized this way, ER is a key feature of neoliberal selfhood. In contemporary education discourse, behavioral and academic problems are treated as consequences of emotional dysregulation, which is the inability to display the emotions that are appropriate in a given context. This way of reasoning about school success is a modern invention, one that has taken a strong hold in schools over the last three decades.

Emotions are used as a way to organize the private lives of persons in ways to achieve particular goals. In neoliberal discourse, the regulation of emotions is to signify particular character traits and support persons' efforts to conform to emotion rules. Students are expected to turn their gaze inward and outward. They must read environmental demands and discern emotion rules. They must evaluate themselves to judge whether or not their emotions are enabling them to conform to emotion rules. If there are maladaptive emotions, the management must be exercised to suppress those emotions. Or if certain contexts require the presence of emotion, students must evoke and harness those emotions. In this description of the process of ER, there is a good deal of prescription and conformity. It is a mistake to assume that the pedagogical efforts to shape ER are unequivocally for the good of students and are about recognizing students' humanity independent of a governing agenda.

CHAPTER 5

Lifelong Learning
Sentencing Learners to Life

5.1 Introduction

Researchers refer to the modern context as a *learning society* (Field, 2000; Illeris, 2018; Jarvis, 2008; Oliver, 2019). This characterization captures the idea that contemporary economic, political, technological, cultural, and institutional structures rapidly change. In conjunction with the purported pace of change, availability of and access to information continues to increase. Taking these conditions together, the assumption is that persons must acquire, display, and perform learning competence by upskilling and reskilling to meet changing demands. In a learning society, knowledge acquisition alone is inadequate to function. Without continuous, flexible, and adaptable learning, persons may find themselves obsolete to meet the demands of the twenty-first century. Harari (2016) warns that rapid structural change without corresponding, adaptable persons threatens to give rise to what he calls the *useless class*. In this narrative, the notion of lifelong learning (LLL) has appeal.

LLL can be defined as the self-directed, intentional, and strategic pursuit of the acquisition of knowledge, skills, and dispositions that enable one to pursue goals throughout the lifespan (Field, 2000). Being a lifelong learner is regarded as the normal, healthy, and desired condition for people, irrespective of age, class, gender, ethnic background, or other preconditions (Berglund, 2008). Although most notably lauded for its economic value, the prevailing assumption is that LLL supports civic engagement, improvement of health, achievement of happiness, and self-determination in ill-defined and changing contexts. Given the value and broad appeal, there tends to be general acceptance of the imperative to support LLL in both formal and informal educational environments from early childhood through adulthood.

Although critical discourse is related to LLL, this ideological underpinning tends to be ignored in policy and practice, especially surrounding NCS. The purpose of this chapter is to highlight the alignment between the modern conception of the lifelong learner with neoliberal selfhood, showing that LLL functions to normalize, validate, and support a problematic vision of being, schooling, and opportunity. The argument advanced in this chapter is that LLL reflects a specific type of learning that is instrumentally tied to producing persons who are infinitely flexible and governable. The ideal lifelong learner analyzes action and calibrates qualities to ensure that the consumption of experience renders one flexible, adaptable, and useful – making it possible to be infinitely responsive to structural conditions and demands.

Learning throughout life cannot be whimsical, capricious, and presumed but must reflect strategic and flexible adaptations, which are responsible for productivity, efficiency, economic prosperity, happiness, health, and democratic engagement. LLL normalizes the trope of the self-governing and strategic agent who is attuned and responsive to environmental configurations. In order to be considered a lifelong learner, this agent must develop, acquire, and perform certain competencies, qualities, and dispositions to pursue learning goals. LLL is a kind of cognitive capital that purportedly enables persons to take responsibility for their place in the socioeconomic hierarchy. This conception of the lifelong learner normalizes and prescribes a way of being that aligns with neoliberal selfhood and validates a specific perception of economic structures.

5.2 From Adults to Children

It might seem strange to associate LLL with neoliberal selfhood, especially given that researchers and theorists argue that people naturally learn throughout their lives and do not need any particular intervention to cultivate this process. Learning throughout life can be considered a presumed and definable feature of persons that can help realize multiple visions of persons and purposes of schooling. Field (2000) captures this position by stating: "Lifelong learning is a beautifully simple idea. It is obvious that people learn throughout their lives. From our earlier attempts to walk and talk, our capacity to adapt and learn extends through a remarkable variety of new abilities and knowledge, and it can be almost as unconscious as breathing" (p. 1).

It is difficult to find a definition or theory of learning that does not assume a lifelong, continual process. Jarvis (2007), a well-known researcher on adult education, admits that his definition of learning is not much different from his definition of LLL, which he defines as:

the combination of processes throughout a lifetime whereby the whole person – body (genetic, physical and biological) and mind (knowledge, skills, attitudes, values, emotions, beliefs and senses) – experiences social situations, the perceived content of which is then transformed cognitively, emotively or practically (or through any combination) and integrated into the individual person's biography resulting in a continually changing (or more experienced) person. (p. 1)

Jarvis notes that this definition was slightly adapted from his conception of learning in order to explicitly include the lifespan component but did not change the processes and components involved. According to Jarvis, the learning process is the same for young children and adults, and although it plays out differently across the lifespan, this process is continual. Jarvis argues that as long as there is consciousness, there is learning. Although the conception of consciousness is philosophically complex, Jarvis makes this distinction in order to avoid privileging the view that learning happens only when we can articulate its occurrence. The idea is that learning happens all the time even if not immediately articulated.

Despite the arguable naturalness of learning throughout life, the notion of LLL as a goal for which to strive in formal and informal contexts has been around for decades. Researchers and policy makers are committed to understanding and implementing structures to support the development of LLL. Formal study began in the 1970s but some researchers contend that there is evidence of LLL in policy and practice as early as the 1920s (Centeno, 2011). Regardless of the time of its emergence, the discourse of LLL has primarily been about adults. The focus was on figuring how to structure programs for adult learning and to understand the factors that affected participation and success in those programs. This work tended to be about economic productivity, which involved learning new content to switch careers, learning to adapt to technological changes for current careers, or merely learning to improve performance in relation to current work structures. The image of the economically useful adult informs this discourse. Although generally centered on supporting adult learning for economic usefulness, Fejas and Nicoll (2008) argue that the notion of LLL has surfaced and resurfaced in policy and research over the last several decades with varying emphases, connotations, and versions of the adult learner.

5.2.1 *A Vision for the Ideal Adult*

In the modern narrative of LLL, persons must operate beyond unfocused curiosity, caprice, and passivity and display behaviors that are recognized as intentional, active, and strategic (Bollington, 2015; Laal & Salamati, 2012; Pearse & Dunwoody, 2013). Strategic and intentional learning must be directed at the development of twenty-first century competencies, which include critical thinking, creativity, self-direction, problem-solving, and collaboration (Boyatzis, 2009; Collins, 2009; OECD, 2012; P21, 2009; Pearse & Dunwoody, 2013). In addition to these features, the ideal adult learner is persistent, entrepreneurial, risk-taking, and a *willing* learner (Buckinham-Shum & Crick, 2016; Kakouris, 2015). Pearse and Dunwoody (2013) describe the lifelong learner as tenacious, reflective, metacognitive, a divergent thinker, self-efficacious, and collaborative. The Organisation for Economic Development (OECD) has long endorsed educational commitments to fostering LLL (OECD, 2001, 2012, 2019). In an OECD (2012) report, lifelong learners are described as exhibiting or working toward higher-order thinking skills, such as (1) generating, processing, and sorting complex information; (2) thinking systematically and critically; (3) making decisions while weighing different forms of evidence; (4) asking meaningful questions about different subjects; (5) being adaptable and flexible to new information; (6) being creative; (7) justifying and solving real-world problems; (8) acquiring a deep understanding of complex concepts; (9) demonstrating media literacy; and (10) fluency with social and communication skills. These features are supposed to enable persons to be adaptable and flexible – two quintessential features of the lifelong learner.

It is clear that in contemporary discourse the lifelong learner has specific competencies and dispositions that resemble representations of ideal persons for twenty-first century environments. The alignment with these competencies immediately reveals an entanglement with neoliberal selfhood. Twenty-first century competencies detail the cognitive capital that is required for persons to make themselves useful for and responsive to modern conditions (Partnership for 21st Century Skills, 2009; Vassallo, 2014; World Economic Forum, 2017). There is a general acceptance of the representation of the twenty-first century as rapidly changing and in need of flexible persons. Concomitantly, there is generally the acceptance of the representation of ideal persons for this context. With an established representation of the modern world and ideal persons, researchers are focused on how to support the development of LLL so that persons can approximate the ideal learner. The question with which policy makers and researchers grapple is: how can formal and informal experiences be structured to support the enactment and development of LLL so that persons can govern their flexible adaptations to environmental conditions?

Increasingly, early childhood formal and informal educational experiences have become answers to this question (e.g., see Allvin, 2017; Bollington, 2015; Kautz et al., 2014; OECD, 2012; Park, 2019).

5.2.2 Realizing That Vision: Cradle to Grave

Emerging strongly in the discourse is the emphasis on early childhood experiences. In the mid 1990s and continuing through today, the target for LLL interventions has broadened to include young children prior to entering school, in addition to extending throughout formal K-16 contexts. As Bollington (2015), who is Vice President of Research and Learning at the Lego Foundation, claims:

> There is a growing understanding that the gap between the outputs of our education system and the needs of employers are not a failure of the last few years of formal schooling alone, but the cumulative consequence of years of education built upon a *foundation* set down in early childhood. In other words, the problem – and the answer – starts early. (emphasis added, p. 28)

The foundation metaphor is used frequently in the LLL discourse when it refers to targeting young children. Like Bollington, the OECD (2012) contends, "Laying a foundation that cultivates lifelong, self-directed learning starts at an early age . . . it is actually the knowledge, skills, values and attitudes acquired during the early life-stages that provide the foundation for the lifelong learning habit. Schools are pivotal organisations for laying such foundations" (p. 9).

The logic is that carefully structured educational environments with teachers trained in a specific way are essential for cultivating those qualities needed to be adult lifelong learners. Along with the myriad other teacher responsibilities, they are now tasked with implementing environments that will lead to the cultivation of a specific set of dispositions and competencies that have a lifelong impact.

It is not just in schools, however, that LLL must be cultivated. The OECD charges that learning it must extend from the "cradle to the grave" in both formal and informal contexts (p. 2). Realizing the vision of LLL is not just about expanding the ages in which interventions are implemented but creating conformity of purpose across all spheres of life, including vertical and horizontal commitments. The former are organized and orchestrated efforts to foster LLL that start at home, continue through K-16, and extend to vocational and professional settings. Efforts to develop and practice LLL must happen across the lifespan. Horizontal commitments are organized and orchestrated efforts to shape all contexts in that given moment. Depending on age, these efforts might involve teachers, parents, community members, employers, and coaches. The idea is that LLL develops through concerted efforts across domains of life. The call for vertical and horizontal commitments is about expanding the reach of LLL to occur throughout the lifespan and in every social sphere.

5.2.3 Pedagogical Structure

Although there is a call for vertical and horizontal alignments, the sphere that researchers and policy makers can most influence is schools. There are repeated calls to shape schooling practices and curricula to target the cultivation of students' self-directed LLL (Bollington, 2015; Boyatzis et al., 2019; London, 2011; OECD, 2012). London (2011) characterizes such initiatives as informed by commitments to empower students. The logic is that preparation for the learning society involves creating specific types of environments in order to develop students' competencies, dispositions, and capabilities to learn in and outside of school. In this paradigm, the transmission of knowledge is treated as counterproductive. Pedagogically, researchers and policy makers generally agree that LLL best develops in child-centered contexts (Ali, 2019; Allvin, 2017; Bollington, 2015; Yehia & Gunn, 2018).

This commitment is predicated on the ontological assumption that students have natural dispositions and proclivities that if expressed, guided, and disciplined can help realize the vision of the ideal learner. Bollington (2015) captures this line of thinking. He states:

> The youngest children have an in-built curiosity to learn and ask questions, to learn through play. When a toddler repeatedly asks 'why' or works with other children to create a city using building blocks, they are setting down the basic foundations of inquiry-based, active learning. They are learning by asking their own questions rather than learning rote answers to other people's questions. This is the foundation of lifelong learning, an approach that should continue throughout school, not stop at the kindergarten. (p. 28)

This view of children as naturally curious and inquisitive is fairly common in learning theories and assumptions about persons (e.g., Allvin, 2017; Montessori, 1948; Piaget and Inhelder, 1969). If children naturally display these behaviors, then the pedagogical task is to identify and create environments that recognize, validate, reward, enhance, and discipline those dispositions. This commitment is referred to as *child-centered* because what is presumed as natural in students drives the learning process.

Ontological assumptions are important for thinking about teaching LLL. If one concludes that the dispositions for LLL are natural, then supporting LLL is about limiting pedagogical constraints so that those dispositions can be expressed. The idea is that expression of dispositions will turn into a lifelong habit if students are given choice, autonomy, and control. This way of thinking is not unlike a Montessorian philosophy that is based on the idea that students' will develop cognitive skills and self-regulation if teacher direction and control is limited. For this view, the less restrictive the environment, the more likely natural dispositions will manifest and develop in valued ways. Others might not be as trusting of the developmental process and argue that children have natural dispositions and competences for LLL but they need structure and explicit guidance. Curtis and Carter (2011) capture this way of thinking:

> Children are natural learners, but they need to have their internal, intrinsic motivation to be lifelong learners reinforced. You see their eagerness to learn beginning in infancy. Supporting this eagerness should be our real readiness agenda! As children become preschoolers, initial academic experiences should fill them with joy, not dread or boredom. Watch them for signs of eager desire to learn, and look for everyday ways to support these dispositions as you embed literacy, math, and science into everything children do. (p. 183)

Curtis and Carter attribute certain dispositions to learning as natural. However, as the authors contend, teachers must validate those dispositions and direct them toward the learning of school subjects. In this context, effective teaching for LLL involves associating the "natural" love for learning to school subjects. The so-called desire, joy, intrinsic value, and eagerness for learning are not enough to count as a lifelong learner.

5.2.4 *Training Educators*

Although there are different ontological and pedagogical assumptions, researchers and policy makers tend to agree that children have natural dispositions that are relevant for LLL and that teaching environments need to be set up to ensure those dispositions develop in certain ways. There is not a great deal of debate and controversy on pedagogical structures and LLL. Allvin (2017), who is the Chief Executive Officer for the National

Association for the Education of Young Children (NAEYC), argues that the challenge for facilitating LLL is not knowing the pedagogical structures but implementing them. Allvin contends that cognitive psychology and neuroscience have illuminated truths about at which points in life the necessary neurological structures develop for LLL. In conjunction, she contends that research reveals in what types of environments these structures form. The problem lies in training persons, whether parents or early childhood educators, to create the conditions that support that development during those periods. Allvin (2017) states, "initiative, curiosity, motivation, engagement, problem solving, and self-regulation are at their height of development in the early years . . . ..capitalizing on the opportunities provided by these years doesn't happen by accident. Attending to a child's development in child care and preschool requires knowledge, skills, and competencies from early childhood educators" (p. 58).

With critical periods and neural plasticity, Allvin suggests that there is a small window for creating certain types of experiences that optimize LLL development. Like other researchers, Allvin advocates child-centered contexts. This pedagogical commitment reflects the trope of the educator as facilitator who can create the conditions that lead students to construct a specific understanding and a way of being without explicit direction. Generating the perception that students are in control and governing their learning activity is the goal of child-centered structures. Allvin claims that failure to create and protect child-centered contexts will impede efforts to take full advantage of natural dispositions and the critical periods that are implicated in LLL development.

To recapitulate, there is a particular vision for the ideal adult lifelong learner. This learner is intentional, strategic, and responsive to rapid economic, democratic, technological, and cultural shifts. This learner is treated as necessary to meet the demands of the twenty-first century. Given its importance for the modern world, educators propose expanding the pedagogical reach of policy and practice to support the development of LLL for all. There is a focus on starting with early childhood education and continuing throughout schooling and employment spheres. However, given the suggestion that the foundation for LLL forms early in life, there is a strong push to be intentional with developing LLL in young people. Proponents suggest that teachers, parents, coaches, and community members must be coordinated to support the manifestation and development of the natural dispositions in children that are foundational to the modern version of the lifelong learner. These dispositions include joy in learning, curiosity, inquisitiveness, creativity, and problem-solving, which are supposed to support flexibility and adaptability in twenty-first-century contexts. The so-called foundational dispositions must be manifested and developed in child-centered contexts.

Initiatives to foster LLL are thus directed at educating parents, early childhood educators, and teachers to implement certain types of learning environments. Crafting these environments requires consistency, uniformity, and conformity. Various persons working with children must be aligned with their understanding of LLL and the conditions that support it. They must learn how to create contexts that validate, reward, and discipline the foundational psychological components of LLL. Educators must see their roles in a particular way and learn how to recognize, evaluate, and develop certain dispositions and competencies in students. There is a need for structural conformity and buy-in from multiple partners who agree on the ideal representation of the student and adult. Whether rhetorically framed as disciplining, cultivating, supporting, validating, or rewarding, LLL discourse is informed by a specific and well-defined image of the ideal adult, which can be realized through carefully structured learning experiences starting early in life.

5.3 Function and Purpose: Market, Democratic, and Humanistic

LLL often appears in policy and research with little allusion to critical contours and complexities. Part of the reason is its broad appeal and the rhetorical inclusion of various functions and purposes (Centeno, 2011). It is not uncommon for proponents to justify and rationalize LLL on three bases: market, democratic, and humanistic. A market basis emphasizes the importance for changing market reconfigurations, technological advancement, global competitiveness, corporate efficiency, and economic productivity. Like the perception of economic structures, democratic institutions are also treated as changing and capable of change. Therefore, those who support a democratic vision of schooling emphasize LLL for participating in, contributing to, and helping to create and improve democratic structures. The humanistic purpose is about personal transformations in modernity. The idea is that the modern context requires persons to perpetually learn in order to self-direct their choice-making to pursuit fulfillment, self-actualization, and general well-being. Knowledge about health and well-being constantly change. Arguably, LLL can support efforts to learn about and make choices in relations to those changes.

5.3 Function and Purpose: Market, Democratic, and Humanistic

5.3.1 Market: Transforming for Economic Conditions

There has been particular interest in LLL in the past thirty years because of representations of economic reality as rapidly shifting, competitive, and unpredictable. Since the 1970s and continuing today, manufacturing jobs are in decline and machines continue to take on more of the work of humans (Harari, 2016). With technological advancements and shifting economic conditions, Harari (2016) raises concern that there will be a rise of an economically useless class. Ostensibly, in order to be economically useful, relevant, and wage-earning, adults have to be ready and committed to renewing their skills according to economic conditions and demands. Even if one was not changing occupations, which is a common occurrence in modern worklife, technology, knowledge, and corporate structures change and require workers to be attuned and adaptable to those changes. The assumption is that with learning competence, coupled with the desire to perpetually learn, persons can re-skill and upskill in order to participate in the economy and compete for well-compensated positions, as well as remain competitive in their current position. As Field (2000) argues, those without LLL commitments and skills are less likely to find reasonable and sustainable employment than those who are engaged in LLL. Although some researchers raise doubt about the causal link between LLL and economic prosperity and competitiveness (Fejes & Nicolls, 2008; Lee & Morris, 2016), the contemporary narrative overwhelmingly peddles this relationship.

The potential or promised economic value of LLL may not warrant critical concern from those who endorse economic justice. Part of the acceptance of a market rationalization of LLL results from the perception of mutual benefit. One might conclude that the economic reality is one of change and unpredictability, requiring persons to perpetually learn in order to be efficient and productive. Thus, intentional and strategic LLL can support persons' ability to compete and participate in an economic structure. Fejes and Nicoll (2008) state:

> There is a sense that lifelong learning is being promoted as 'the' solution within a new policy rationality of capitalism, whereby those who do not conform will be left out of the next phase. The question of who is included and excluded is therefore significant – for whoever rejects this new rationality may potentially miss, as the policy narrative goes, the economic boat. (p. 2)

Fejes and Nicoll do not endorse this narrative, but are merely commenting on its pervasiveness in the discourse. In the research and policy narrative,

LLL serves as an economic equalizer, providing opportunities for persons to develop the competence, skills, and dispositions that will be rewarded in a learning society.

5.3.2 *Democratic: Transforming Institutions*

In addition to serving economic interests, LLL is associated with democratic participation and civic virtue. The democratic purpose can be informed by the pursuit of self-actualization, which is realized not through the expression of personal identity nor economic attainment but through solidarity, mitigation of inequality, and fair political processes. Schön (1983) nicely captures this purpose. He argues that institutions, which are implicated in producing and reproducing inequality and injustice, are unstable and capable of transformation through collective action. Given this apparent state, Schön argues:

> We must learn to understand, guide, influence and manage these transformations [institutional and social change]. We must make the capacity for undertaking them integral to ourselves and to our institutions. We must, in other words, become adept at learning. We must become able not only to transform our institutions, in response to changing situations and requirements; we must invent and develop institutions which are 'learning systems,' that is to say, systems capable of bringing about their own continuing transformation. (p. 28)

Although Schön does not specifically name LLL as a goal for schooling, his representation reflects the notion of the learning society and he alludes to the need for continuous learning by others in order to ensure that institutional transformations are steered in democratic and just ways.

In the democratic picture, the learning society must orient persons to pursue learning for the purposes of security, fairness, and well-being for all. In order to realize this purpose, as Olssen (2008) argues, LLL must be directed toward "a progressive deepening of the political arts of democratic communication and negotiation through the skills of deliberation, contestation and debate. Learning must move away from a concern with quantitative addition of cognitive and metacognitive skills to a concern with qualitative transformation of the subject through their active engagement in the democratic process" (p. 44).

Olssen's suggestion requires that researchers and teachers define and teach LLL in a different way than what currently informs the discourse. Olssen writes that this approach "requires a theory of learning that teaches

5.3 Function and Purpose: Market, Democratic, and Humanistic 95

how powers are formed, harnessed and sustained; how compositions are brought into being, or avoided, how encounters are influenced and how institutional and collective politics are negotiated productively" (p. 44). The author is optimistic that LLL does not inherently have to be economic but can serve a broad social good that is not solely about individual economic attainment. In the democratic vision, persons are arguably "empowered" through their ability to continually learn about and participate in political, economic, and cultural institutions in order to adapt to and change. This particular vision connects with Freire's (1968/2000) emphasis on *integration* rather than adaptation.

5.3.3 Humanistic: Transforming Oneself in Postmodernity

As a condition of late modernity or postmodernity, Field (2000) reasons that life trajectories are not linear and well defined. Starting early in one's life and extending through adulthood, Field argues that persons must make choices and adapt to ever-changing conditions in one's personal and social life. These changes are driven by the need to remake identity and learn about subjects that have relevance for making choices and self-directing one's adaptations. The cultural, political, and ideological makeup of the modern era, Field argues, requires reflexivity about knowledge, choices, and goals. LLL can support consumption of knowledge and the pursuit of self-directed learning to manage change. This purpose of LLL can be referred to as *humanist*, or what Fejes and Nicol (2008) call *soft economics*. A strong economic purpose is about reskilling and upskilling to produce an efficient, productive, and competitive workforce. A soft economic purpose is associated with progressive individualism. Rhetoric surrounding this orientation is about perpetual self-management and strategic organization for the purpose of self-guided improvements in the modern age. The humanist, or soft economic, purpose is about the continuous pursuit of learning for personal completeness and self-actualization, as understood in terms of the expression of identity and the attainment of happiness.

As an example of illustrating the humanistic vision of LLL, consider the discourse on health and well-being. There is a perpetually shifting discourse on the norms and practices that support optimal health. The health implications for types of activity, schedules for activity, what foods to eat, when to eat, and how often to eat, to name a few, change frequently. There is a great deal of changing and, oftentimes, contradictory information on how to live a life that supports optimal health and well-being. There are such vastly differing views, with empirical bases underpinning those views, about what to do to pursue and consume. Given this landscape, LLL can support efforts to remain current on research and to evaluate knowledge claims and sources of knowledge to figure out what is trustworthy. LLL can enable persons to ascertain the information to make choices that can bring about health and wellness for them.

5.3.4 Rhetoric and Subsumption

If LLL can function to serve all three purposes, persons might be remiss if they did not adopt all the recommendations to cultivate persons into lifelong learners. Failure at LLL can be implicated in psychological, economic, and democratic problems. As London (2011) argues, "If we fail to learn and fail to make the transformational change, we are likely to be mired in the past, perhaps stuck alone on a plateau while others move away and ahead of us, or worse yet, we face loss and a life of self-doubt or unhappiness" (p. 3).

London paints a bleak picture of persons who "fail" to make "transformational change." Unwilling or ineffective learners are problems to themselves, organizations, and the economy. Not only faced with being economically obsolete, irrelevant, unproductive, complacent, passive, and uncompetitive, persons who do not engage in LLL face a great deal of psychological danger. Conversely, those who engage in LLL not only face psychologically healthy lives, but can also be used to solve a range of economic and democratic problems. The narrative is that LLL can avoid all the ills that result from "complacency" and "inflexibility" of being.

The broad appeal of LLL can make it difficult to generate, sustain, and center critical conversations. However, there is reason to question the genuineness of the varied purposes and functions. Some theorists suggest that the market-based rationalization is most pervasive and serves as the driving force for shaping persons into lifelong learners (Field, 2000; Fejes & Nicoll, 2008; Smith, 2000). The inclusion of humanistic and democratic purpose may simply be rhetorical and designed to make LLL palatable to a broad range of persons. This assessment of the discourse makes sense. If the democratic vision of LLL was realized, then workers and students might commit to structure and restructure contextual conditions in ways that run counter to the mission and purpose of an institution. The democratic vision of LLL is that persons have a voice in creating new structures, not adapting to them. It is more likely, however, that LLL is recognized as such when persons direct themselves in ways that render

5.3 Function and Purpose: Market, Democratic, and Humanistic

them adaptable. If a corporate structure changes, the lifelong learner changes in accordance with that structure rather than engaging in dialogue with others to critically interrogate those structures and potentially present different ones that might compete with a specific agenda.

It seems that LLL is endorsed mainly for economic purposes and for cultivating the disposition to change oneself to function within a context. Notwithstanding, researchers and policy makers often include all three purposes of LLL. Explicit and sole economic instrumentalism might incite resistance if not rationalized as supporting citizenship and personal growth. It is reasonable to conclude that democratic and humanistic purposes are simply rhetorical and function to generate buy-in from persons from a variety of ideological camps. Despite the rhetorical inclusion of various purposes, LLL is generally about shaping persons in specific ways so that they can be useful and productive for the economy. This strong economic basis reveals a clear alignment with neoliberal selfhood.

Even if the varied purposes were realized in the discourse, humanistic and democratic purposes can also be subsumed under neoliberalism. The humanistic purpose is about the self-management of personal growth amid rapid cultural, historical, and technological changes. Consider again the example of health and well-being as an area that persons need to manage. Persons are responsible for acquiring the knowledge to make the choices that optimize their well-being. The imperative to manage health is arguably driven by economic purposes. Health and well-being are increasingly taken up in work settings because of the impact on productivity and healthcare costs. Some policy analysts treat health as a potential drain on the economy and on organizations. Good health is sold as reducing strain on the healthcare system, reducing healthcare costs, increasing worker energy, and improving worker productivity. The lifelong learner might be construed as one who is committed to this imperative and stays informed about ideal health in order to make choices about which products and experiences to consume. In this vision, however, the lifelong learner recognizes that practices and knowledge associated with optimal health frequently change and, therefore, must change in accordance with the evolution of the discourse. Fejes and Nicoll (2008) refer to this purpose as *soft economic* because the focus is about the consumption of experience and knowledge to make choices that bring value to one's being.

Although the democratic basis for LLL potentially stands as a counter to an economic purpose, there is a concern that the democratic vision of LLL can also validate neoliberal selfhood, despite the emphasis on contributing to structural change. As Cruikshank (1999) has shown, institutional programs that are intended to serve a democratic purpose can align with neoliberalism. Although a democratic vision of LLL has a different purpose – citizenship over economic instrumentalism – there is a specific vision for ideal citizenship that is not unlike the economic ideal. The democratic vision of LLL still requires self-governing, consumption, flexibility, and adaptability in order to realize the ideal democratic citizen. Shifting the endpoint still preserves a key function of LLL, which is to generate organizational conformity, adaptability, and consumption.

A difference with the democratic vision is that persons are expected to use LLL to shape – not respond to conditions – democratic, social, and political institutions. Rather than merely adapting, the democratic vision reflects what Freire (1968/2000) describes as *integration* which captures the dual requirement to adapt and contribute to forming organizational structures. Although the democratic vision emphasizes integration, there is still a predetermined vision for persons, one that is informed by the self-governing, responsible, choice maker. The broad concern with LLL is that this way of being functions to generate conformity to social, political, and economic conditions and organizations. LLL is an instrument to realize visions and goals for being, tying it to frameworks for improvement. LLL used as a tool to calibrate and measure persons in specific ways in accordance with those visions and improvements. LLL for whichever purpose still reflects state management of learning by instilling those dispositions that render persons amenable to organization structures and commitments. LLL is about embodying a particular type of learner and strategically organizing oneself in order to always pursue value-added consumption.

It is unlikely that researchers, policy makers, school administrators, and CEOs want LLL to be instrumentally tied to critically interrogating contextual demands and structures. Those who endorse a democratic vision see LLL as having value for producing the type of learning and learners who have the knowledge, skills, and dispositions to participate in and transform policy and practice. Achieving this brand of LLL, however, can negatively impact organization operations. Although the language of democracy, equity, and justice is included in the contemporary narrative, there is reason to doubt that researchers and policy makers want LLL to be directed at examining power structures and working in solidarity with others to transform them. The inclusion of the democratic purpose seems rhetorical. With that said, regardless of the purpose and function, there are neoliberal currents that run throughout the discourse. Whether humanistic, democratic, or economic, LLL functions as an instrument to realize a particular vision of persons.

5.4 A Particular Type of Learner

In the contemporary discourse, it is not enough to have certain dispositions, propensities, or proclivities to learn. Demonstrating behaviors and thoughts that one might recognize as curiosity, caprice, wonderment, and inquisitiveness is alone inadequate to count as LLL. Learning without "consciousness" and intention might be construed as passivity. LLL is recognized as self-generating the thoughts and actions that can be recognizable as strategic pursuit of learning. This counts as such if it is recognized and articulated as conscious, managed, and controlled in ways that support flexible adaptations. The discourse is not about celebrating and validating what is presumed in persons but harnessing what one might believe are natural psychological and cognitive characteristics in order to realize a particular vision for persons.

There is a specific representation of the lifelong learner that informs research and policy. Bollington (2015) captures this representation by describing what children need to think and do to be recognized as lifelong learners. He states that children must:

> be able to ask questions and relate the knowledge gained to real-life challenges. We need to stick at the challenge even when the work gets hard. We need to be prepared to try something; fail; adapt; then try again until it works. We need to network with other students, sometimes virtually, often across cultures. We need to critically analyse and evaluate the content we find in seconds on the internet, not memorise it. We need to play creatively with ideas and solutions. (p. 28)

Although not using the terminology, Bollington's vision of the lifelong learner, which is common in policy discussions, involves curiosity, grit, GM, collaboration, and critical thinking, which are included in representations of the ideal twenty-first century person. Some researchers and policy makers treat these behaviors, dispositions, and competencies as instances of LLL, as well as the foundation of LLL in adulthood. Even if one presumes that the foundations of LLL are natural, there is a specific vision for what LLL is supposed to look like and how it is supposed to function; pedagogical efforts are designed to realize that vision.

5.4.1 *Strategically Flexible and Adaptable*

The vision for the ideal lifelong learner aligns with neoliberal selfhood. The alignment is evident not only in the similarity to twenty-first-century competencies, but also regarding the emphasis on adaptability and flexibility. As Fendler (2001) argues, those who can perform and enact scripts that are interpreted as flexible inform the image of the educated person, who is also the good lifelong learner – the learner necessary for the twenty-first century. Researchers and policy makers use the notion of flexibility to describe the acts of evaluating contextual conditions and needs, and then responding by taking action to acquire the knowledge and develop the cognitive and behavioral tools to adapt to those conditions. One who is flexible recognizes that such adaptations are subject to change, as contextual demands and needs are unstable. To achieve this type of flexibility, learning must be an iterative and perpetual process of self-examination and context analysis that must lead to the consumption of experience to make oneself useful and relevant.

Two criteria and expectations for flexibility are relevance and use. Those who read contextual demands incorrectly, are unresponsive to change, miscalibrate their competence, or fail to pursue and achieve personal transformations may find themselves obsolete and irrelevant. In order to be useful and relevant, persons must be conditioned in particular ways and learn specific scripts for engagement and self-management. To count as flexible and adaptable lifelong learners, persons must (1) be attuned to environmental demands; (2) assess the demands correctly; (3) calibrate their knowledge and competencies; (4) determine which types of experiences support adaptability to demands; (5) take action to consume those experiences; and (6) assess whether those actions led to adaptations.

In this vision, persons are expected to live an examined life with constant, iterative evaluations of context and selfhood. Although thought about as breaking down barriers to learning and supporting self-determination, critical theorists contend that this type of examined and scripted life is double-edged. Falk (1999) argues, "learners ... continue their 'schooling' and engage a highly-scripted scenario that increasingly finds them sentenced to an unending search for the Holy Grail of 'value-added' learning, a grail that is

5.4 A Particular Type of Learner

proving more ephemeral in this era of post-Fordist labour displacement" (p. 22).

The use of the word *sentenced* is notable. By using this term, Falk points to the normalization and requirement for a specific type of learning that one must practice throughout life. Learning has moved beyond the confines of schooling walls and years. While breaking down associations between learning and schooling, Falk makes the point that LLL discourse extends the reach of institutional power to shape the engagement and activity of persons throughout life. As Falk aptly put it, learners are sentenced to life. He means that "Lifelong learning ... has become mandatory if one is to participate in the redundant and highly-stylised performance piece referred to as labour today" (p. 23). Falk does not deny the economic value, but \ does not see LLL as an expression of autonomy, freedom, and will but a scripted and obligatory way of being that must be carried out throughout life.

Researchers and policy makers typically treat LLL as an expression of and a way to realize empowerment, autonomy, and personal control. However, regardless if associated with democracy, economic participation, and personal transformation, the embodiment of the lifelong learner reflects a docile position. If one embodies the ideal lifelong learner, that person is malleable and docile. If persons merely respond to shifting contextual circumstances, then their activity is governed by their reading of contextual conditions and the enactment of behaviors that are deemed appropriate for those conditions. To influence thoughts and behaviors, all one needs to do is change an organizational structure to invite persons to change themselves in order to function within that structure. LLL can serve to make persons controllable from a distance by instilling dispositions for them to be infinitely responsive to contextual demands.

Like Falk, Fendler (2001) challenges the meaning of flexible persons that is presented in the LLL literature. She argues that strategic and self-managed flexible adaptations are not a level of personal freedom but rather "an effect of power and constitutive of current patterns of social governance and self-discipline" (p. 125). Fendler argues that "fixed" roles are not valued and normalized. Persons must be made so that they can make themselves function within a changing social matrix. In order to achieve that type of being, the goals of schooling are to shape aspirations, competencies, dispositions, and learning scripts so that persons can change themselves in ways that appear useful and relevant for a social matrix. Failure to be flexible and do so in a particular way is interpreted as cognitive and psychological inadequacies. Those who are unresponsive to environmental conditions might be constructed as an "unwilling learner" or a "maladaptive learner."

5.4.2 The "Unwilling" Learner

Herein lies a major concern with LLL. The discourse of LLL invites teachers to construe learning activities as problematic and persons as deficient if they do not change themselves to fit and function within a context. In this regard, the notion of LLL functions as both exclusionary and pathologizing. If persons fail at persuading themselves and others that they are relevant, useful, and flexible, then they can be treated as problems, unwilling, maladaptive, stuck, complacent, left behind, or ineffective lifelong learners. A contradiction in the discourse is apparent. Persons are treated as active, strategic, empowered, and self-governing when they are responsive to conditions in ways that render them useful and valuable. They can be treated as complacent and unwilling if they do not. For example, in schools, persons are likely to be interpreted as lifelong learners if they show intrinsic interest to pursue school objectives and use every opportunity to master those objectives without the perceived presence of coercive sources. If students "give up" on academic goals, are performance oriented, are motivated by rewards, or show signs of physical and cognitive withdrawal from school, they are open to critiques of their LLL ability, competencies, and dispositions. If not recognized as adaptable and flexible, then persons can be treated as problems that need to be addressed with targeted interventions.

One can argue that all persons are lifelong learners but may not exhibit the kind of LLL that renders them adaptable to certain contexts. Those who do conform to valued types of LLL that lead to flexible adaptations are subject to criticisms of their character. For this reason, Ahl (2008) comments that concerns about LLL emerge when "someone wants someone else to do something and this person does not" (p. 160). If one is not pursuing economic relevance and usefulness, participating in specific types of learning to contribute to a democracy, or consuming knowledge and experiences to manage personal transformations, then they could be subject to negative evaluations of their LLL. LLL functions to pathologize those who do not conform to what might seem to be appropriate change for contextual conditions.

Such evaluations are a matter of perspective and can be product oriented. If one conforms to context and can show productivity and efficiency in activity, then those persons are likely to be perceived as good lifelong learners. If one resists or changes in "unproductive" ways, then those persons are likely to be perceived as lifelong learners who need some type of intervention. Persons have to correctly interpret contextual needs to choose experiences to consume in order to show responsiveness and conformity to those needs. The promise is that if persons calibrate themselves and contexts correctly, as well as have access to all learning opportunities, then they can make choices for consumption that supports their adaptability and flexibility. This type of technically rational thinking contributes to the perception that personal choice is responsible for socioeconomic conditions. This perception is made possible by the assumption that persons have limitless opportunity for engaging in LLL.

5.4.3 A Narrative of Personal Control

LLL is entangled in the narrative of personal responsibility. Bollington (2015) argues that technology has increased access to information and learning opportunities. Differences in persons' economic positions result from their ability and effort to take advantage of those opportunities. Bollington argues that economic disparities result from schooling structures that fail to shape motivation, persistence, learning competence, and problem-solving. If schools target these cognitive characteristics, then the assumption is that all persons can take advantage of LLL opportunities. Although not solely responsibilizing persons, Bollington contributes to a conception of schooling that is based on targeting persons' capacities, competencies, and dispositions for LLL. The assumption is that the more one engages in LLL, the more likely they are to be competitive for well-compensated and prestigious positions in the economy. The more likely they can function in and contribute to a modern corporate structure, the more likely they are to be entrepreneurial.

Field (2000) acknowledges that an unintended consequence of the LLL discourse is the responsibilization and individualization of inequality. The LLL narrative supports a certain consciousness about the structural positions of labor and capital. Problems with economic prosperity and competitiveness are understood and addressed at the level of individual motivation, aspirations, and dispositions. Economic problems are a consequence of persons' ability, capacity, and propensity to engage in LLL opportunities. If neurological structures can be shaped early in life, then there will be no impediments to take advantage of wide-open opportunity. Researchers and policy makers are not likely to conclude that missed critical periods for developing the foundations of LLL are deterministic. However, with decreasing neural plasticity with age, one might argue that it is more difficult to reconfigure psychological and cognitive qualities to align with a particular vision for being. Knowledge claims about brain development form the basis for interventions to create a particular type of person. Researchers and policy makers implicate educational settings in the realization of the vision. If educators create the foundation for LLL and one believes educational opportunity is available to all, then the explanation for economic position is personal choice, individual effort, and aspirations.

The prevailing belief is that LLL will benefit persons by ensuring that they have the skills, dispositions, and knowledge to strategically and intentionally develop themselves to secure gainful employment and contribute to work organizations. Given this narrative, LLL is featured in a social and economic justice agendas. Accepting the need for productivity and the inevitability of change make LLL an important subject position for which to strive and achieve. However, some researchers raise doubt that there is a causal connection between participation in LLL activities and economic prosperity (Fejes & Nicoll, 2008; Hughes & Tight, 2008; Lee, 1997; Lee & Morris, 2016). In addition, Hughes and Tight (1995) raise doubt that the modern economy requires more productivity and efficiency than it did in the past. The authors encourage their readers to examine the data that suggest that economic structures are amid unprecedented change and that persons must engage in self-directed LLL in order to be a part of that structure. In addition to questioning that representation of economic structures and that continued learning will lead to better economic positioning, Hughes and Tight also raise the question about empowerment and exploitation. They question whether LLL is about generating participation from all members of a context or an effort to maximize efficiency and productivity of workers. In a neoliberal context, this query is not an either/or but a simultaneous requirement. All persons are construed as empowered when they can maximize their productivity and efficiency.

5.5 Conclusion

The image of the self-driven, tenacious, curious learner who pursues learning in and out of school is a romantic one. Aside from realizing this romantic image, there are compelling reasons for persons to pursue learning throughout their lives. The notion of LLL can break down barriers and expectations about age-related categories, such as child and adult, that designate when learning happens. Breaking down these barriers and binaries can open possibilities for understanding oneself and possibilities for engaging in and contributing to a democracy and economy. The concern with LLL, however, is that it functions to render persons amenable and adaptable to contextual demands, making them governable. LLL is not just about learning through the lifespan, which persons arguably automatically do. LLL is about rendering persons effective, efficient, and productive in relation to technological, economic, and democratic changes. Persons must develop the disposition, aspirations, and competencies to respond to changing contexts. They must be flexible, adaptable, and responsible for their consumption of knowledge and experiences to be relevant and useful. LLL extends institutional power beyond formal K-12 experience to a the lifespan in order to make them self-determined, flexible, and adaptable.

Ahl (2008) recommends that rather than buying into the ideal visions of the lifelong learner and structuring schooling to realize this vision, research and practice should be centered on two questions: (1) Why is not engaging in what is recognized as LLL a problem? (2) On what grounds is it a problem? Typically, researchers and policy makers do not consider these questions. LLL is considered an unequivocal good and associated with the image of the educated person, the ideal for which to strive and the type of being to embody. If there is focus on the aforementioned questions, there is opportunity to illuminate the way neoliberal ideology runs throughout the LLL discourse. Even if for humanistic and democratic purposes, LLL is instrumental and prescriptive in trying to normalize and validate the self-governing, consumptive being who is committed throughout life to pursue value for oneself.

CHAPTER 6

Creativity
An Organizing Value

6.1 Introduction

Researchers and theorists tend to argue that schooling does little to foster students' creativity (Azzam, 2009; Mohr, 2017; Newton & Newton, 2014; Soh, 2017). Although there are debates about the conceptualization and pedagogical approach, few are likely to disagree that policy and practice should be explicitly organized around this commitment. Aside from being considered a quintessential human expression, researchers and policy makers associate creativity with democratic and economic participation (Ooi & Stöber, 2011). Theorists reason that resistance to conformity and the imagination of new realities to mitigate injustice are important for democratic participation (Greene et al., 2010; Griese, 2016; Schön, 1983). Others emphasize the economic value, citing the modern context as competitive, global, fast-changing, uncertain, and unpredictable (BIAC, 2004; Gerguri & Ramadani, 2010; Mohr, 2017; Trilling & Fadel, 2009). Consequently, there is a need for persons to be innovative, entrepreneurial, adaptable, and adept at problem-solving. Given such conditions, creativity is an important feature of the ideal twenty-first-century democratic and economic participants.

Given the value, researchers and policy makers argue that schools have an obligation to take up creativity as an educational aim (Robinson, 2015; Soh, 2017). Soh (2017) nicely captures this reasoning:

> The school has the obligation to produce students who display creativity now and, more importantly, later when they go into the adult world. Although the school uses a lot of resources to perpetuate the society's accumulated knowledge, it is also obvious that much of this knowledge is going to be soon obsolete as new ones keep replacing the existing ones, exponentially at that. Hence, Einstein's 'The true sign of intelligence is not knowledge but imagination.' (p. 58)

This reasoning is commonly featured in policy and research discussions. The underlying rationale is that the acquisition of declarative knowledge is not adequate to prepare students to navigate and participate in ill-defined and fast-changing contexts. Instead, schooling should be centered on teaching students to critically think, problem-solve, self-regulate, and create. These thinking skills, of which creativity is featured, can serve as signs of intelligence and preparedness for twenty-first century contexts.

There are diverse and compelling reasons to support the explicit focus on creativity. Raising critical questions might seem counterintuitive, misguided, antihuman, undemocratic, and economically detrimental. Notwithstanding, a critical pause is necessary as the contemporary discourse is entangled in neoliberal values for selfhood. A starting claim is that researchers and policy makers use creativity as an identity marker to assign value to persons in relation to their approximation to an ideal vision of being, whether democratic, economic, or humanistic. The longing of adults for a type of citizenry informs deliberations, rationalizations, and structures surrounding creativity (Ogata, 2013). As a result, creativity has become something to be technically managed in and through educational environments. Although there are diverse ideological underpinnings, making for vastly different ethical justifications, the economic motivation for creativity seems to be the most pervasive.

Contemporary value for creativity tends to be framed in terms of ideal visions for modern economic participants. Robinson (2015) reasons that chief executive officers overwhelmingly want their employees to be creative, which can be linked to product development, innovations, problem-solving, and adaptability. Furthermore, the emphasis on entrepreneurialism and enterprise makes creativity a valuable asset and a feature of human capital that optimizes one's value in the marketplace. For this reason, creativity is referred to as a skill that can be technically developed and managed, even in ill-defined pedagogical contexts. Directing creativity toward different endpoints or supporting it for its own sake does little to divorce this concept from technical management and neoliberal selfhood. Although humanist and democratic visions can potentially stand in contrast to a neoliberal one, there are still commitments to the strategic and intentional orchestration of environments and experiences that are directed at realizing a creative being. The neoliberal entanglement is not only about the economic benefit but also about representations of creativity as internal features of persons that must be displayed and developed through carefully managed environments.

6.2 Definition: Novelty and Use

To be integrated into schooling discourse and featured in ideal representations of persons, defining and measuring creativity is important in order to stand as a marker of capacities, value, and potential. Definitions tend to include the production of an object or idea that is novel and useful (Azzam, 2009; Cropley, 2000; Howkins, 2011; NACCCE, 1999; Newton & Newton, 2014). Novelty and use (or value) are commonly featured in conceptualizations across disciplinary perspectives and fields (Benedek et al., 2014; Lubart, 1994; Plucker et al., 2004; Runco & Jaeger, 2012). From this understanding, any idea that has no use or exists elsewhere does not count as creative. Likewise, the production of something deemed new but with no use or value is not creative. Given the emphasis on novelty and use, which centers the interpretation of a product, Cropley (2000) describes creativity as "productive fluency" (p. 73). Persons must have a sense of what can be of use, what is already in use, what product can be developed that has value, and how to create that product.

Novelty and use can pertain to different spheres: individual, relationships, and social and economic systems. To capture these possibilities, Boden (1996) makes the distinction between H-creativity and P-creativity. In terms of individuals, creativity can manifest in the production and performance of identity, the production of strategies to achieve learning goals, and the use of various media for therapeutic purposes (Arfken, 2014; Boden, 1996; Ziegler & Kapur, 2018). Broadly, P-creativity is about the production of novel ideas that can be useful for facilitating personal transformations and goal attainment. This form has the potential to justify the classification of a vast array of ideas and objects as novel and useful. Unlike P-creativity, H-creativity, which is the production of ideas or products that are novel and useful for relationships and systems, is subject to the evaluation and negotiation from others. H-creativity is generally regarded as an idea or product that is brand new to the human race. This type of creativity involves agreement from others about the value and novelty of a product.

The distinction between P- and H-creativity is not unlike the designation between little-c and big-C creativity, respectively (Beghetto & Kaufman, 2014; Craft, 2005). With these semantic choices, researchers make it possible to justify a wide range of activities and products as creative, while simultaneously producing a basis for excluding other activities and products. Although seemingly not trying to privilege one form over others, the use of terms big and little can invoke evaluative judgments.

6.2 Definition: Novelty and Use

Notwithstanding these classifications, it seems reasonable to conclude that the majority of creative moments are of the P and little kind. It is not common to produce an idea or product that is brand new to the human race and has never been present in history or culture. If in schools, for example, teachers valued, rewarded, and recognized only H-creativity, most students would likely be branded as uncreative.

Although classifications can work to broaden justifications of action and products, novelty and use are bound to perceptions and imaginations of others. P-creativity might seem like a purely subjective evaluation, but the recognition of novelty and use is bound to contexts. Structures and persons comprise a social field and contribute to such evaluations. One of the complexities with this dual requirement is that persons are encouraged to judge and evaluate their outputs in relation to a context. Such evaluations can be governed by personal interpretations of the immediate use or value, as well as by the imaginations and evaluations of others in the social field. Products themselves are not inherently creative. While objects or ideas may seem irrelevant or hackneyed in one context and historical moment, they can be interpreted by others in a different time and place as novel and useful.

The point is that, especially for the P and little-c type, it is challenging to determine which objects are new and useful and to distinguish between products that are indicative of creativity. The institutionalization of creativity, however, orients persons to form and apply criteria for classifying products. If one creates something that others find to already be in existence or of no value, then one might be deemed as lacking creativity or at least not being creative at that moment. The level of value and novelty is determined in a social field and the authority granted to certain voices may function to legitimize and delegitimize creative activity. The determination of use and value might be a result of limits in knowledge and imagination by those who produce and evaluate the idea or object.

Concerns with the definition relate to practices of exclusion, authority in evaluation, effects of social fields, and consequences for identity. In this exploration, the assumption is preserved that products can be novel, just that criteria are bound to persons, perceptions, and social fields. However, there are those who claim that no idea or product is ever really novel (e.g., see Amabile & Pratt, 2016; Ashton, 2015; Bilton, 2010). The line of reasoning is that all things or ideas exist already and the creation of products or ideas that appear novel is merely reconfigured products of the already existing objects or ideas. Creativity is, therefore, the expression of reconfigured concepts and materials that is recognized as new and useful. If one believes that creativity is reconfiguring existing objects or ideas, then access to materials and experiences are responsible for novel and useful production. One might argue, however, that creative persons can take any materials and reconfigure them to create something new and useful. Conversely, access to certain materials for reconfiguration could be implicated in shaping possibilities for creative output. This way of understanding has socioeconomic class implications.

The complexities with novelty and use are vast. A full exploration is beyond the scope of this chapter. A major concern here is that if creativity is defined in terms of novelty and use, then the production of new ideas and products, whether treated as brand new or reconfigured, is subject to interpretations and perceptions about those products. What counts as novel and useful become gauges to determine who is and who is not creative. Although persons can debate the criteria for what counts as novel and useful, if creativity is defined by these terms then persons are prompted to seek criteria to brand products as creative or not. Novelty and use are evaluative terms, held as unproblematic norms and defining features that can be used to classify products and persons. Furthermore, these defining criteria make creativity instrumental, tied to capitalist values for devaluing existing products in search of new ones, or perhaps using old products in new ways (Pope, 2005). Pope (2005) argues that capitalism requires the continual diminishing of market value for products and the desire to replace those products with those not yet known. Novelty and use are criteria that lend themselves well to this feature of capitalism.

6.3 Realizing the Creative Student

Ideology circulates not only in the definition but also in the ontology of creativity. The prevailing narrative is that creativity results from individuals' actions, characteristics, behaviors, attitudes, perceptions, and dispositions. Oftentimes, biographical studies of historical and contemporary figures who are associated with inventions are intended to reveal character profiles, origins, experiences, processes, and the evolution of being. The purpose of such studies is to identify the potential for creativity in others and to inform interventions to shape developmental trajectories. The question guiding this line of thinking is: What are the qualities of creative people and how can those qualities be recognized, cultivated, and nurtured in others? The hope is that by answering this question, creativity can be fostered on a broad scale. One of the reasons for this imperative is that creativity is conceptualized as a form of human capital that can be exchanged in the economic market. Creative people can be identified to fill roles in the socioeconomic hierarchy that require innovation, enterprise, product development, organizational efficiency, and institutional restructuring.

6.3.1 Natural Proclivity

As a feature of human capital, researchers and policy makers cannot conclude that creativity is featured only in a select few nor that it cannot be developed. Such a conclusion would serve to characterize opportunities as predetermined and preselected, whereby students have no control over their academic and life outcomes. If valued as a twenty-first century skill and disposition, then the belief that all persons are or can be creative endorses a level playing field for economic competition and participation. Thus, a common assumption in the discourse is that creativity is a natural proclivity of all persons. This assumption is not just held by proponents of economic instrumentalism. In fact, researchers and theorists from a variety of academic and ideological camps tend to endorse this naturalist view. If bound to visions for ideal personhood, there must be a commitment that all persons can embody the ideal. Despite this common assumption, there is not always agreement on the necessary dispositions, character traits, skills, knowledge, and behaviors, as well as the structure for pedagogical environments.

For example, Robinson (2015) is a strong proponent of the view that children are naturally creative and that schooling structures can suppress this proclivity. He argues that modern schooling tends to educate creativity out of students. From this perspective, the pedagogical task is about structuring environments that allow students to express what is innately a part of their being. Like Robinson, Sullivan (2017) argues that all persons are creative but emphasizes diversity of expression and time of manifestation. Expressive differences pertain to domains such as music, play, problem-solving, performance, cooking, and building, to name only a few. In terms of time, Sullivan reasons that creativity can manifest in persons at different points in their lives and at different moments. As a result, any classification of persons as not creative is a failure to recognize and validate the various possible expressions and temporal emergent properties. This perspective provides justifications for endorsing pedagogical commitments to choice, autonomy, exploration, discovery, and experimentation. Informing this view is the claim that persons are naturally curious, experimental, and motivated to produce novel and useful products. Given autonomy and limited adult intervention, these proclivities can be expressed, nurtured, and developed.

Whereas some researchers endorse the view that persons are innately creative and need the right context to express it, others contend that all persons can be creative with the right structures to support the development of procedures, dispositions, and traits. Although natural, the thinking is that persons need discipline, structure, and guidance in order to realize their potential. Sawyer (2012) expresses this view by arguing that all students have the potential to create if they follow a methodology and practice disciplined engagement. In addition to methods and discipline, Sawyer also contends that persons must also have certain traits, attitudes, and perceptions, which can also be fostered with targeted interventions. This treatment of creativity is part of an effort to dispel the creativity myth, which is the idea that production of novel and useful ideas is spontaneous, whimsical, and possible only from a few (Ashton, 2015). The perspective is that creativity is ordinary with nothing happenstance about it. All persons can produce novel and useful products if they have certain knowledge, habits, skills, and dispositions.

Beghetto and Kaufman (2014) present a view that might appear to diverge from the characterization of ordinariness. They describe creativity as a higher-level mental process and contend that creative products require extraordinary abilities, interests, and learning styles. This description can function as exclusionary in that persons must resemble processes that count as "higher" and "extraordinary," as well as have particular interests and perform certain "learning styles." Although potentially divergent, herein lies the importance of GM. It is possible that students believe that they do not have "higher" mental processes and "extraordinary" abilities, and, therefore, conclude that creativity is stable, immutable, and featured only in a select few. This belief might be characterized as a fixed mindset, which can be linked to avoiding efforts to develop the necessary processes and abilities for creativity. Therefore, the conception that Beghetto and Kaufman present must be accompanied by a commitment to persuade students that they can acquire, develop, and improve extraordinary abilities through their own efforts. If successful, this view of creativity can be ordinary in that all persons can produce novel and useful products with the right attitude, belief, and work ethic.

6.3.2 *Character, Attitudes, and Dispositions*

Although generally regarded as a natural proclivity, researchers identify specific dispositions, traits, and processes as necessary for creativity to be expressed and developed. For example, Knox (2011) lists the following qualities: (1) original, (2) venturesome, (3) persistent, (4) proficient, and (5) complex. In a similar characterization, Sawyer (2012) contends that creativity results from persons who persist, take risks, embrace failure, and are comfortable with incremental change. Sternberg and Lubart (1991) contend that creative people are curious, tolerant of ambiguity, and intrinsically motivated. They have the desire and ability to work for recognition and are willing to surmount obstacles, grow, and take moderate risks. The discourse is saturated with claims about dispositions, perceptions, attitudes, and character traits. It is possible to glean interconnectedness with other NCS, such as grit, GM, and ER. The values for embracing failure and risk-taking are emphasized through the literature on NCS. If creativity is to be institutionalized in schooling and featured as human capital, constructing this profile and developing measurements and pedagogical strategies to support the realization of that profile make sense. Although the profile can potentially be exclusionary by identifying those who display these traits, researchers conclude that all persons can develop those qualities and schools should be focused on them.

The teachability of creativity is subject to debate. If featured in visions for ideal twenty-first century persons, then there must be optimism for its teachability, which depends on assumptions about the malleability of a person's character and the degree to which pedagogical environments can be shaped to cultivate those traits. If one concludes that creativity requires certain personality or character traits, then teachability must be underpinned by the assumption that traits can be changed and the pedagogical environments can, and should, produce that change. If viewed as strictly a skill or procedure, some of the ethical and pedagogical complexities are avoided. Brinkman (2010) captures this point:

> The idea of teaching someone to be creative can strike people as an impossible task, which is a realistic response if we imply that we can teach someone to become another Beethoven or Einstein. However, we can teach people to approach their jobs or their study with creativity in mind. We can teach and model techniques for generating ideas, for being sensitive to personality traits that might encourage creative expression and risk-taking in their work. We can help people allocate time to creative activity. We know that 'incubation' is a part of the creative process. We can structure teaching and creative situations so that the student will understand the value of letting an idea simmer. (p. 48)

Brinkman thinks about creativity as an ordinary activity that involves a set of skills and strategies. As such, creativity can be taught and applied daily to work and life by all persons. Milić et al. (2018) validate this commitment by suggesting that all persons can engage in creative thinking using a strategy they call "control list" (pp. 204–205). They describe this type of thinking as flexible, fluent, original, and imaginative and suggest a procedural process to practice these qualities. The strategy is based on trying out different applications of ideas, analyzing similar ideas, modifying the idea, considering what can be added and removed, editing, and combining. Consider the title of an article written by Wilson (2013) in the popular psychology magazine *Psychology Today*. The title is, *Surprise: Creativity is a Skill, not a Gift: You can Reacquire your Natural Creative Ability with these Steps*. In this article, Wilson highlights that the economy requires all persons to be creative regardless of their position in the socioeconomic hierarchy. Like Robinson's ontological assumption, Wilson contends that persons are naturally creative but have been conditioned to believe that creativity comes only from a select few. He promises that persons can realize their natural ability with steps and procedures.

Not all researchers, theorists, and practitioners support procedural display and well-defined methods but rather endorse approaches characterized by autonomy, choice, and nonspecific methods. Among these differences, researchers and policy makers also disagree about what teachers need to know and be able to do in order to support creativity in their classrooms. The discourse is not only about shaping students into particular types of beings but also shaping teachers so that they are better able to shape students. Whether optimizing choice, instilling procedural knowledge, or targeting attitudes, the discourse is centered on efforts to create the conditions that will enable persons to be creative. Although the argument here is that neoliberal ideology contributes to accepting a procedural narrative, this ideology also normalizes the technical management of creativity even in seemingly less structured and prescriptive ways. Neoliberal ideology is implicated in strengthening the educational resolve to make creativity a pedagogical target, a measurement of personhood, an internal trait with exchange value, an inevitable subject position, and an instrument to realize an ideal type of being.

6.4 Individualism, Politics, and Ideal Citizenry

Although educational philosophers and researchers have theorized creativity and discussed its role in schooling for centuries, the explicit, formal, and

6.4 Individualism, Politics, and Ideal Citizenry

broad attention emerged in the past sixty years (Ogata, 2013). Ogata (2013) highlights specific reasons for the emergence during this time. She contends that the creative child reflected ideological and political interests to produce a specific type of citizen. Critical researchers increasingly point to the ways creativity is bound to history, culture, politics, and ideology (Glăveanu, 2018; Gormley, 2018). This feature of the discourse tends to be ignored in educational conversations in favor of ontological, pedagogical, methodological, and conceptual controversies. In other words, researchers and policy makers are committed to improving students' creativity through the development of conceptualizations, measurements, and pedagogical structures. One line of critical interrogation, however, is to examine the ideological underpinning for institutionalizing creativity, as well as how ideology shapes a particular narrative. While considering debates and controversies is important, there must be critical reflections about the source and function of targeting interventions to realize a vision of the creative child.

6.4.1 Emergence of the Creative Child

Research on creativity and its related concepts such as curiosity, divergent thinking, risk-taking, and innovation are expanding at exponential rates (Newton & Newton, 2014). Although there is considerable debate about the degree to which schools support creativity, there is little question about its importance. As Ogata (2013) argues, this schooling imperative did not emerge until the latter part of the twentieth century. Post–World War II, Ogata contends, American propaganda was centered on a narrative of Russian oppression, restriction, and compliance as a counterpoint to American ideals of autonomy, imagination, and democracy. It was during this time that creativity became formally centered in discussions about children and schooling. The notion of the creative child entered public and institutional discourse to steer policy and practice for the purpose of promulgating the American trope of the hopeful champion of democratic and economic innovation and technological advancement.

To realize this vision, Ogata (2013) contends that there were concerted and multipronged efforts in various spaces. She contends that psychologists, anthropologists, teachers, policy makers, and toy manufacturers all contributed to practices to "design" the creative child. Ogata uses the notion of *design* to point to the systemic efforts to realize a particular vision for children. These efforts involved social science research to inform the production of toys, parenting manuals, and curricula. The purpose was to develop the knowledge to strategically manage learning environments and experiences so that children can move toward the ideal representation of the creative child. Although prior to the 1950s creativity was part of educational conversations, Ogata argues that it was not until this time that creativity functioned as scientific management, was institutionalized to realize an ideological agenda, and served as evaluative tools of children, parents, and teachers. These commitments still persist today, but the purpose is rationalized differently.

6.4.2 Economic Participation

In contemporary discourse, the significant driving force for creativity in schooling is economic. In the late twentieth and early twenty-first centuries, funding for school activities and curricula that were associated with creativity was being cut. Investments in Science, Technology, Engineering, and Math (STEM) were on the rise as these areas were associated with economic development and productivity. However, the discourse changed when researchers and policy makers bought into the instrumentalism of creativity for STEM fields. Consequently, the acronym went from STEM to STEAM (Science, Technology, Engineering, Arts, and Math) – a shift that gives legitimacy to the attention to arts, which is one means for developing and expressing creativity. The value for arts is driven by the association with creativity, which is instrumentally tied to the production of human capital to support global competition, technological innovation, entrepreneurialism, community vitality, and worker competence (Howkins, 2011; Robinson, 2015; Sullivan, 2017).

Given the association with economic participation, productivity, and innovation, Howkins (2011) argues that schooling can no longer ignore creativity. He contends that the nature of the modern economy has changed from one established by information, knowledge, and automation to one based on the transactions of creative products. He argues that the economy is fueled by ideas and innovation. Howkins, like other proponents of making creativity a pedagogical target (e.g., Robinson, 2015; Sung, 2015), believes that corporate vitality and emerging business, along with environmental, political, and personal problems, require creative solutions. In this so-called new economy, the need for creativity is not specific to certain rungs on the socioeconomic hierarchy nor to positions conventionally referred to as the creative fields, such as engineering, design, marketing, and programming. Policy makers in general contend that all jobs in the modern economy require some degree of creativity (Howkins, 2011; Robinson, 2005; Sung, 2015; Wolfe & Bramwell, 2008). For example, fewer workers are needed on assembly lines because of automated machinery, but persons are needed to troubleshoot dysfunctions with those machines. Creativity can potentially support the understanding and solving of those dysfunctions.

Researchers and policy makers argue that the imperative to institutionalize creativity can help with cultivating the kind of human capital that can support functioning on all rungs of the socioeconomic hierarchy. However, there is a hierarchical value placed on certain expressions and outcomes of creativity. Perhaps a machine technician can benefit from an explicit emphasis on developing creativity, but the person designing the machines might be more valued and compensated than the technician. Creativity can function to evaluate those who can show that they are the most qualified to fill certain economic positions, thus operating as a sorting tool and rationalization for access to opportunity. Creativity is marketed as a form of human capital that is necessary to identify, cultivate, and develop in persons so that they can navigate any emerging conditions and drive development. Creativity is supposed to signify value to one's being to fulfill certain roles on the socioeconomic hierarchy. If creativity is required for the twenty-first century environment and schools are responsible for cultivating it, then schools are also responsible for determining who has adequately displayed creativity in the ways that are required in modern contexts.

6.4.3 Individualism and Skill

As a form of human capital, persons must be seen as more or less creative, which is an internal feature that can be mobilized and transferred to any context regardless of actors and tools. Demonstrating this quality and transferability signals value and readiness for participation in the twenty-first century economy. Thus, institutionalizing creativity makes sense to level the playing field and support the types of human capital accumulation that are rewarded in the opportunity structure. This economic instrumentalism reveals an explicit relationship to neoliberal selfhood. This relationship is further evidenced by characteristics, behaviors, and dispositions of the creative person: (1) works hard to develop novel and useful products; (2) strategizes efforts to improve creative capacity; (3) persists with efforts to improve the self and create products regardless of failures and setbacks; and (4) takes risks in the transformation of being or the production of ideas and objects. Creativity is entangled in other neoliberal values.

The neoliberal narrative is that all persons can be creative with grit and GM. The belief in the value of persistence and effort must be accompanied by the emphasis on skill and technical management. If creativity was treated as a natural disposition of only a few or something that cannot be explicitly and strategically cultivated in all children, then those who can convince others of their creative prowess will have access to certain positions by virtue of nothing that was personally controlled. That position does not lend itself well to the neoliberal values of ideological individualism in which individuals can develop themselves with hard work and consequently compete for positions in the socioeconomic structure. Those persons who show the most creativity, which can be expressed and developed through persistence and hard work, will be rewarded with corresponding opportunities to fill roles in the economy. The neoliberal narrative requires a conceptualization that is based on internal, controllable attributes that can be managed, developed, and directed. The narrative requires a skills-based understanding, as all persons can learn and apply the strategies to create. This narrative communicates an optimistic appraisal of the potential for displaying creativity. As Glăveanu (2018) notes, such a treatment democratizes the notion by suggesting that all persons can develop and practice the skill.

Creativity is not necessarily inherently a feature of neoliberal selfhood, but when understood and applied in a particular way, it aligns with values for that selfhood. In a context in which neoliberal influence is pervasive, a specific narrative takes form that is based on skill, economic instrumentalism, personal value, internal characteristics, and individual controllability. Critique here is not about taking a position on the definition, ontology, and value, but ways in which neoliberal ideology is entangled in the modern discourse of creativity. Much contemporary discourse has explicit neoliberal currents. Some of the most widely known proponents explicitly tie the imperative to teach creativity to human capital accumulation, economic instrumentalism, and individual responsibility (Howkins, 2011; Newton & Newton, 2014; Wolfe & Bramwell, 2008). Researchers may resist this imperative only to supplant the purpose and endpoint. If rhetorically associated with humanity and democratic goals rather than solely about economic production, educators and researchers might find the pedagogical imperative appealing. The different endpoints and purposes, however, do not necessarily disentangle creativity from neoliberal values for being.

6.4 Individualism, Politics, and Ideal Citizenry

6.4.4 Neoliberal Means to a Democratic End

Although the economic dimension of neoliberal values is pervasive in the discourse and shapes the narrative, researchers also emphasize a seemingly opposing democratic vision. Rather than emphasizing preparation for the economy, researchers contend that creativity is essential for democratic engagement (Greene et al., 2010; Hetland, 2013; Pope, 2005). Hetland (2013) captures this vision:

> Creativity, at its core, pushes against the edges of the known and bursts open new perspectives, shifting the sense of what is possible or even real. I am reminded of the creative legacies of Paulo Freire (1996, 2005) and bell hooks (1994), who envisioned transforming education's role to a transgressive intent: to oppose oppression and move toward liberation. Creativity makes new things and makes old things new – new problems, new solutions, new realities – things not conceived before. (p. 68)

Critical theorists such as Paulo Freire and bell hooks (also known as Gloria Jean Watkins) are known for advocating for the participation in the production of reality, which means to shift, change, dismantle, and create just, economic, and democratic processes. Arguably, creativity can support this goal by challenging existing structures, imagining new ones, and envisioning a world, not merely adapting to an existing one. In this regard, conformity, habitual engagement, and perception of the immutability of structures – all of which can be avoided through creative capacities – are antithetical to democratic citizenry. John Dewey (1938/1991) also advocates this view. He emphasizes the importance of developing tools of inquiry to direct at undemocratic and unjust situations. Dewey contends that when habit no longer works to support democracy, persons must have the skills to work with others to support inquiry in relation to and develop solutions for democratic problems. Inquiry is practical judgment that involves reflecting on and revising ends, which requires the creative transformation of values and processes, and the production of new possibilities.

Maxine Greene (1988), a well-known education philosopher and proponent of a democratic vision of schooling, argues that the arts, imagination, and creativity are foundational to freedom, independence, and meaningful democratic participation. From this view, an understanding and cultivation of creativity and its counterparts are a basis for a strong democratic learner who participates meaningfully in society and is oriented toward the social good (Greene, 1988; Sullivan, 2017). As Tanggard and Glăveanu (2013) contend, a key reason for interest in creativity is the association with being a "well-rounded" person who can think "outside the box" in situations that require creative solutions. From a democratic vision, institutionalizing creativity is foundational to realizing the liberal-democratic citizens who can engage in dialogue to form, reform, and transform democratic structures.

Although there seems to be widespread agreement that creativity should be formally integrated in schools, not all agree on the purpose. There are two seemingly opposing rationales: democratic and neoliberal. One reason for perceiving these purposes as oppositional is that neoliberal policies are accused of exacerbating inequality, preserving oppressive institutional structures, requiring conformity to market structures, and normalizing self-interest (Apple, 2017; Di Leo et al., 2015; Harvey, 2007; Sugarman, 2015). In the context of this analysis, neoliberal ideology is implicated in validating an economic instrumentalist approach to creativity and rendering it a skill to realize market values of novelty and usefulness, which are judged in terms of efficiency, productivity, and identity development. However, from a democratic vision, creativity is supposed to support resistance, subversion, and transformations of oppressive structures and practices in order to realize a social good. Although opposing endpoints, there are a few critical issues to consider.

From both perspectives, creativity is an instrument to realize an ideal person. Having a predetermined representation makes technical management possible and suggestive. Furthermore, a governing vision for creativity necessarily binds it to practices of conformity, despite its rhetorical deviation from it. The discourse can be homogenizing and universalizing by encouraging persons to calibrate themselves in relation to an endpoint and to make strategic choices to move incrementally toward that goal. That image can shape self-regulatory processes and practices, as well as inform pedagogical rationalizations, assessments, and interventions. For example, some people might inundate children with STEM toys hoping that they develop disposition and passion for creation in the sciences. Or others might encourage the learning of an instrument given its positive association with mathematical and scientific reasoning. In these examples, there are specific pedagogical choices for materials and experiences that are bound to the STEM fields which reflect economically instrumental commitments.

However, if hoping to foster creativity for a democratic purpose, one might embed students in discussions about local problems and guide them through deliberations over and enactments of solutions. These contexts can be further differentiated through a spectrum of commitments ranging from maximizing autonomy to direct strategy instruction. Regardless of purpose and structure, creativity is a normalized and assumed feature of persons that is targeted in pedagogical rationalizations, decisions, deliberations, and evaluations. Students' dispositions, traits, and goals become targets and are tied to neoliberal language of performance and maximization (e.g., see Greene, 1988). Even if educators rationalized their teaching as informed by a commitment to value creativity for its own sake, there are still governing ideas about what counts as creativity and pedagogical management remains intact as persons are interpreted and acted upon based on their approximation to an ideal type.

Herein lies a key critical complexity. Researchers and educators may rationalize the integration of creativity for different purposes. A democratic purpose may appear more palatable than an economic one. With each purpose, certain pedagogical commitments might make sense to realize the corresponding vision. Although an explicit and targeted purpose may not be immediately discernible in schooling structures and activities, the notion of creativity is taken for granted as a concept to (1) make sense of students, products, and ideas; (2) assign value to being in relation to an ideal endpoint; and (3) technically manage. Furthermore, invoking different purposes does not obscure the need for the function to make persons adaptable and amenable. Although rhetorically distinguished from conformity and implicated in the production of novel and useful products, ideas, and identities, creativity involves the shaping of cognitive capacities to function a certain way. Glăveanu (2018) points to a contradiction in the discourse. He argues that educators, business leaders, and policy makers tend to value obedience to existing orders rather than the instability, uncertainty, and inefficiency of constant organizational change and negotiation. In this regard, creativity may be tolerated to the degree to which it aligns with and enhances an organizational agenda.

6.5 Sociocultural Perspectives

Regardless of endpoint, the discourse tends to be informed by individualist or cognitive conceptualization. A cognitive approach is characterized by a commitment to transform mental operations into an algorithm for creativity (Arfken, 2014). From this perspective, researchers dissect and compartmentalize cognitive capacities so that interventions can be shaped to target the sources of creativity, such as divergent thinking, emotions, individual dispositions, values, imagination, motivation, and intellectual style (e.g., Sternberg & Lubart, 1991). This type of cognitive mapping aligns with neoliberal values for selfhood, as psychological characteristics are targeted to look a certain way, where students can reflexively perform valued and validated forms of creativity. Although this narrative tends to circulate in policy and research, other ways of understanding creativity are emerging that have the potential to divorce this notion from neoliberal selfhood. Sociocultural theorists tend to emphasize relationships, context, processes, interactions, and negotiated meanings (Amabile, 2018; Glăveanu et al., 2014; Jaramillo, 1996). From a sociocultural perspective, creativity is a product of persons acting together with available tools wherein certain products of that activity are agreed to be novel and useful (Glăveanu, 2015; Simonton, 1975). Theorists who endorse this view contend that even acting in physical isolation from others, persons are operating in a historical moment in which certain tools, practices, ideas, and products are available. Thus, they are likely to argue creativity is not the result of isolated actors with particular traits but rather the result of interaction with others, historically embedded tools, collaborations, artifacts, and agreed-upon values for novelty and usefulness. As Glăveanu (2018) argues, individualist models ignore the context of how creativity emerges, is practiced, and gets branded as such.

Sociocultural theorizing invites a shift away from the narrative of the creative individual to creativity as practice. This way of thinking dispels the myth that individual persons are solely responsible for creative products, a view that can undermine the neoliberal emphasis on human capital accumulation and isolated individualism. As Glăveanu (2018) contends, a sociocultural view does not ignore individual actors but situates them in a historical, social, and cultural network. There are different lines of sociocultural theorizing that are organized around the commitment to embed creativity in context. One perspective is called *distributed creativity* (Glăveanu et al., 2014). From this view, activity and products are conceptualized as connected in virtual, global, and physical spaces wherein ideas and products emerge because of shared cognition. Ideas and products exist and are continuously shared that elicit other ideas and the materialization of useful and novel products. From this line of thinking, products and ideas would not have materialized without existing and shared contributions.

Another line of sociocultural theorizing emphasizes the effects of the material world on cognitive processes. Research centered on this line involves analysis of how socioeconomic class, culture, and educational structures affect individual dispositions and traits. From this view, context is responsible for cultivating traits and dispositions that can be transferred to other contexts. Although seemingly counter to an individualistic model, Glăveanu (2018) warns that this line remains focused on individual dispositions and treats context as a separate entity that affects those dispositions. Glăveanu argues that to adequately capture a sociocultural view, persons must be understood within a context, not merely affected by it. Those who draw from a sociocultural perspective see that whatever counts as creative has emerged because of interactions, relationships, and meaning. If one makes or remakes an identity that is novel, it is only branded as such in relation to those identities that are perceived to exist around that person. If one creates a product that is novel and useful, that person does so with available tools and in reference to what exists in that context. Furthermore, products and ideas themselves that count as creative will be recognized as such given historically bounded values, frameworks, assessments, and imaginations.

Although a sociocultural view can potentially depart from a neoliberal narrative, there is concern with preserving creativity as a normalizing and evaluative concept. A sociocultural view can present different ontological possibilities and help to overcome some of the limitations of individualist models by shifting from personal attributions to activities, relationships, and teaching structures. Sociocultural theories may offer examples of good practice surrounding aims to foster creativity by showing its social origins and its evolution within a setting. Such insights might provide teachers, policy makers, and researchers with the tools to strategically manage situations, relationships, and material in ways that most optimally invite and recognize creativity from all participants in a context. A sociocultural shift may function to preserve creativity as an evaluative tool for activity, products, and relationships.

From cognitive and sociocultural perspectives, creativity can be treated as a natural category and descriptor of actors, actions, and products. A primary concern is that neoliberal ideology contributes to the normalization of creativity as a phenomenon that is out in the world and consequently measurable, observable, controllable, and valuable. A commitment in this critical interrogation is that creativity is not a natural, inherent descriptor of persons and activities. Rather, creativity is being brought to bear on the evaluations of persons, activity, and context for specific reasons and functions to assign value and inform interventions. This way of thinking can be described as a constitutive perspective.

6.6 A Constitutive Perspective

From this perspective, creativity is not a natural category of persons, activities, and products. Glăveanu (2018) captures this way of thinking when he writes:

> Creativity is, essentially, a social construction and not a natural category. This means we should not expect to 'find' creativity in the genes, the brain, the inner mental states of the person, for as much as any of these contribute to ongoing creative activities. Ideation, for instance, is a mental process supported by neural networks, but no idea is creative in a universal, contextual manner. This is because creativity is first and foremost a social label we apply to ideas, objects, people, actions, performances, and so on; as a cultural sign, it is variable across historical time and geographical place. In other words, nothing is creative because it just is, and to realize this we should only remember the fact that the notion of creativity itself has a history. (p. 119)

This perspective opens up certain possibilities for critical interrogation. The argument is that neoliberal ideology influences the acceptance of certain narratives about creativity, ones based on individualist models, human capital, instrumentalism, and novel and useful products or ideas. Gormley (2018) makes this argument and suggests that alternative narratives may get silenced that do not align with neoliberal values and assumptions. Sociocultural perspectives can potentially offer a counter-narrative that is focused on activity, relationships, and context – troubling attributions of personal value, traits, and NCS. Although this potential exists, considering a sociocultural narrative may do little to problematize the use of creativity as an evaluative tool and means for managing persons and activity. If treated as a discursive construction, the ideological and political forces that circulate in different narratives can be explored.

Creativity is a historically specific way to brand certain actions, activities, and products. Observations and interpretations of persons in context do not have to be governed and informed by creativity. Their actions and products do not have to be conceptualized as indicative of or resulting from a phenomenon known as creativity. A key insight of Ogata's historical analysis is that the trope of and efforts to cultivate the creative child are embodied by the ideals and longings of adults who operated within historical, cultural, and economic context. Ogata does not engage in debate about whether or not children are naturally creative or if it can be taught. She also does not support the claim that teachers or parents can operate outside of historical context to recognize, realize, and cultivate a form of creativity in children that is abstracted from history, culture, politics, and ideology. The fact that creativity is a concept that is used to make sense of persons, activity, products, and processes is itself a historical artifact.

There is no trope of the creative child that reflects a conception that is neutral or objective. The use of creativity itself is historically dependent in that it is used specifically to govern the conduct of persons around a goal to produce particular types of persons. In other words, children were not always treated as persons with creative capacities that can be measured and calibrated. Creativity was not always a way to judge character, skill, and value. The concerted effort to cultivate creativity did not always exist in the schooling discourse and the calibration of persons. However, at some point that changed and it changed for political, ideological, and cultural reasons. Historical context not only shapes what counts as creative but also shapes the propensity to use creativity as a marker of students' value, capacity, and character.

6.7 Conclusion

Debates and controversies can detract from the ideological implications of formally making creativity a pedagogical target. The analysis here is intended to avoid ontological and pedagogical certainty. Researchers, policy makers, and educators may believe that creativity is natural, learned, developed, or acquired. They may disagree about ideal environments, some emphasizing autonomy while others emphasize discipline and procedures. Endpoints and functions are another point of contention. This burgeoning interest has led to the abundance of methodological, conceptual, pedagogical, and ontological debates, which are driven by efforts and hopes to improve experiences, interactions, and contexts that are associated with creativity. As part of that effort, creativity as a normalizing framework for persons, contexts, and products is preserved. The notion of creativity is centered as a pedagogical target, which is informed by visions of the creative child. Even if this vision is democratic, neoliberal ideology is entangled in this discourse. The economic rationalization reveals a clear alignment as creativity tends to be treated as a calculable feature of persons that signals potential for participation in the so-called creative economy. However, though democratic and humanistic conceptualizations may seem more palatable than an economic purpose, creativity is still bound to neoliberal values of instrumentalism, management, and prescription.

CHAPTER 7

Whole Child
Leave No Part Behind

7.1 Introduction

In contemporary education discourse there are calls to teach the whole child (WC), which is intended to shift focus away from the overemphasis on test performance to target students' physical, affective, social, spiritual needs and states. The narrative is that narrowly committing to cognitive abilities ignores the complexities of being and directs attention away from other parts of children that researchers deem just as important, if not more so, for academic success (Darling-Hammond et al., 2018; Duckworth et al., 2007; Dweck, 2006; Garcia &Weiss, 2016; OECD, 2006; Shechtman et al., 2016; Tough, 2012). WC education typically includes practices that target ER, personality development, self-regulation, creativity, civic engagement, and physical health. Researchers and policy makers argue that successfully creating a classroom climate that takes into account these parts will lead to economic preparedness, self-sufficiency, democratic participation, good character, conscientiousness, aesthetic sensibilities, and overall wellness (ASCD, 2020; Darling-Hammond et al., 2018; Griffith & Slade, 2018; Noddings, 2005; Soder et al., 2002).

In contrast to schooling dedicated to only a partial or fragmented child centered on cognitive abilities, centering wholeness seems like an appealing alternative. The promises of WC education can potentially dissolve ideological, political, and philosophical debates and controversies about the purposes of schooling. Schooling that prepares children for the economy, supports civic virtue, nurtures love for art, and promises safety and health can be embraced by persons who endorse humanistic, democratic, and neoliberal visions of schooling (see the bipartisan report by the American Enterprise Institute and Brookings Institute, 2015). The broad appeal can help explain the burgeoning interest in WC education. In 2007, the Association for Supervision and Curriculum Development (ASCD), which comprises 113,000 members worldwide, launched an effort to redefine academic achievement called the "Whole Child Initiative." A commission produced a report as a call to action to encourage schools, districts, and states to adopt WC education. Edsurge (2019) reports interest in the WC schooling continues to grow exponentially. Although seen across all grade levels, this commitment is explicit and pervasive in early childhood and elementary schools (Jenkins et al., 2018).

Even if not part of educational structures and practices, as reported in the EdSurge (2019) research report, teachers are not likely to disagree with organizing the classroom in accordance with wholeness, notwithstanding the different perceptions about what that means. The thought of fragmenting students can seem dehumanizing and a throwback to the time when standardized testing rhetorically mattered a great deal. The range of benefits for WC schooling is compelling. Given the conceptual and ethical appeal, along with a broad range of values, there tends to be an absence of critical dialogue on the discourse of the WC. Debates and controversies tend to be about conceptualization and pedagogical structures. Seldom are there explorations into the ideological context and consequences of the WC. Advancing such a dialogue is not about defending structures that reward, center, and cultivate so-called cognitive abilities. Critical analysis is not an endorsement to fragment children or preserve the validity of standardized tests to predict academic success and signify intelligence and ability. Conversations and visions for children and schooling can move beyond the binaries of cognitive/noncognitive and fragmented/whole.

The purpose of this analysis is to highlight ways that the notion of the WC is used in contemporary discourse to normalize, validate, and reward neoliberal selfhood. Implicating neoliberal ideology in this discourse might seem counterintuitive. Often, neoliberal selfhood is associated with economic instrumentalism and, therefore, may appear to compartmentalize persons in ways that enable a strategic and targeted focus on a limited subset of attributes, traits, dispositions, and skills. A common criticism of neoliberalism is that it supports schooling policies and practices that target qualities of selfhood for economic productivity at the expense of well-being, happiness, physical health, community engagement, civic virtue, and democratic participation. However, qualities for economic productivity are broad and include a variety of characteristics that are featured in conceptualizations of the WC. The modern narrative is that to be economically productive one must regulate emotions and be passionate, entrepreneurial, creative, innovative, conscientious, persistent, adaptable, and engaged. The ways in which wholeness is constructed and the desired manifestation of it align with visions of ideal twenty-first century persons.

Another line of critical engagement is about the increased institutional reach for shaping all parts of children. Simply stated, in WC education no part of the child is to remain unaffected by institutional power (Fendler, 2001). For this point, let us bracket debates about the contents of children and what the ideal WC looks like. In addition, let us assume that the promises of WC education can support democratic, economic, and humanistic visions of schooling. The pedagogical focus on the WC is directing the educative gaze on all parts of children in order to subject those parts to institutional lessons. WC schooling is about creating pedagogical structures and contexts to target children's character, emotions, body, attitudes, personality, and dispositions. The desired effect of this type of education is to shape what was once thought about as a part of private life, self, and self-regulatory actions to align with institutional objectives. WC schooling provides a good example of ways in which neoliberal governance works. These lines of critical inquiry are offered in order to invite educators, researchers, and policy makers to consider the ideological context for the understanding and value of wholeness and to recognize the ethical implications of broadening institutional reach to achieve the production of a certain type of wholeness.

7.2 Contents of the Whole Child

Throughout history, schooling has been charged with targeting different features of persons. As Fendler (2001) points out, at different moments in history, schooling policy and practice centered on morality, aesthetics, economic participation, spirituality, and intellect. With such charges, schooling was open to accusations of favoring some features while ignoring others. Centering certain characteristics results from a key function of schools to shape persons in ways to realize an ideal vision for a citizenry, whether that means cultural assimilation, economic productivity, civic engagement, or happiness. Although there are various reasons to target certain features of students, philosophers, practitioners, and researchers generally believe that fragmentation does students a disservice by limiting the possibilities for learning, as well as denying their humanity (ASCD, 2020; Darling-Hammond et al., 2018; Johnson, 2015; Lee & Lee, 2020; Noddings, 2005). In the literature, not integrating wholeness in schools is associated with anxiety, stress, resistance, and disconnectedness to schools, teachers, and peers (e.g., Darling-Hammond et al., 2018).

Despite long-standing concerns about fragmentation, there are disagreements in the discourse about the contents of the child, ways the WC is understood, and the pedagogical structures for validating and developing the child. Although there is a general consensus that wholeness as an organizing concept for pedagogical possibilities is favorable, there is not always agreement on what that means. The focus of this section is on some of the variations which make it possible to consider that wholeness is not a neutral, objective, ahistorical, and natural depiction of persons.

7.2.1 Historical Ontology

Before delving into differences in the contents of wholeness, it is important to note a foundational commitment in this analysis. Wholeness is not treated here as a natural category of persons but rather a concept that is (1) a specific representation of persons that is underpinned by philosophical assumptions about being; (2) entangled in ideological context; and (3) deployed in a time place for specific reasons. This last point is informed by a historical ontological position that descriptions of psychological phenomenon are informed by available instruments, accepted methods for knowledge production, frameworks for being, ideology, philosophy, and language. Historical ontology is predicated on the assumption that there are many possible ways to be a person and that features of a historical moment help to constitute being in particular ways. The notion of whole is abstract but rendered concrete through well-defined and elaborated descriptions about contents of humanness. As Sugarman (2009) urges, rather than accepting psychological description as a given, historical analysis needs to examine the context wherein psychological description occurs, the purposes it serves, how it is implemented, and the possible consequences.

From a historical ontological perspective, the notion of the WC is not a depiction of an essential, existing category that is named. Rather, the notion of whole is historically contingent and takes form in a particular historical moment for certain reasons. The historical boundedness is not only about the contents of the WC but also about the notion of wholeness itself. Philosophers have been contemplating the ideas of wholeness for centuries. *Mereology* is a field of study organized around articulating and delineating ideas of and relationships between parts and wholes. This type of philosophizing is traced back to Plato and Aristotle and persists in psychology and philosophy today. Typically, the purpose of studying wholeness is to articulate natural laws about the composition and relationships of material and immaterial things. In contemporary policy documents and research, proponents of WC schooling believe that advancements in science have revealed parts of children and how they work together to form an entire being. In this discourse, scientific advancement is implicated in (1) mapping the various components of students; (2) articulating healthy forms of wholeness; and (3) revealing the types of environments to support the recognition and development of wholeness (e.g., ASCD, 2020; Darling-Hammond et al., 2018; Garcia & Weiss, 2016).

A historical ontological perspective invites one to question the certainty of this picture in order to situate wholeness in a particular moment. In order to challenge such certainty, it is helpful to consider different perspectives. Given its long-standing presence in philosophy and subsequently in emerging disciplines of science and psychology, there is a vast literature that cannot be exhaustively reviewed here. Rather, three different perspectives are presented: Jungian psychoanalytic, Christian (as per Friedrich Froebel), and posthuman. These perspectives were chosen because they represent different ways of thinking about wholeness. The purpose of discussing these views is to show that there are multiple ways of thinking about wholeness and that the representation in contemporary discourse is not the only possibility. Once open to variations of wholeness, the question becomes: why adopt, endorse, normalize, and validate one vision over another? One possible answer is that the modern vision for the WC appeals to neoliberal sensibilities about the types of people who are desired for the modern world.

7.2.1.1 Harmony of the Conscious and Unconscious: A Jungian Perspective
Carl Jung is a well-known psychoanalyst who is often compared to Sigmund Freud in terms of level of importance for informing a specific form of therapy. Like other psychoanalysts, Jung was concerned with articulating differences between the relationship of conscious and unconscious elements in order to achieve mental and physical health (Jung, 1954/2014; Smith, 1990). It is in this relationship that wholeness is understood and achieved. Jung is well known for theorizing a quest for wholeness, which was not a given but something achieved through analytical work. Wholeness is a psychological state of being that results from distinguishing oneself from others and ensuring that one's conscious and unconscious drives are in harmony (Jung, 1954/2014; Smith, 1990). Jung called this a process of *individuation*.

In order to facilitate this process, one must explore fears, dreams, and desires that have been ignored or denied. According to Jung, all persons have a psychic center, which is represented in dreams by a mandala. Each person has their own symbol for their psychic center that appears in messages from the unconscious and the spiritual realms through dreams, word associations, and the interpretation of symbols, play, metaphors, and creative activities. Wholeness for Jung is achieved through the recognition of this psychic center, which is the self, and the analytical work to produce harmony between the conscious and unconscious. For Jung, persons have a persona, shadow, anima, animus, and ego. These psychological features are parts of a whole and through psychoanalytic work, persons can reconcile these parts around their psychic center. Although one is distinguishing self from others in the process of individuation, making this sense of self is in some sense relational Wholeness is identifying a unique psychic center and generating harmony with several unconscious parts.

7.2.1.2 Divine Unity: Froebel and Unification of Life

Although some researchers contend that Jung's psychoanalytic view of wholeness has spirituality at its core, his view stands in contrast to the Christian view espoused by Friedrich Froebel. Whereas Jung emphasized the exploration and articulation of a self, around which all other psychological phenomena must be organized, some theorists contend that wholeness is measured by liberation from a sense of self (Albahari, 2016; Lindgren, 2019). This liberation can be played in at least a couple of different ways. As will be discussed later, posthumanists think about this in terms recognizing one's being in relation to all living creatures and ecological contexts. Another way is in relation to God.

German philosopher Friedrich Froebel, who is associated with the start of the kindergarten movement, explicitly bound the concept of wholeness to God, despite the fact that this association is seldom acknowledged in his theorizing about early childhood education. Froebel (1885/2005) endorsed a specific vision of wholeness that cannot be embraced in public schooling, which, unlike private schools, often excludes any allusion to spirituality or religion. For Froebel, wholeness is bound to "Divine Unity"; to omit this part is a source of fragmentation, a denial of one's wholeness (Froebel, 1885/2005; Marenholtz-Bülow, 1895). Like Jung, Froebel argues that all persons have an essence, which is a stable and continuous core of being. This essence, however, is unity with God. Froebel writes:

> It is the destiny and life-work of all things to unfold their essence, hence their divine being, and therefore, the Divine Unity itself – to reveal God in their external and transient being. It is the special destiny and life-work of man, as an intelligent and rational being, to become fully, vividly, and clearly conscious of his essence, of the divine effluence in him, and, therefore, of God; to become fully, vividly, and clearly conscious of his identity and life-work . . . . (p. 2)

For Froebel, wholeness extends beyond emotion, mental, and physical attributes; modern descriptions of wholeness do not apply to Froebel's theorizing. In his annotations for Froebel's well-known book *Education of Man*, Hailmann (1885/2005) describes wholeness as "unification of life," which means: (1) harmony in feeling, thinking, willing, and doing (achieved through recognition of unity with God); (2) subordination of self to common welfare; (3) subordination to laws of nature (which are laws of God); and (4) perfect faith in Christianity. For Froebel, schooling based on wholeness is a specific developmental pathway for full unification of life, which means living according to God's plan.

7.2.1.3 Relationality in an Ecosystem: A Posthumanism Perspective

Although in different ways, the previous two accounts of wholeness assume an internal life and reality. For Jung, persons have a composite of unconscious and consciousness parts that must be recognized, analyzed, and harmoniously organized around a psychic center. For Froebel, persons have an inner, spiritual life through which God flows outward. Wholeness is recognizing that inner life, discerning the divine unity in one's being, and living a life of faith. In a perspective under the rubric of posthumanism, wholeness is not bound to so-called internal phenomena. Keeling and Lehman (2018) identify three assumptions about being that informs posthumanist philosophy: (1) persons are physically, chemically, and biologically enmeshed and dependent on the environment; (2) persons move to action through interactions that generate affects, habits, and reason; and (3) persons possess no attribute that is uniquely human but is instead made up of a larger evolving ecosystem. From this view, persons are not composed of parts that make them an entire being. Rather, persons are part of an ecosystem in which action and a sense of being only take form in relations to others and the broad material context. The entirety of one's being is simply a part of a relationship that perpetually evolves. Posthumanists are not likely to argue that persons are bundles of attributes, attitudes, traits, qualities, and dispositions that are inherent and internal to them. Rather, they are likely to contend that treating persons in that way is actually a practice of fragmentation by severing identity, being, and action from others and the natural world.

7.2.1.4 Psychologism: Educational Psychology and Policy

Martin (2014) contends that the idea of wholeness that informs education and psychological discourse is informed by a style of reasoning that he calls psychologism, which is the idea that persons are a composite of internal and knowable features that serve as causal explanations for thoughts, behaviors, and outcomes. Martin explains that psychologists tend to apply the methods of the so-called natural sciences in order to inform this understanding. The underlying assumption is that children have wholeness that is composed of knowable parts. In this regard, there is a simultaneous fragmentation and unification of personhood that can be known. Although the notion of the WC is an attempt at unification of persons to include in educational spaces, the belief is that the children have psychological lives that are predetermined, knowable, and, in carefully controlled environments.

It is not uncommon for psychologists and educators to separate persons from their brains, emotions from rationality, behavior from personality, and cognitive from NCS while at the same time claim that these features are part of all children. The notion of the WC is based on this type of fragmentation but with the added theorizing about how parts work in concert. Teaching the WC does not necessarily mean challenging fragmentation, but ensuring schooling is adequately attuned, in a concerted way, to those various parts. According to proponents of WC schooling, problems arise when some parts of the child are ignored while others are targets of pedagogical structures.

This position is informed by several assumptions that critical psychologists tend to reject: (1) there is an innate wholeness to persons; (2) improved methods can represent wholeness; (3) there is a coherent wholeness that is stable across time and place; and (4) structures can predictably target and effect that wholeness to make it into a desirable state (Amsel, 2015; Freeman, 2015; Martin, 2015). Martin (2015) challenges the assumption that scientific methods can be employed to present an objective representation of students. Even if one assumed persons had an inherent wholeness, Freeman (2015) contends that subjecting persons to particular methods and frameworks for articulating and developing that wholeness actually competes with that state. The idea is that measuring, calibrating, and delineating parts, even if there are many, undermine representations of a whole being. Freeman points to the potential limiting factor of applying predetermined frameworks, measurement, and technical rationality to make sense of persons. The same concern can be raised about evaluative tools and mechanisms that are intended to provide information about the contents of children. Critical psychologists tend to take the position that instruments used to measure psychological phenomena help to give form to that phenomena rather than simply stand as a representation of what is preexisting (e.g., Brenner, 1978; Burman, 2008; Sugarman, 2009). There is a tendency to assume that with new perspectives, improved instruments, and expanded frameworks, children can be known wholly and that the right types of environments can ensure that wholeness manifests in desirable ways.

7.2.2 Contemporary Narrative

There are numerous conflicting, contradictory, and competing ideas about wholeness. Debates exist even if it makes sense to use parts and wholes to describe persons. The varying viewpoints are informed by the conceptualization of parts and wholes, and merely scratch the surface of a complicated philosophical, ethical, and pedagogical landscape. Attention to these examples can serve four purposes: (1) invite one to consider a complex picture of what counts as wholeness; (2) consider how certain perspectives can be viewed as fragmentation from another perspective (e.g., omitting God and historical-situatedness from wholeness can be viewed as fragmentation); (3) provide counter-narratives that exist in education discourse; and (4) consider how modern context might influence the acceptance of one narrative of wholeness over others.

For the fourth point, consider that the separation of church and state makes it unlikely to realize Froebel's vision for wholeness. Many researchers who cite Froebel to justify WC education omit his emphasis on Divine Unity and rather use his theorizing to argue for the importance of play and learning in nature during the early years of a child's life (Bruce, 2015). Pragmatically, adopting a Jungian perspective requires that teachers have an entirely different skill set and for educational practices to dramatically change. A posthumanist account competes with existing school structures and practices that are based on calibrating, measuring, and targeting students' psychology in pedagogical interventions. There are pragmatic, structural, and philosophical conditions that contribute to accepting certain visions for wholeness. The argument here is that the dominant narrative that pervades education discourse is adopted and accepted because it aligns with a particular ideological vision for persons and societies.

Researchers often cite the deleterious effects of the *No Child Left Behind* (NCLB) legislation, which is responsible for increased high-stakes testing. During its enactment, critics accused school policy and practice of primarily focused on transmitting knowledge and cultivating the types of reasoning ability that support test performance. This emphasis was branded as a focus on cognitive ability, which for many years was believed to predict success in- and outside of school. Against this backdrop, WC education is advanced, justified, and promoted as an appealing educational paradigm. Proponents often remark that children are more than their test scores. Not only is there more to persons than reasoning abilities, researchers and policy makers argue that the additional substance is more predictive of success than test scores. In addition to its predictive value, educating the WC is associated with satisfaction, civic engagement, productivity, creativity, adaptability, and self-regulation.

7.2.2.1 Parts of a Whole

There tends to be consensus on the contents of children. Generally, researchers and policy makers refer to children as consisting of physical, social, emotional, and intellectual parts (ASCD, 2020; Darling-Hammond et al., 2018; Garcia & Weiss, 2016; Noddings, 2005). Taking these parts into account, the ASCD (2020) describes WC education as committed to health, safety, support, engagement, and intellectual challenge. For the Learning Policy Institute, Darling-Hammond et al. (2018) published a report that captures the WC narrative. The authors state:

> New knowledge about human development from neuroscience and the sciences of learning and development demonstrates that effective learning depends on secure attachments; affirming relationships; rich, hands-on learning experiences; and explicit integration of social, emotional, and academic skills. A positive school environment supports students' growth across all the developmental pathways – physical, psychological, cognitive, social, and emotional –while it reduces stress and anxiety that create biological impediments to learning. Such an environment takes a 'whole child' approach to education, seeking to address the distinctive strengths, needs, and interests of students as they engage in learning. (p. v)

Darling-Hammond et al. suggest that new, valid, objective, scientifically informed knowledge has revealed and unlocked the mysteries of being and the causal determinants of that being. In this report, the authors use the notion of *pathways* to depict parts of children that must be integrated into the pedagogical act in order to count as WC schooling.

Major educational organizations and influential policy figures adopt this version of wholeness, including the ASCD, Educational Testing Service (ETS), Learning Policy Institute, Brookings Institute, and American Enterprise Institute. Although there tends to be a broad framework, there can be subtle variations and emphases. For example, some researchers, policy makers, and schools emphasize arts, creative practice, and aesthetic sensibility as quintessential to wholeness (ASCD, 2020; Ferrandino, 1999). ASCD (2020) supports this view and agrees that cultivating an affinity for arts is key for realizing WC education.

The ETS developed an assessment for teachers to test their knowledge of the WC. In their study guide (2018), they not only cite physical, cognitive, and emotional components but also included linguistic, cultural, and familial components. These features are not likely to be disputed as parts of children but might rather be subsumed under broad categories. For example, some researchers and policy makers may reason that linguistic and cultural parts of children are necessary for emotional and social development, as well as feeling supported, engaged, and safe. The broad parts – social, emotional, psychological, and cognitive – organize several subsets of parts.

Kyllonen (2005), who is a Distinguished Presidential Appointee at the ETS, provides an elaborate picture, which was created to inform the production and defense of measuring wholeness. He uses the broad category of psychology, which includes personality such as conscientiousness, agreeableness, and emotional stability. Another category is affective, which includes creativity, cognitive style, and emotional intelligence. Kyllonen also includes what he terms performance factors, which include leadership, management, organization, effort, and discipline. Despite variation, specificity, and elaboration of components, he includes features that align with the broad categories of physical, psychological, emotional, social, and cognitive being.

Although there tends to be agreement in the policy arena about wholeness, there are subtle differences that suit a particular vision for schooling, personhood, and society. A function of wholeness is to justify pedagogical structures to cultivate, reward, value, validate, and normalize a particular type of person, yet conceal that operation by framing that representation as wholeness. A particular reading of the literature can reveal various agendas around the concept of the WC, which is used to produce and reproduce a particular citizenry.

7.2.2.2 *Prescribing the Right Kind of Wholeness*

WC schooling is not only about a commitment to recognize and integrate all of the "parts" and "pathways" of children into schooling. There is another less explicitly stated purpose: to shape attitudes, dispositions, personalities, emotions, and traits in ways to realize visions for being and social systems. Researchers and policy makers have ideas about good character, ways of relating, work ethic, and emotional expression. WC education is informed by those ideas. For example, in the ETS Open Notes by Michael Nettles, who is a Senior Vice President of ETS's Policy Evaluation & Research Center, he endeavors to build a case for WC education by asking questions that point to potential problems with children's character. He asks, "Are we [children] patient? Are we respectful? Are we tolerant of our differences in appearance, values, belief, habits and behavior? Do we persevere through adversity, and even failure? Can we empathize with the suffering of others? Are we able to work collaboratively and creatively toward shared goals? Can we keep our tempers in check?" (Nettles, n.d.).

There can certainly be fruitful debates about the understanding, evaluation, and the ethics of the qualities captured in those questions. One can problematize what counts as respect, patience, and failure, for example, as well as debate if such qualities should be included in representations of whole persons. Putting aside those ethical and metaphysical questions, the purpose here is to highlight that WC schooling is about realizing a particular representation of being.

Schooling today is focused on character, personality, dispositions, desires, and attitudes. In part, this focus results from negative assessments of young people and by representations of the types of people that are needed for the twenty-first century. Pushing for educational programs to cultivate certain states and to realize a specific vision for persons is framed as teaching the WC. In fact, much of the WC schooling centers on a certain expression of social and emotional development. What counts as an emotion, and an acceptable one at that, is complex. However, if one accepts that persons have emotional lives and that certain behaviors indicate an expression of that emotion, it is clear in the WC discourse that social emotional health is associated with specific behaviors, dispositions, and perspectives.

For example, Darling-Hammond et al. (2020) argue that WC schooling needs to include a focus on "Social and emotional learning that fosters skills, habits, and mindsets which enable academic progress and productive behavior. These include self-regulation, executive function, intrapersonal awareness and interpersonal skills, a growth mindset, and a sense of agency that supports resilience and perseverance" (p. 99).

There is a specific set of behaviors, cognitive functions, and perceptions, as well as norms for engagement, that signify the types of social and emotional learning that support "progress" and "productive" behavior. In another reading of this quotation, the authors contend that persons are recognized as emotionally and socially developed if they embody and perform subject positions that align with neoliberal selfhood. Self-regulation, GM, and resilience are key features of neoliberal selfhood. Successfully targeting social and emotional lives of children is evidenced by the approximation to this brand of self. If one does not embody such a self, then schooling practices must be shaped to produce them in order to support the realization of this representation of wholeness.

Social and emotional learning is included in the broad category of NCS. Although researchers recognize the limitations of this term, noncognitive is still used to emphasize the importance of WC education. Herein lies a major point of concern: NCS are entangled in neoliberal values for selfhood. WC schooling is not just about what children are but what they need to be and what they need to be is informed by values for twenty-first century persons. Representations of the ideal twenty-first-century person align with ideal neoliberal selfhood. A broad concern is that the modern narrative of wholeness is used to normalize, propagate, value, and validate neoliberal selfhood. The inclusion of grit and response to failure are illustrations of these values.

Grit and Wholeness   In an interview with Perkins-Gough (2013), Angela Duckworth encouraged educators to take up grit in schooling as a way to realize WC education. This suggestion makes sense; children's psychological lives are purported to extend far beyond reasoning abilities to include so-called NCS, of which grit is an oft-referenced feature. Researchers and policy makers argue that grit is a NCS that must be targeted as a way to realize WC schooling (Duckworth & Yeager, 2015; Gold et al., 2016; Michelman, 2015; Tough, 2012). The ASCD fully endorses this view, as evidenced by the inclusion of grit in the lexicon for WC education (Michelman, 2015). In order to encourage cohesion and precision, Michelman (2015) put out an information brief for the ASCD to define key terms associated with WC schooling. In this brief, she discusses the distinctions between grit, resilience, and perseverance. Michelman acknowledges that there is potential for conceptual differences in these terms but does not question their place in the representations of wholeness. As a NCS, grit is generally accepted as a component of WC schooling.

If one were to commit to educating the WC, then one must use grit as a way to measure and evaluate students, as well as inform pedagogical interventions. Such inclusion in wholeness can make resistance to adopting the grit imperative a challenge. If educators disagree with grit as representing a feature of whole persons and, consequently, refusing to inform pedagogical decision-making to foster its development, they can be accused of ignoring wholeness and fragmenting children. One can suggest that those educators dehumanize students by denying natural parts of their being. The label of noncognitive, in addition to the classification of grit as a NCS, solidifies grit among representations of wholeness. Given that wholeness is generally regarded as humanistic, if one wanted to educate with this ethical commitment, they must calibrate students in terms of their grittiness and commit pedagogical resources to its development.

Although researchers and policy makers tend to believe that supporting the development of grit in schooling indicates WC education, Kohn (2014), who is an outspoken critic of grit, argues the contrary. He contends that a focus on grit is about pushing behavior without considering the satisfaction and moral direction of that behavior. For Kohn, WC schooling must include these dimensions. He critiques the grit narrative for overly emphasizing behaviors (e.g., spending time on a task, pursuing a particular outcome, practicing, and being tenacious) and outcomes. Kohn (2008) stated, "if we're interested in the WC – if, for example, we'd like our students to be psychologically healthy – then it's not at all clear that self-discipline should enjoy a privileged status compared to other attributes" (p. 3). Although Duckworth believed she endorsed a multidimensional view of persons, Kohn contends that the child in the grit narrative ignores morality, satisfaction, and happiness.

Although there are problems with both Kohn's and Duckworth's reasoning, this difference highlights an important consideration of wholeness. Ideological and political commitments shape what is accepted as whole and what children should be. Kohn operates from a liberal-democratic perspective and endorses a view that centers on self-expression, happiness, and orientation to the communal good. However, Duckworth operates from a neoliberal perspective that emphasizes self-control, goal attainment, personal responsibility, and self-interest. Political perspective, historical moment, spiritual commitments, disciplinary tradition, and culture are implicated in the representation of what children are and should be.

Integrating grit in this representation normalizes and validates neoliberal selfhood. Grit is used to judge character and inform pedagogical interventions to normalize a specific work ethic, set of behaviors, and attitudes.

Seemingly contradictory, an educator is not permitted to accept quitting as part of wholeness. A human flight response is pathologized and signals deficits in character. Quitting signals poor character and stunted social and emotional development. The implicit reasoning in the research and policy is that persons who quit have not been exposed to the right types of schooling structures that help them realize their wholeness. That reasoning makes WC schooling a serious concern. If children are not recognized as self-regulated, they may not be considered whole. If they are not recognized as expressing aesthetic and creative sensibilities, children might not be considered whole. Being branded as having a fixed mindset, not perpetually oriented to progress, uninterested in school, and distrusting of school personnel are all pathologies. Such attitudes and behaviors do not signify political resistance, nor are valid and rational responses, but rather are consequences of inadequate experiences that deny wholeness. Wholeness is about endorsing quite specific subject positions that align with neoliberal values for being. Such an alignment is clear in a healthy social and emotional response that is related to grit.

Response to Failure Students' response to failure is featured in the WC discourse. Students count as whole based on their perception of and response to failure, both of which, as the narrative goes, indicate social and emotional health. First a caveat: the term *failure* here is used as an evaluation of a performance event that exists only in a framework and is known by available instruments. Students act and engage in a fluid way. However, at a particular moment in time, performance is rendered static through the use of an instrument that enables one to represent a person on a trajectory. For example, standardized cognitive tests render intelligence and ability static and knowable by situating a score on a hierarchical framework. Measurements of NCS also function this way. Failure is the perception that a representation of a performance did not produce the intended outcome or does not align with expected norms for that performance. From this understanding, the notion of failure is not inherent as it requires an evaluative system, tools for measurement, certain perceptions, intentions, and norms. However, in the WC discourse, failure stands as an unproblematized representation of a performance event. In this discourse, students fail and their perception and response indicate wholeness.

A sign of social and emotional health is persistence in the face of failure. Such persistence is made possible, however, if one has certain perceptions and attitudes. One such perception is the branding of failure as "good" or "bad." Hoerr (2013), who was invited to speak at an ASCD conference on the WC, states:

> We need to teach and embrace the term *good failure*. No one wants to fail, but a *good* failure can help us learn and become stronger. Employing the term *good failure* lets everyone know that failing isn't the end of the world. What matters most is what we do after we fail. With that in mind, we need to go beyond measuring and rewarding students' results and also applaud their effort, trajectory, and progress. (emphases added, p. 84)

This way of thinking about performance and a response to it is fairly common in the WC discourse. Researchers and policy makers are committed to ensuring that children seek out, learn from, and embrace failure (Diamond, 2010; Hoerr, 2013; Tulius et al., 2016). This message is foundational to the GM narrative. Normalized, healthy visions of students are that they should pursue discomfort, seek challenges, and take risks. In doing so, failure is a real possibility and should not be a deterrent, but the motivation to persist with goals. The socially and emotionally healthy WC is energized by failure, which is used as a source of learning and strategic choice-making. The idea is that an indication of wholeness is using a performance event, in which one did not experience a desired outcome, to guide efforts to improve. Thinking about failure in this way encapsulates the idea of GM and the perpetual orientation to improvement. Failure only counts as such if the performance event does not have value for progressing on a trajectory of betterness.

There are several issues with this perspective. First, even if not branded as failure, but rather a *stepping stone* students must accept that some instrument can validly render their performance static in some quantitative or qualitative way. The meaning and rhetorical description (e.g., failure or stepping stone) of the performance event might be problematized, but not the representation of performance. Cultivating the character trait to embrace failure is about protecting frameworks, norms, values, tools, and instruments to represent a performance event. This way of thinking preserves the legitimacy of systems of evaluation to designate a moment in time as a failure or a point on a trajectory. If a student fails a test, in order for this performance event to be counted as failure or a reference to inform choices to improve, the test, test structure, grading scale, and cutoff for failing must be afforded legitimacy. Failure exists in well-defined, predetermined frameworks for performance. Conceptualizing oneself as failing in relation to these frameworks helps to justify personal responsibility for outcomes and supports efforts to calibrate and act on oneself. As a result of failure, one must make choices that can be situated on a path of improvement. Without the static rendering of being, one might not know one's qualities and what needs to be improved. The calibration of being, valuation of experience, and movement toward betterness are essential for neoliberal selfhood

Successfully cultivating this way of thinking about and responding to a performance event indicates good character and an achievement of WC schooling. It is not enough, however, to cultivate this way of thinking. Children must concede to the legitimacy of a performance event to count as failure, analyze that event to extract value, and inform action for a trajectory of improvement, all the while maintaining a positive attitude. It is important not to forget that the WC is optimistic and happy with this perspective and life ethic. A healthy response to failure is to analyze experiences to extract as much value as possible. An experience for the sake of an experience is unacceptable. One must analyze an experience to maximize the value for growth and improvement. Pessimism, quitting, denying that some type of performance indicates failure, and resisting the valuation of experience are not valued perceptions and behaviors as they indicate problems with wholeness. One is whole if they have a GM, remain optimistic, persist, and legitimize institutional frameworks to stand as representations of performance.

7.2.2.3 Neoliberal Values for Being

There are several qualities included in WC schooling, which is not only about integrating all parts of children but also ensuring that those parts develop in a certain way. WC discourse is prescriptive and normative. Such prescription is problematic more so because the representation reflects neoliberal values for self. From the above examples, the WC perseveres, uses failure to inform perpetual growth, and strategically manages life by making choices to pursue improvement. In addition, researchers and policy makers emphasize features of wholeness as including self-regulation, collaboration, and adaptability. These characteristics are featured in representations of ideal twenty-first century persons which are instantiations of neoliberal selfhood. Although these qualities might be construed as positive, they are driven by economic purposes. In a bipartisan working group from the American Enterprise Institute and the Brookings Institute, the authors write:

> Increasingly, economists, employers and corporate leaders are recognizing how vital "soft skills" are to success in the labor market and to the nation's productivity. In an information and service economy, a variety of what some researchers (mistakenly) call "non-cognitive traits" are especially important. These include workplace skills such as the ability to follow directions and take feedback from supervisors, cooperate with co-workers, and focus on tasks and complete them on time. They also include more personal skills like managing one's own feelings and making responsible decisions about one's personal life. These and other characteristics influence people's educational attainment, employment and earnings as much as or more than academic achievement as measured by standardized achievement tests. In education policy and practice, these soft skills go by many names, most commonly social-emotional learning or character development. (p. 61)

This quotation is from a consensus plan on reducing poverty and restoring the American Dream. One might see how it makes sense that policy makers focus on cultivating skills and dispositions that arguably make persons marketable and functionable within modern workplaces. Although this approach to poverty reduction is certainly questionable, the main concern here is that the development of character, dispositions, adaptability, amenability, and self-management for the modern workplace is framed as WC schooling. In this regard, the WC vision is prescriptive, normative, and instrumental, and it invalidates a range of behaviors, attitudes, dispositions, beliefs, and perceptions. A vision of WC schooling that is both exclusionary and prescriptive seems counterintuitive, especially when neoliberal values inform representations of wholeness.

7.3 No Part Left Uneducated

There tends to be a consensus that WC schooling reflects a departure from the NCLB legislation by shifting testing away from so-called cognitive abilities to noncognitive ones. In the WC discourse, testing is acceptable if measuring children's NCS and the teacher's ability to teach them. There is a shift away from leaving no child behind by measuring cognitive abilities to leaving no part of the child behind by developing and testing character, dispositions, personality, perceptions, desire, and attitudes. No part of the child is to be untouched by institutional lessons and unmeasured by psychological instruments. Regardless if one can defend a conception of wholeness that can be scientifically and humanistically defended, the WC discourse is about subjecting the entire child to schooling. Although one might treat such a pedagogical commitment as progress in humanism, WC schooling is also about extending institutional power to infiltrate what one might think of as personal life.

Humanism and the extension of institutional reach are not incompatible if one believes the lessons from schooling are about protecting and realizing that which makes one whole. In contemporary discourse, WC education, humanism, and twenty-first century skills all center around a similar vision for being. That alignment is an achievement of neoliberalism and the naturalization of a particular type of being. Moving toward a WC structure, thus, can be defended on many grounds, including validating and recognizing those things that make persons distinctively human, while supporting preparation for the modern world.

However, WC schooling can be thought about in a different way, which can challenge assumptions about progress, humanism, and ethics. As Fendler (2001) points out, the targeting of broad psychological substances in children is less about progress in discerning and realizing wholeness, and more about rendering children susceptible to scientific management. If the imperative was to know students in terms of their composite parts and that such knowledge made it possible to shape environments to develop those parts, then children are in a position to be managed. Fendler states:

> The thrust of whole child education is that the child's entire being – desire, attitudes, wishes – is caught up in the educational process. Educating the WC means educating not only the cognitive, affective, and behavioral aspects, but also the child's innermost desires. There must be no residue of reluctance to learning; success for whole child education means not only that the child learns, but the child desires to learn and is happy to learn. No aspect of the child must be left uneducated; education touches the spirit, soul, motivation, wishes, desires, dispositions, and attitudes of the child to be educated. (p. 121)

One can read this assertion and applaud the the commitment to leave no part of the child "uneducated." However, Fendler does not use the term *educated* as unequivocal good that signifies freedom, empowerment, and humanness. In the context of WC schooling, being educated means convincing others that through performance standards one embodies valued ways of thinking and being that signify wholeness. Furthermore, persons are *educated* (i.e., whole) if they think about failure a particular way, persist with goals, are optimistic, are emotionally regulated (as evidenced by docility to school learning), seek challenges, are attached to teachers and peers, show evidence of aesthetic sensibilities, and remain excited and enthusiastic about learning.

Educating the WC means limiting any type of resistance to schooling objectives, generating positive attitudes from students in their pursuit of objectives, and ensuring that they eventually self-regulate their engagement. WC schooling is about educating all parts of children so that certain attitudes, perceptions, and beliefs will lead them to self-regulate and become lifelong learners. This purpose is lauded as a valued goal of WC schooling. Darling-Hammond et al. (2018) state:

> Emotions and social relationships affect learning. Positive relationships, including trust in the teacher, and positive emotions – such as interest and excitement – open up the mind to learning. Negative emotions – such as fear of failure, anxiety, and self-doubt – reduce the capacity of the brain to process information and to learn. Students' interpersonal skills, including their ability to interact positively with peers and adults, to resolve conflicts, and to work in teams, all contribute to effective learning and lifelong behaviors. (p. 17)

The authors point to key purposes of WC education: to target broad substances of children and to ensure such lessons are continuous. The effects of WC schooling are achieved by tying aspirations, motivations, and sense of fulfillment to school success. Fendler (2001) asserts that, "In order to be recognized – or recognize oneself – as 'educated,' the subject understands and reflexively disciplines desires, feelings, loves, wishes, and fears" (p. 124). WC education is about shaping pedagogical environments to cultivate certain perceptions, attitudes, and commitments in order to ensure that persons in an automatic and self-regulated way govern themselves to happily achieve a particular vision of academic success. As Fendler contends, this commitment is about discipline. She states, "The construction of the 'WC' is a relatively new configuration in educational discourse, and inscribes a new target – or substance – for pedagogical technologies and self-discipline" (p. 124). Not only is the purpose to target a particular substance but also that the impact is long-lasting by merging desires, aspirations, meaning, fulfillment, and happiness with institutional objectives. As Rose (1999) contends, the merging of aspirations and desires with institutional objectives is a key goal of neoliberal governance.

Aside from aligning with a particular rationality of government, there is an ethical paradox. As either a part or a whole, children likely do not experience themselves in these terms. However, WC schooling is about providing frameworks of being to shape pedagogical environments to target a broad range of psychological substances in children. Emotions, aesthetic sensibility, democratic engagement, empathy, grit, desires, and attitudes are the targets of schooling. In WC schooling, these parts are used to make up and make sense of students. To be whole and to be educated is to have all psychological substances look a certain way that policy makers believe comprise good character, which should reflexively be performed. The paradox is that regardless of the dispositions, qualities, behaviors, and traits with which students enter a classroom, they are supposed to form into a specific being. There is no opportunity for other subject positions to be valued and validated. There is no opportunity to leave parts of being unaffected by lessons. All of being is under the gaze in WC education. It is humanistic, democratic, and whole, not at all invasive, obtrusive, or controlling.

Researchers and policy makers may argue about the validity of different representations of wholeness. Theorists might conclude that the entire picture of wholeness is not quite captured and that the improvement of instruments and conceptual frameworks might lead to a complete picture. Many researchers assume that with the label *noncognitive* and all its features, an improved picture of wholeness is offered, one with implications for mitigating inequality. Some theorists might argue that there are too many parts or not enough parts included in WC frameworks. Although questions about the ontology of wholeness are important to consider, there is a particular commitment that underlies efforts to get wholeness right. The discourse is entangled in neoliberal forms of governance by targeting all aspects of children in ways to produce particular types of persons. Taking up the aim to teach the WC is an effort to extend the reach of institutional power to normalize, value, validate, and reward a kind of self that aligns with neoliberalism.

7.4 Conclusion

The notion of the WC is not a natural category but a way of reasoning about children that is bound to historical, political, philosophical, cultural, and ideological contexts. Thought about that way, the critical question to consider is: What are the contexts that inform ideas about wholeness? WC schooling is often endorsed as an imperative to realize economic justice, humanness, democratic engagement, and an overall good life. Although not dismissing these possibilities, there are critical concerns not often considered. The key points of this analysis are: (1) wholeness is not an inherent category to describe persons; (2) there are different ways of conceptualizing wholeness; (3) the contemporary narrative is informed by a scientific commitment to fragment and unify; (4) the parts and whole of children are prescriptive and normative; and (5) the features that comprise the WC align with visions for ideal neoliberal selfhood.

It is dangerous to assume that there is a monolithic representation of the WC and that such representations are neutral and value-free. However, in the modern narrative of wholeness, researchers and policy makers normalize a framework for thinking about and educating the WC. The intention here is not to offer a polemic about whether children are whole, the contents of wholeness, and the knowability of wholeness. Rather, there is consideration of how neoliberal ideology contributes to truths about the contents of wholeness. WC schooling is tied to norms for what children should be, and that image closely resembles ideal neoliberal selfhood. It is with this notion that many of the topics in this book come together. The WC is creative, gritty, emotionally regulated, has a GM, and through character development has long-lasting dispositions to engage in a specific way in- and outside of school. The discourse of the WC provides a justification for reproducing, normalizing, and propagating institutional values by targeting the entire being.

CHAPTER 8

Conclusion

Schools have long been charged with forming persons in particular ways to achieve social, economic, democratic, and political purposes. However, at different moments and in various climates, the educational substance and desired outcomes vary. Regardless, the making up of persons happens in schools. The phrase *making up* is not to suggest that schools determine selfhood. Rather, a certain kind of selfhood circulates in schooling discourse and serves as a reference point for educators to make sense of and act on students, as well as for students to make sense of and act on themselves. The analyses are not intended to serve as justifications for categorizing persons as having or lacking certain qualities. Instead, the purpose is to examine how certain psychological constructs align with a particular vision for being and to consider the consequences of applying those constructs in school settings.

Given that schools are ideological spaces, the type of being that is endorsed in them is also ideological. Whether visible or unnoticed, visions about ideal ways of being circulate in pedagogy, practice, and policy. The vision for what students need to be and for what purposes may not always be shared by stakeholders. Coherent and consistent messages about selfhood are not always communicated. Furthermore, there can be competing and contradictory visions across teachers, parents, administrators, students, and policy makers. Despite the variations, students tend to be treated as sites of ideological battles. Researchers and policy makers endeavor to structure policy and practice to realize, endorse, validate, and develop a particular type of person. Along with disagreements about the ideal self, the consequences that schooling discourse has on selfhood are debatable.

The overall argument is that grit, GM, ER, creativity, LLL, and WC, which can be grouped under NCS, circulate in, contribute to, and take a certain form in relation to neoliberal selfhood. Typically, these NCS are associated with a broad range of benefits. Thus, researchers and policy makers work to formally integrate instruction around them. These efforts tend to be endorsed and embraced because of the alignment with diverse ideological and philosophical visions of personhood. Furthermore, the formal integration of NCS reflects a discursive shift in the educational target of students. Rather than directly cultivating intelligence, talent, and behavior, there is a growing commitment to shape students' attitudes, traits, desires, perceptions, and beliefs. This focus emerged as resistance to the overemphasis on cognitive testing and intelligence as predictive measures of students' academic performance, economic success, and democratic participation. NCS function as a framework for delineating the optimal states of students' psychological substance, as well as informing pedagogical structures and interventions to realize that ideal.

The formal integration of NCS in schooling ostensibly democratizes success by pointing to personal responsibility and individual control. In this line of reasoning, talent, intelligence, ability, potential, and success are not predetermined, static, and immutable. A foundational assumption is that with the right beliefs, attitudes, perceptions, behaviors, emotions, and thought processes, students can exercise control over the forces that are implicated in academic performance, economic productivity, and democratic engagement. In addition to these benefits, proponents emphasize the value for attaining happiness, satisfaction, and ethical citizenry. Without the rhetorical inclusion of these benefits, the discourse of NCS is open to democratic, humanistic, and ethical concerns. However, with claims to align with seemingly opposing visions, these constructs can be reasonably defended and promoted by those from various ideological, political, and academic camps.

Critical theorists tend to be pessimistic that, for example, an economic vision of personhood is compatible with and achievable by the same means as a democratic one. Typically, an economic vision of personhood is associated with self-interest, competition, and radical individualism, which are implicated in exacerbating inequality, obscuring the effects of systemic inequalities, and exploitation. These values and consequences misalign with democratic and humanistic ideals about personhood. However, proponents of NCS reveal optimism for realizing multiple visions by invoking humanistic and democratic rationalizations and consequences. This rhetoric is especially prevalent in the discourse of the WC, grit (with the inclusion of passion), creativity, and LLL.

In relation to the broad benefits of NCS, two questions require consideration: (1) What counts as democratic selfhood and engagement? (2)

What is the vision of the human? These visions might justifiably align, pointing to an effect of neoliberal ideology. The realization of humanity, democratic engagement, and economic value has become entangled in one vision of selfhood. For this reason, critical interrogation requires consideration of the forms of democratic citizenship and humanness, as well the mechanisms required to embody those forms. As a result of such consideration, one might conclude that the democratic and humanistic appeal of NCS is rhetorical, with the effect of promoting and normalizing neoliberal selfhood. Resistance to the economic instrumentalism of schooling discourse is more likely to occur when it is explicit and threatens civic virtue and humanity. Although the broad benefits of NCS can reasonably be described as rhetorical, the analyses point to ways that this group of skills serve as a basis to merge various visions of being. As a unifying framework, humanism, civic virtue, democratic engagement, and economic participation take a neoliberal form. Consequently, the analyses in this book complicate the position that humanistic and democratic visions of being in the NCS discourse adequately serve to resist neoliberal selfhood, and cannot adequately be connected to broad visions of being. Even if directed toward different endpoints, the conceptualizations, applications, and functions of NCS are entangled in neoliberal ideology.

Neoliberal structures require persons to embody, perform, and normalize a particular way of being, referred to as neoliberal selfhood. The reasoning is that in contexts that are ostensibly characterized by competition, autonomy, and choice, persons must have certain desires, skills, dispositions, beliefs, and attitudes to function within, adapt to, and arguably be successful in those contexts. The requirement is for persons to engage in the strategic management of their lives to increase their value, which can be measured in relation to ideal representations of an economic participant, democratic citizen, or human. Regardless of endpoint, these neoliberal practices and mechanisms for self-management are preserved. This neoliberal self is: (1) constantly calibrated and examined; (2) evaluated in terms of personal value; (3) expected to make choices that increase value; (4) focused on the consequences of choices; (5) flexible and adaptable; (6) useful; and (7) enterprising and entrepreneurial. Even if researchers and policy makers invoke values for the social good over individual betterment, self-actualization over economic instrumentalism, and community accountability over individual responsibility, one of the dangers, aside from serving as a rhetorical device, is that the process, practices, and mechanisms of selfhood are similar.

The analysis of creativity reveals a robust illustration of this point. Proponents of humanism, democracy, and economic productivity tend to rally behind pedagogical efforts to foster students' creativity. However, creativity might be endorsed and practiced in ways that seem more justifiably aligned with one commitment than with others. It is reasonable to resist the instrumentalism of creativity and rhetorically evaluate it for its own sake. Along with this type of treatment, one might resist a skills-based conceptualization and adopt pedagogical strategies to maximize autonomy, choice, experimentation, and discovery. Although seemingly aligned with a humanistic view, creativity is still treated as a phenomenon to be named, targeted, managed, and developed. Even with different rationalizations and conceptualizations, the attention to creativity is gaining momentum because of its instrumental value for participation in twenty-first-century contexts – whether about producing the best version of oneself through creative self-management, engaging in dialogue to imagine just institutional structures, leading entrepreneurial activity, or developing innovate products in a corporate setting. Consequently, creativity is entangled in technical and human management, regardless of the conceptual, pedagogical, and methodological differences.

Educators researchers, and policy makers do not always agree about the consequences that schooling practice and policy have on selfhood. Notwithstanding ontological, conceptual, pedagogical, and methodological debates, researchers and policy makers tend to agree that formally integrating NCS in schooling indicates progressive thinking that has a broad range of benefits for students. The analyses in this book, however, present a different narrative. NCS are entangled in neoliberal selfhood, which is a brand of being associated with several problematic consequences. Herein lies the main objective of this book. Researchers, educators, and policy makers may endeavor to resist neoliberal values but inadvertently endorse them through the normalization, validation, and integration of NCS. The association of NCS with humanism and democratic engagement can conceal the neoliberal entanglement, making resistance a challenge and possibly absurd. By pointing to ways that neoliberalism operates in and through NCS, ethical reflections are possible about whether they should guide schooling practice and policy.

Resistance to neoliberal selfhood and concern over NCS are not necessarily an endorsement of opposing binaries that are featured in the discourse. In addition to the attraction that results from the alignment with democratic, humanistic, and economic visions, each of the constructs in this book appear to have an unappealing, opposing binary. The word *appear* is used to suggest that binaries are seldom adequate for making sense of persons and opposing positions may not necessarily reflect an unequivocally negative subject position. For example, although committing to the present is pathologized in GM discourse, philosophers have long argued for the value of this life ethic. If one concludes that only two mindsets exist and that students fall into one or the other, then it is important to acknowledge the potential benefits and desirable qualities of a fixed mindset. In the LLL discourse, the unwilling learner is pathologized as the one who resists flexible adaptations to changing institutional structures. However, this so-called unwillingness can also be viewed as politically informed resistance to problematic systemic structures and refusal to be governed through a proxy under the guise of self-management. Situating the discourse of the WC in neoliberal visions of selfhood is not an endorsement of fragmenting students. Nor is the analysis intended to suggest that a better, scientific, neutral, or elaborated version of wholeness needs to be envisioned. Concern about the conception of wholeness is a call neither to improve this construct nor to fragment students. The hope is that the critical analyses invite an openness to rethink the binaries altogether as inherent descriptors and organizations of persons and to invite critical conversations about the norms and values operating in and through binaries.

The perception that these binaries are not natural descriptions of students is necessary to move beyond them. A critical commitment in these analyses is that NCS do not describe natural and inherent qualities of persons. These skills do not have to be used to make sense of students, inform interventions, and comprise an ideal type. There are many ways to make sense of persons and conceptualize being which can have varying effects. Psychological categories and descriptions are not assumed, inherent, objective, and natural representations of being. The ways students are understood and how they understand themselves are bound to history, culture, politics, philosophy, and ideology. Psychological language, ways of reasoning, instruments, and tools used to describe students are not the result of scientific progress for representing and measuring them. A foundational assumption is that no vision of personhood is neutral and value-free. However, one of the effects of neoliberalism is to render certain constructs and a particular narrative for being as natural and inherent to persons. An important goal of this book is to denaturalize NCS by situating them within a neoliberal vision for selfhood. The constructs analyzed in this book were chosen because there is growing discourse on them; they tend to be defended as natural descriptions of students, and are mobilized to defend a vision of personhood that ostensibly resists neoliberal selfhood.

8.1 Form of Entanglement

The analyses show three ways that NCS are entangled in neoliberal selfhood. The first relates to the alignment between values for the conceptualization of selfhood, a valued life ethic, and desirable attitudes, perceptions, and beliefs. To this point, NCS serve as a framework to instantiate neoliberal selfhood. Another form of entanglement relates to the interpretation and practice around psychological constructs. A critical position is that students do not have to be defined, measured, and calibrated, in general, and specifically in relation to NCS. However, if adopted, these constructs tend to be understood, applied, and take form in relation to neoliberal values. A third form of entanglement relates to the need for NCS to cope with and render neoliberal selfhood tolerable. The idea is that NCS capture certain attitudes, beliefs, and regulatory abilities to counteract the effects of the confrontation with neoliberal values.

8.1.1 Instantiation of Selfhood

A foundational assumption is that there is not an invisible hand operating to propagate neoliberal selfhood in policy and practice. Proponents of neoliberalism did not create the terms analyzed in this book. Notions such as creativity, ER, LLL, and WC had been considered in education discourse decades before the dominance of neoliberal ideology. It is difficult to find persons who self-identify as proponents of neoliberalism. There is not a centralized group of persons committed to protect market operations by plotting to normalize and propagate a self that aligns with a specific ideological vision. In fact, NCS tend to be endorsed by researchers and policy makers with various ideological commitments. A contention is that NCS are appealing and accepted because they align with a particular vision of ideal students and fears over potential deficiencies. With hegemonic status, this narrative is informed by neoliberal values.

In a neoliberal ethos, certain psychological constructs, theories, methods, and descriptions are likely to be endorsed, valued, and accepted because they align with ideas about what forms of being to embody. This modern narrative tends to emphasize personal responsibility, choice-making, strategic self-management, management of affect, perpetual growth, maximizing value, and optimizing productivity. The discourse of NCS instantiates these commitments and can stand as a framework to normalize, validate, and reward this brand of selfhood. Putting the NCS together in a coherent narrative reveals many of the alignments with neoliberal selfhood.

Taking all the constructs together, the ideal student pursues passion to achieve long-term goals for the purpose of attaining a prescribed and recognizable level of mastery and success. The challenge of achieving greatness requires that the student be bound to a life ethic of improvement and have the requisite belief that effort and hard work are necessary to improve. It is through passion, tenacity, and commitment to improvement that persons can impact local and global communities through creative problem-solving, reimagining of democratic arrangements, technological innovation, entrepreneurialism, and personal transformations. As this trajectory will likely be accompanied by setbacks, failures, frustrations, and anxiety, the ideal student must emotionally regulate to ensure that the right emotions are experienced and expressed in order to support the continued pursuit of success, mastery, and greatness. This type of engagement must be intentionally practiced in- and outside of schooling; it must be prevalent in all spheres of life continuing from the "cradle to the grave." Achieving or demonstrating this way of being indicates wholeness.

Embodying this type of personhood is foundational to the discourse on NCS, which aligns with ideal representations of neoliberal selfhood. As part of this narrative, there are fears about students' character deficiencies that threaten the normalization and validation of neoliberal selfhood. Defense and justification for formally integrating NCS in schooling reveal concerns about the potential for contemporary schooling structures and practice to exacerbate, produce, and ignore students' problems with character, dispositions, traits, beliefs, and attitudes. Each of the constructs in this book is associated in some way to the mitigation and avoidance of such deficiencies. A key critical commitment is that students do not have inherent flaws. Instead, the articulation of and fears over character exist in a framework and are recognizable in relation to a vision for ideal being, norms, forms of evidence, interpretations, and systems of measurement.

For example, the notion of complacency exists in relation to constructs such as grit, GM, and LLL, which normalize certain types of motivation, behavior, goal pursuit, and outcomes. Such a notion that does not inherently exist nor is inherently negative, but can be used to categorize persons who do not perform certain types of engagement that align with a particular narrative for being. However, complaceny competes with fundamental tenets of neoliberal selfhood. The normalization of NCS supports the pathologization of complacency, as well as provides criteria and legitimacy to categorize persons as stagnant. From this instance, a key function of NCS is to normalize particular ways of being, to mitigate fears of deficiencies for embodying that being, and to serve as a compass for realizing a particular brand of self.

In another example, risk-taking, persistence, and responses to failure are themes that appear in much of the discourse on NCS. Researchers and policy makers repeatedly raise concerns that students are deterred by and may not maximize learning from failure, mistakes, and risks. As a psychological quality to be calibrated and targeted, risk-taking is a fairly modern invention that is formally integrated in contemporary pedagogical rationalizations and assessments. The reason for this integration results from the association with creativity, innovation, and entrepreneurialism. Given the value for this disposition, accompanied by fears of risk avoidance, which in a neoliberal narrative signals character deficiency, NCS serves an important function.

Risk increases chances for failure. To support the kinds of risk-taking that are acceptable and valued in school, students must develop the right attitudes, perceptions, and responses to failure. They must develop the disposition and commitment to extract all the possible knowledge from an event that some normative structure deemed a failure. The norms for students are that if they take risks and fail, they must not quit. Quitting or shifting goals too often and frequently is pathologized. To foster grit, other processes, perceptions, and beliefs are necessary. Students must use emotional regulatory strategies to remain calm by rationalizing the event as part of a lifelong process of growth that is situated on a trajectory of a normative view of success.

In contemporary discourse, risk-taking is a desirable and measurable feature of students that requires specific psychological dispositions, behaviors, and emotions. Risk-taking is featured in pedagogical rationalizations and is encouraged to inform interventions to target students' disposition to take risks. In addition to targeting the disposition, specific scripts must be developed so that students can practice and manage those risks. In this example, NCS are associated with and defended because of the modern value for risk-taking. With this value, students are calibrated using this term, subject to a system of measurement, and targeted for specific dispositions, attitudes, and perceptions. Grit, ER, GM, and LLL support acceptable instances of risk-taking, which can be associated with a variety of purposes, including self-actualization and democratic engagement.

Regardless of the reason, the practices surrounding risk-taking and its role in twenty-first century personhood have their roots in neoliberal ideology.

8.1.2 Interpretation of Constructs

Another way NCS are entangled in neoliberal ideology is in the interpretation of constructs. A key goal is to denaturalize NCS as inherent descriptors of students. However, if applied, these constructs can take on a certain form in a neoliberal climate. For example, consider LLL. Regardless of the definition, conceptualization, and measurement, educational psychologists and philosophers are not likely to conclude that persons do not learn throughout their lives, essentially supporting the idea that persons are naturally lifelong learners beyond any intentional orchestration and commitment. Although a theory of learning is required to support this conclusion, it is difficult to find any that counter this assumption. This point is not necessarily to endorse an inherent substance to persons that validates the naturalization of neoliberal selfhood. In contemporary discourse, there is a specific way of thinking about LLL that normalizes assessments of intention, strategy, and adaptability.

The opposing and seemingly undesirable binary of LLL might be described as whimsical and unintentional learning, which signifies unacceptable forms of engagement. Not renewing a skill set in relation to shifting economic conditions signifies unwillingness. Resistance to changing features of oneself in relation to shifting economic and institutional structures signifies inflexibility and maladaptiveness. LLL is perpetual, intentional, strategic, and managed in ways that support adaptability and amenability to shifting social, economic, and democratic structures. This construct is used to categorize learning, to assign value to that which is recognizable as intentional, and to pathologize those who seemingly do not perform that type of engagement. The neoliberal values of intentionality, flexibility, perpetual growth, and strategic management give form to LLL.

The notion of the WC reveals another example of the neoliberal influence on NCS. The narrative in education policy discussion is that students are composed of parts, all of which must be integrated into pedagogical deliberations. Success of WC schooling is demonstrated by students who are adaptable, self-regulated, emotionally regulated, open to teacher's guidance, committed to learning goals, conscientious, and gracious. The idea of wholeness as psychological parts and the vision for wholeness are embedded in a specific way of thinking about persons and what they should be. The compartmentalization reflects a scientific understanding of psychology that is composed of nameable and measurable parts that can be technically managed. This way of understanding aligns with neoliberal selfhood. There are vastly different versions of wholeness that can impact conceptualizations and treatments of students, as well as inform pedagogical rationalizations. The idea of a whole is a metaphor that takes form in relation to neoliberal values for being. Even with new possibilities for wholeness, this concept is not an inherent descriptor of being. New ways of conceptualizing an entire being may still function to extend institutional reach by targeting a broad range of educational substance.

8.1.3 Coping, Tolerability, and Preservation

A third way to view the entanglement of NCS in neoliberal discourse is instrumental. Critical theorists point out that confrontation with discourses of neoliberal selfhood can have several negative psychological consequences that include anxiety, stress, withdrawal, and feelings of lack, isolation, and emptiness. Values for individual responsibility, perpetual improvement, risk-taking, performance standards, self-management, choice-making, and self-examination can generate angst, uncertainty, and pressure. NCS can be mobilized to mitigate possible consequences related to the confrontation with and efforts to embody neoliberal selfhood.

In this regard, NCS function as a coping mechanism to preserve and make tolerable a vision for being. NCS target dispositions, beliefs, and attitudes that can mitigate the consequences associated with neoliberal selfhood. For example, a GM supports acceptance and comfortableness with failure by promoting a belief in process and individual control. Thus, students can engage in acceptable forms of risk-taking without suffering derailment from emotions that might emerge in response to setbacks and failures. A conception of growth can support the types of ER needed to perform and pursue risk-taking. The integration of passion in grit can also function to render neoliberal selfhood tolerable. A feature of the grit narrative is that if one identifies a passion, one will be gritty in its pursuit. Passion is a natural human response and gritty pursuit is the natural corollary. Grit is positioned then as a natural product of the emergence, identification, discovery, or ignition of a strong emotional connection to a goal. Passion can potentially weather or justify the suffering, emptiness, and stress that result from the pursuit of a normative form of greatness.

Students who are optimistic, gracious, emotionally regulated, always in process, and committed to improvement can avoid the negative psychological consequences associated with neoliberal selfhood. Problems with underlying values of selfhood, however, can remain obscured and invisible by normalizing, naturalizing, and formally integrating NCS in schooling. The commitment to NCS in this role further validates the functioning of neoliberal ideology by targeting students' emotions, attitudes, and perceptions to mitigate the consequences of a problematic representation of being. To resist neoliberalism, instead of working with students to cope with the consequences of a particular brand of selfhood, values for being can be shifted and rethought.

8.2 Contextualizing Values for Selfhood

There are subtle ways in which neoliberal selfhood circulates in school discourse. At times, this way of being can be masked by humanistic and democratic rationalizations. If one wants to resist neoliberalism in schools, then it is important to consider ways that the constructs analyzed in the book are entangled in this ideology. The acknowledgment of such entanglement is not intended to invite rejection of constructs in favor of neutral and value-free ones. The promise of psychological discourse to depict inherent, objective, and unequivocally beneficial student profiles is false. Any act of naming and measuring students is bound to history, power, culture, politics, and ideology. These acts will have both unintended and intended consequences which are reflected in the interpretation of experience, the formation of selfhood, pedagogical structures, and forms of self-regulation. The hope is to present a narrative on NCS that represents contextual conditions and to invite conversations about the values for being that circulate in this discourse. The purpose is to show ways in which NCS contribute to the normalization of certain subject positions and pathologization of others, both of which are organized around neoliberal selfhood. From these analyses, constructs that are accepted as objective depictions of students can be denaturalized, opening up new possibilities for thinking about students. With that said, it is dangerous to assume that such possibilities are progressive and free from ideological and political constraint. New possibilities can still align with neoliberal values or justifiably align with different ideological commitments. Critical work involves making these commitments explicit in order to invite conversations about the ethical implications for the values of being that circulate in school discourse.

References

Adams, G., Estrada-Villalta, S., Sullivan, D., & Markus, H. R. (2019). The psychology of neoliberalism and the neoliberalism of psychology. *Journal of Social Issues, 75*(1), 189–216.
Ahl, H. (2008). Motivation theory as power in disguise. In N. Fejas & K. Nicoll (eds.), *Foucault and Lifelong Learning: Governing the Subject* (pp. 151–163). Routledge.
Ainsworth, J. (2018). *Inheriting Possibility: Social Reproduction and Quantification in Education*. Oxford University Press.
Albahari, M. (2016). *Analytical Buddhism: The Two-Tiered Illusion of Self*. Palgrave Macmillan.
Ali, S. S. (2019). Problem based learning: A student-centered approach. *English Language Teaching, 12*(5), 73–78.
Allvin, R. E. (2017). Early childhood educators and the American economy: A new story. *Young Children; Washington, 72*(5), 56–59.
Amabile, T. M. (2018). *Creativity in Context: Update to the Social Psychology of Creativity*. Routledge.
Amabile, T. M. & Pratt, M. G. (2016). The dynamic componential model of creativity and innovation in organizations: Making progress, making meaning. *Research in Organizational Behavior, 36*, 157–183. https://doi.org/10.1016/j.riob.2016.10.001
American Enterprise Institute & Brookings Institute (2015). Opportunity, responsibility, and security: A consensus plan for reducing poverty and restoring the American dream. American Enterprise Institute and Brookings Institute. www.brookings.edu/wp-content/uploads/2016/07/Full-Report.pdf
Amsel, E. (2015). Conceptual and pedagogical challenges in understanding the whole person. *New Ideas in Psychology, 38*, 1–3.
Amstadter, A. (2008). Emotion regulation and anxiety disorders. *Journal of Anxiety Disorders, 22*(2), 211–221. https://doi.org/10.1016/j.janxdis.2007.02.004
Apple, M. W. (2006). Understanding and interrupting neoliberalism and neoconservatism in education. *Pedagogies: An International Journal, 1*, 21–26. https://doi.org/10.1207/s15544818ped0101_4
Apple, M. W. (2017). What is present and absent in critical analyses of neoliberalism in education. *Peabody Journal of Education, 92*(1), 148–153.
Arfken, M. (2014). Creativity. In T. Teo (ed.), *Encyclopedia of Critical Psychology* (pp. 325–327). Springer-Verlag.

Arnold, L. E. (1990). *Childhood Stress*. John Wiley.

Ashton, K. (2015). *How to Fly a Horse: The Secret History of Creation, Invention, and Discovery*. Anchor Books.

Association for Supervision and Curriculum Development (2020). *The Learning Compact Renewed: Whole Child for the Whole World* (pp. 1–48). Association for Supervision and Curriculum Development. Retrieved August 2nd from http://files.ascd.org/pdfs/programs/WholeChildNetwork/2020-whole-child-network-learning-compact-renewed.pdf

Association for Supervision and Curriculum Development (2007). *The Learning Compact Redefined: A Call to Action* (pp. 1-32). Association for Supervision and Curriculum Development. Retrieved August 2nd from www.ascd.org/ASCD/pdf/Whole%20Child/WCC%20Learning%20Compact.pdf

Atasay, E. (2014). Neoliberal schooling and subjectivity: Learning to desire lack. *Subjectivity*, 7(3), 288–307. https://doi.org/10.1057/sub.2014.12

Azzam, A. M. (2009). Why creativity now? A conversation with Sir Ken Robinson. *Educational Leadership*, 67(1), 22–26.

Beghetto, R. A. & Kaufman, J. C. (2014). Classroom contexts for creativity. *High Ability Studies*, 25(1), 53–69. https://doi.org/10.1080/13598139.2014.905247

Benedek, M., Jauk, E., Sommer, M., Arendasy, M., & Neubauer, A. C. (2014). Intelligence, creativity, and cognitive control: The common and differential involvement of executive functions in intelligence and creativity. *Intelligence*, 46, 73–83. https://doi.org/10.1016/j.intell.2014.05.007

Berglund, G. (2008). Pathologizing and medicalizing lifelong learning: A deconstruction. In A. Fejes & K. Nicoll (eds.), *Foucault and Lifelong Learning: Governing the Subject* (pp. 138–150). Routledge.

Business and Industry Advisory Committee to the OECD (2004). Creativity, innovation and economic growth in the 21st century: An affirmative case for intellectual property rights.

Bialostok, S. & Kamberelis, G. (2012). The play of risk, affect, and the enterprising self in a fourth-grade classroom. *International Journal of Qualitative Studies in Education*, 25, 417–434.

Bilton, H. (2010). *Outdoor Learning in the Early Years: Management and Innovation*. Taylor & Francis.

Blackwell, L. S., Trzesniewski, K. H., & Dweck, C. S. (2007). Implicit theories of intelligence predict achievement across an adolescent transition: A longitudinal study and an intervention. *Child Development*, 78(1), 246–263. https://doi.org/10.1111/j.1467-8624.2007.00995.x

Boddice, R. (2017). The history of emotions: Past, present, future. *Revista de Estudios Sociales*, 62, 10–15.

Boden, M. (1996). *Dimensions of Creativity*. MIT Press.

Boler, M. (1999). *Feeling Power: Emotions and Education*. Psychology Press.

Bollington, A. (2015). *Why Isn't Everyone Lifelong Learning?* Organization for Economic Development. https://search.proquest.com/openview/9efc974bf187bd7f55c4a119b372ae6f/1?pq-origsite=gscholar&cbl=35885

Bonneville-Roussy, A., Vallerand, R. J., & Bouffard, T. (2013). The roles of autonomy support and harmonious and obsessive passions in educational persistence. *Learning and Individual Differences, 24*, 22–31.
Bourdieu, P. (1977). Cultural reproduction and social reproduction. In J. Karabel & A. H. Halsey (eds.), *Power and Ideology in Education* (pp. 487–511). Oxford University Press.
Bowles, S. & Gintis, H. (1976). *Schooling in Capitalist America*. Basic Books.
Boyatzis, R. & Boyatzis, R. E. (2009). Competencies in the 21st century. *Journal of Management Development, 28*(9), 749–770. https://doi.org/10.1108/02621710910987647
Boyatzis, R., Smith, M. L., & Van Oosten, E. (2019). *Helping People Change: Coaching with Compassion for Lifelong Learning and Growth*. Harvard Business Press.
Bradberry, T. (2020). *The Massive Benefits of Boosting Your Emotional Intelligence*. World Economic Forum. www.weforum.org/agenda/2020/02/emotional-intelligence-career-life-personal-development/
Braunstein, L. M., Gross, J. J., & Ochsner, K. N. (2017). Explicit and implicit emotion regulation: A multi-level framework. *Social Cognitive and Affective Neuroscience, 12*(10), 1545–1557. https://doi.org/10.1093/scan/nsx096
Brenner, M. (1978). Interviewing: The social phenomenology of a research instrument. In: M. Brenner, P. Marsh, & M. Brenner (eds.), *The Social Contexts of Method* (pp. 122–139). Croom Helm.
Brinkman, D. J. (2010). Teaching creatively and teaching for creativity. *Arts Education Policy Review, 111*(2), 48–50. https://doi.org/10.1080/10632910903455785
Bröckling, U. (2015). *The Entrepreneurial Self: Fabricating a New Type of Subject*. Sage.
Bruce, T. (2015). Friedrich Froebel. In T. David, K. Goouch, & S. Powell (eds.), *The Routledge International Handbook of Philosophies and Theories of Early Childhood Education and Care* (pp. 43–49). Routledge.
Buckingham Shum, S. & Crick, R. D. (2016). Learning analytics for 21st century competencies. *Journal of Learning Analytics, 3*(2), 6–21.
Burman, E. (2008). *Deconstructing Developmental Psychology* (2nd ed.). Routledge.
Burns, E. & Martin, A. J. (2014). ADHD and adaptability: The roles of cognitive, behavioural, and emotional regulation. *Journal of Psychologists and Counsellors in Schools, 24*(2), 227–242. https://doi.org/10.1017/jgc.2014.17
Burstein, R. (2019). *Educators Don't Agree on What Whole Child Education Means. Here's Why It Matters.* – EdSurge News. EdSurge.
Calhoun, C. & Solomon, R. C. (1984). *What is an Emotion?: Classic Readings in Philosophical Psychology*. Oxford University Press.
Campos, J. J., Frankel, C. B., & Camras, L. (2004). On the nature of emotion regulation. *Child Development, 75*(2), 377–394. https://doi.org/10.1111/j.1467-8624.2004.00681.x
Centeno, V. (2011). Lifelong learning: A policy concept with a long past but a short history. *International Journal of Lifelong Education, 30*(2), 133–150. https://doi.org/10.1080/02601370.2010.547616

Chamberlin, S. A. & Moon, S. M. (2005). Model-eliciting activities as a tool to develop and identify creatively gifted mathematicians. *Journal of Secondary Gifted Education, 17*(1), 37–47. https://doi.org/10.4219/jsge-2005-393

Chen, X.-P., Liu, D., & He, W. (2015). Does passion fuel entrepreneurship and job creativity? A review and preview of passion research. In C. E. Shalley, M. A. Hitt, & J. Zhou (eds.), *The Oxford Handbook of Creativity, Innovation and Entrepreneurship* (pp. 159–175). Oxford University Press.

Chernyshenko, O. S., Kankaraš, M., & Drasgow, F. (2018). Social and emotional skills for student success and well-being: Conceptual framework for the OECD study on social and emotional skills. https://doi.org/10.1787/db1d8e59-en

Claiborne, L. (2014). The potential of critical educational psychology beyond its meritocratic past. In T. Corcoran (ed.), *Psychology in Education: Critical Theory~ Practice* (pp. 1–16). Springer.

Clark, K. N. & Malecki, C. K. (2019). Academic grit scale: Psychometric properties and associations with achievement and life satisfaction. *Journal of School Psychology, 72*, 49–66.

Claro, S., Paunesku, D., & Dweck, C. S. (2016). Growth mindset tempers the effects of poverty on academic achievement. *Proceedings of the National Academy of Sciences, 113*(31), 8664–8668.

Coleman, L. J. & Guo, A. (2013). Exploring children's passion for learning in six domains. *Journal for the Education of the Gifted, 36*(2), 155–175.

Collins, J. (2009). Lifelong learning in the 21st century and beyond. *Radiographics, 29*(2), 613–622.

Cooper, R. K. & Sawaf, A. (1997). *Executive EQ: Emotional Intelligence in Leadership and Organizations.* Grosset/Putnam.

Corcoran, T. (2016). Ontological constructionism. In A. J. Williams, T. Billington, D. Goodley, & T. Corcoran (eds.), *Critical Educational Psychology* (pp. 26–33). John Wiley.

Craft, A. (2005). *Creativity in Schools: Tensions and Dilemmas.* Psychology Press: London, UK.

Cropley, A. (2000). Defining and measuring creativity: Are creativity tests worth using? *Roeper Review, 23*, 72–79. https://doi.org/10.1080/02783190009554069

Cruikshank, B. (1999). *The Will to Empower: Democratic Citizens and Other Subjects.* Cornell University Press.

Curtis, D. & Carter, M. (2011). *Reflecting Children's Lives: A Handbook for Planning Your Child-Centered Curriculum.* Redleaf Press.

Dahl, M. (2016). Don't believe the hype about grit, pleads the scientist behind the concept. *The New Yorker*, May 9. www.thecut.com/2016/05/dont-believe-the-hype-about-grit-pleads-the-scientist-behind-the-concept.html

Darling-Hammond, L., Cook-Harvey, C. M., Flook, L., Gardner, M., & Melnick, H. (2018). *With the Whole Child in Mind: Insights from the Comer School Development Program.* Association for Supervision and Curriculum Development.

Darling-Hammond, L., Flook, L., Cook-Harvey, C., Barron, B., & Osher, D. (2020). Implications for educational practice of the science of learning and development. *Applied Developmental Science*, *24*(2), 97–140. https://doi.org/10.1080/10888691.2018.1537791

Davidson, A. (2020). *The Passion Economy: The New Rules for Thriving in the Twenty-First Century*. Alfred Knopf.

Davies, B. & Bansel, P. (2007). Neoliberalism and education. *International Journal of Qualitative Studies in Education*, *20*(3), 247–259. https://doi.org/10.1080/09518390701281751

Davies, P. B. & Bansel, P. (2007). Neoliberalism and education. *International Journal of Qualitative Studies in Education*, *20*(3), 247–259. https://doi.org/10.1080/09518390701281751

Davis, V. (2015). 5 Ways of bringing student passions to student learning. *Edutopia*, August 19. www.edutopia.org/blog/bringing-student-passions-to-learning

Day, C. & Leitch, R. (2001). Teachers' and teacher educators' lives: The role of emotion. *Teaching and Teacher Education*, *17*(4), 403–415. https://doi.org/10.1016/S0742-051X(01)00003-8

De Lissovoy, N. (2015). *Education and Emancipation in the Neoliberal Era: Being, Teaching, and Power*. Palgrave Macmillan.

Del Giudice, M. (2014). Grit trumps talent and IQ: A story every parent (and educator) should read. *National Geographic*, October 14). www.nationalgeographic.com/news/2014/10/141015-angela-duckworth-success-grit-psychology-self-control-science-nginnovators/

Denby, D. (2016). The limits of grit. *The New Yorker*, June 21. Retrieved August 2nd, 2020 from www.newyorker.com/culture/culture-desk/the-limits-of-grit

Dewey, J. (1938/1991). *Logic: The Theory of Inquiry,*. Southern University Press.

Diamond, A. (2010). The evidence base for improving school outcomes by addressing the whole child and by addressing skills and attitudes, not just content. *Early Education & Development*, *21*(5), 780–793. https://doi.org/10.1080/10409289.2010.514522

Doyle, O., Harmon, C. P., Heckman, J. J., & Tremblay, R. E. (2009). Investing in early human development: Timing and economic efficiency. *Economics & Human Biology*, *7*, 1–6.

Duckworth, A. (n.d.). Grit Scale. https://angeladuckworth.com/grit-scale/

Duckworth, A. (2016). *Grit: The Power of Passion and Perseverance*. Scribner.

Duckworth, A. L., Peterson, C., Matthews, M. D., & Kelly, D. R. (2007). Grit: Perseverance and passion for long-term goals. *Journal of Personality and Social Psychology*, *92*, 1087–1101.

Duckworth, A. L. & Yeager, D. S. (2015). Measurement matters assessing personal qualities other than cognitive ability for educational purposes. *Educational Researcher*, *44*, 237–251.

Durlak, J. A., Weissberg, R. P., Dymnicki, A. B., Taylor, R. D., & Schellinger, K. B. (2011). The impact of enhancing students' social and emotional learning: A meta-analysis of school-based universal interventions: Social and emotional learning. *Child Development*, *82*(1), 405–432. https://doi.org/10.1111/j.1467-8624.2010.01564.x

Dweck, C. (2006). *Mindset: The New Psychology of Success*. Ballantine Books.
Dweck, C. S. (2000). *Self-theories: Their Role in Motivation, Personality, and Development*. Psychology Press.
Dweck, C. S. & Leggett, E. L. (1988). Ovid: A social-cognitive approach to motivation and personality. *Psychological Review*, 95(2), 256–273.
Eccles, J. S. & Wigfield, A. (2002). Motivational beliefs, values, and goals. *Annual Review of Psychology*, 53(1), 109–132. https://doi.org/10.1146/annurev.psych.53.100901.135153
EdSurge. (2019). *From Vision to Practice: How Educators are Changing Practice to Meet the Needs of All Learners*. EdSurge. https://d3e7x39d4i7wbe.cloudfront.net/uploads/pdf/file/166/K-1587491206.pdf
Educational Testing Service. (2018). *The Praxis Study Companion: Education of Young Children*. ETS Praxis. www.ets.org/s/praxis/pdf/5024.pdf
Eisenberg, N., Cumberland, A., & Spinrad, T. L. (1998). Parental socialization of emotion. *Psychological Inquiry*, 9(4), 241–273. https://doi.org/10.1207/s15327965pli0904_1
Elias, M. J., Zins, J. E., & Weissberg, R. P. (1997). *Promoting Social and Emotional Learning: Guidelines for Educators*. Association for Supervision and Curriculum Development.
Epictetus. (2004). *Enchiridion (G. Long, Trans.)*. Dover Publications.
Falk, C. (1999). Sentencing learners to life: Retrofitting the academy for the information age. *Theory, Technology and Culture*, 22, 19–27.
Fang He, V., Sirén, C., Singh, S., Solomon, G., & von Krogh, G. (2018). Keep calm and carry on: Emotion regulation in entrepreneurs' learning from failure. *Entrepreneurship Theory and Practice*, 42(4), 605–630. https://doi.org/10.1177/1042258718783428
Fejes, A. & Nicoll, K. (2008). Mobilizing foucault in studies of lifelong learning. In A. Fejes & K. Nicoll (eds.), *Foucault and Lifelong Learning: Governing the Subject* (pp. 1–18). Routledge. https://doi.org/10.4324/9780203933411
Fendler, L. (2001). Educating flexible souls: The construction of subjectivity through developmentality and interaction. In K. Hultqvist & G. Dahlberg (eds.), *Governing the Child in the New Millennium* (pp. 119–142). RoutledgeFalmer.
Fendler, Lynn. (n.d.). Fendler, L. (2001). Educating flexible souls: The construction of subjectivity through developmentality and interaction. In K. Hultqvist & G. Dahlberg, (Eds.), *Governing the Child in the New Millennium* (pp. 119–142). RoutledgeFalmer.
Ferree, M. M. & Merrill, D. A. (2000). Hot movements, cold cognition: Thinking about social movements in gendered frames. *Contemporary Sociology*, 29(3), 454–462. https://doi.org/10.2307/2653932
Field, J. (2000). *Lifelong Learning and the New Educational Order*. Trentham Books, Ltd.
Fitzsimons, P. (2011). *Governing the Self: A Foucauldian Critique of Managerialism in Education*. Peter Lang.
Ford, B. Q. & Mauss, I. B. (2015). Culture and emotion regulation. *Current Opinion in Psychology*, 3, 1–5. https://doi.org/10.1016/j.copsyc.2014.12.004

Foucault, M. (2008). *The Birth of Biopolitics: Lectures at the Collège de France, 1978–1979 (G. Burchell, Trans.)*. Palgrave Macmillan.
Framework for 21st Century Learning. (2009). Partnership for 21st century skills. www.p21.org/storage/documents/P21_Framework.pdf
Frank, R. H. (2016). *Success and Luck: Good Fortune and the Myth of Meritocracy*. Princeton University Press.
Freeman, M. (2015). Can there be a science of the whole person? Form psychology, in search of a soul. *New Ideas in Psychology*, *38*, 37–43.
Freire, P. (1968/2000). *Pedagogy of the Oppressed*. Continuum.
French II, R. P. (2016). The fuzziness of mindsets: Divergent conceptualizations and characterizations of mindset theory and praxis. *International Journal of Organizational Analysis*, *24*(4), 673–691. https://doi.org/10.1108/IJOA-09-2014-0797
Fried, L. (2011). Teaching teachers about emotion regulation in the classroom. *Australian Journal of Teacher Education*, *36*(3). https://doi.org/10.14221/ajte.2011v36n3.1
Fried, L. (2010). Understanding and enhancing emotion and motivation regulation strategy use in the classroom. *International Journal of Learning*, *17*(6), 115–129.
Froebel, F. (1885). *The Education of Man (W. N. Hailmann, Trans.)*. Dover Publications.
Gabrieli, C., Ansel, D., & Bartolino Krachman, S. (2015). *Ready To Be Counted: The Research Case for Education Policy Action on Non-cognitive Skills*. Transforming Education. www.casel.org/wp-content/uploads/2016/06/ReadytoBeCounted_Release.pdf
Garcia, E. (2016). The need to address non-cognitive skills in the education policy agenda. In M. S. Khine & S. Areepattamannil (eds.), *Non-cognitive Skills and Factors in Educational Attainment* (pp. 32–64). Springer.
Garcia, E. & Weiss, E. (2016). *Making Whole-Child Education the Norm: How Research and Policy Initiatives Can Make Social and Emotional Skills a Focal Point of Children's Education*. Economic Policy Institute. www.epi.org/publication/making-whole-child-education-the-norm/
Gardner, H. (1983). *Frames of Mind: The Theory of Multiple Intelligences*. Basic Books.
Gendron, B. (2004). *Why emotional capital matters in education and in labour? Toward an optimal exploitation of human capital and knowledge management*. https://hal.archives-ouvertes.fr/hal-00201223
Gerguri, S. & Ramadani, V. B. (2010). The impact of innovation into the economic growth. Retrieved August 2nd, 2020 from https://ideas.repec.org/p/pra/mprapa/22270.html
Gerhards, J. (1989). The changing culture of emotions in modern society. *Information (International Social Science Council)*, *28*(4), 737–754. https://doi.org/10.1177/053901889028004005
Giroux, H. A. (2001). *Theory and Resistance in Education: Towards a Pedagogy for the Opposition* (Revised and expanded edition). Greenwood Publishing Group.
Gladwell, M. (2008). *Outliers: The Story of Success*. Little, Brown.

Gläveanu, V. P. (2015). Creativity as a sociocultural act. *The Journal of Creative Behavior, 49*(3), 165–180. https://doi.org/10.1002/jocb.94

Gläveanu, V. P. (2018). Creativity in perspective: A sociocultural and critical account. *Journal of Constructivist Psychology, 31*(2), 118–129. https://doi.org/10.1080/10720537.2016.1271376

Gläveanu, V. P., Gillespie, A., & Valsiner, J. (2014). *Rethinking Creativity: Contributions from Social and Cultural Psychology*. Routledge.

Gold, J., Kauderer, S., Schwartz, F., & Solodow, W. (2015). The space between. *The Psychoanalytic Study of the Child, 69*(1), 372–393. https://doi.org/10.1080/00797308.2016.11785537

Golden, N. A. (2017). "There's still that window that's open": The problem with "grit." *Urban Education, 52*(3), 343–369.

Goodwin, B. & Miller, K. (2013). Grit+ talent= student success. *Educational Leadership, 71*(1), 74–76.

Gormley, K. (2018). Neoliberalism and the discursive construction of "creativity." *Critical Studies in Education, 61*(3), 313–328. https://doi.org/10.1080/17508487.2018.1459762

Grandey, A., Diefendorff, J., & Rupp, D. E. (2013). *Emotional Labor in the 21st Century: Diverse Perspectives on Emotion Regulation at Work*. Routledge.

Graver, M. (2008). *Stoicism and Emotion*. University of Chicago Press.

Gray, P. (2013). *Free to Learn: Why Unleashing the Instinct to Play Will Make Our Children Happier, More Self-reliant, and Better Students for Life*. Basic Books.

Graziano, P. A., Keane, S. P., & Calkins, S. D. (2010). Maternal behaviour and children's early emotion regulation skills differentially predict development of children's reactive control and later effortful control. *Infant and Child Development, 19*(4), 333–353. https://doi.org/10.1002/icd.670

Graziano, P. A., Reavis, R. D., Keane, S. P., & Calkins, S. D. (2007). The role of emotion regulation in children's early academic success. *Journal of School Psychology, 45*(1), 3–19.

Greenberg, M. T., Weissberg, R. P., O'Brien, M. U., Zins, J. E., Fredericks, L., Resnik, H., & Elias, M. J. (2003). Enhancing school-based prevention and youth development through coordinated social, emotional, and academic learning. *American Psychologist, 58*(6–7), 466–474. https://doi.org/10.1037/0003-066X.58.6-7.466

Greene, J. A., Bolick, C. M., & Robertson, J. (2010). Fostering historical knowledge and thinking skills using hypermedia learning environments: The role of self-regulated learning. *Computers & Education, 54*, 230–243.

Greene, M. (1988). *The Dialectic of Freedom*. Teachers College Press.

Greene, Maxine. (2000). Imagining futures: The public school and possibility. *Journal of Curriculum Studies, 32*(2), 267–280.

Griese, V. (2016). *The struggle for creativity: The effect of systems on principal creativity a systems theory perspective* [ProQuest Dissertations Publishing]. http://search.proquest.com/docview/1777582118/?pq-origsite=primo

Griffin, B. & Hesketh, B. (2003). Adaptable behaviours for successful work and career adjustment. *Australian Journal of Psychology*, *55*(2), 65–73. https://doi.org/10.1080/00049530412331312914

Griffin, C., Holford, J., & Jarvis, P. (2013). *International Perspectives on Lifelong Learning*. Routledge.

Griffith, D. & Slade, S. (2018). A whole child umbrella. *Educational Leadership*, *76*(2), 36–38.

Gross, J. J. (1998). The emerging field of emotion regulation: An integrative review. *Review of General Psychology*, *2*(3), 271–299. https://doi.org/10.1037/1089-2680.2.3.271

Gross, J. J. (2002). Emotion regulation: Affective, cognitive, and social consequences. *Psychophysiology*, *39*(3), 281–291. https://doi.org/10.1017/S0048577201393198

Gross, J. J. (2011). *Handbook of Emotion Regulation, First Edition*. Guilford Press.

Gross, J. J. & John, O. P. (2003). Individual differences in two emotion regulation processes: Implications for affect, relationships, and well-being. *Journal of Personality and Social Psychology*, *85*(2), 348–362. https://doi.org/10.1037/0022-3514.85.2.348

Gumora, G. & Arsenio, W. F. (2002). Emotionality, emotion regulation, and school performance in middle school children. *Journal of School Psychology*, *40*(5), 395–413. https://doi.org/10.1016/S0022-4405(02)00108-5

Hacking, I. (2002). *Historical Ontology*. Harvard University Press.

Hall, N. C. & Goetz, T. (2013). *Emotion, Motivation, and Self-Regulation: A Handbook for Teachers*. Emerald Publishing Limited.

Halliwell, B., Cohen, T., Cruz, T., Gallen, I., Mullarkey, F., & Petrozzino, J. (2017). *The effects of growth mindset intervention on vocabulary skills in first to third grade children*. Retrieved August 2nd, 2020 from https://digitalcommons.sacredheart.edu/cgi/viewcontent.cgi?article=1061&context=acadfest

Hampton, D. (2015). What's the difference between feelings and emotions? *The Best Brain Possible*, January 12. www.thebestbrainpossible.com/whats-the-difference-between-feelings-and-emotions/

Harari, Y. N. (2016). *Sapiens: A Brief History of Human Kind*. Harper Collins.

Harvey, D. (2007). *A Brief History of Neoliberalism*. Oxford University Press.

Heckman, J. & Kautz, T. (2013). Fostering and measuring skills: Interventions that improve character and cognition. NBER Working Paper Series, 19656. https://doi.org/10.3386/w19656

Hetland, L. (2013). Connecting creativity to understanding. *Educational Leadership*, *70*(5), 65–70.

Hochanadel, A. & Finamore, D. (2015). Fixed and growth mindset in education and how grit helps students persist in the face of adversity. *Journal of International Education Research*, *11*(1), 47–50.

Hoerr, T. R. (2013). Principal connection/Good failures. *Educational Leadership*, *71*(1), 86–87.

Hoeschler, P., Balestra, S., & Backes-Gellner, U. (2018). The development of non-cognitive skills in adolescence. *Economics Letters*, *163*, 40–45.

Hoggett, P. (2017). Shame and performativity: Thoughts on the psychology of neoliberalism. *Psychoanalysis, Culture & Society, 22*(4), 364–382.

Holbein, J. B., Hillygus, D. S., Lenard, M. A., Gibson-Davis, C., & Hill, D. V. (2016). The development of students' engagement in school, community and democracy. *British Journal of Political Science*, 1–19. https://doi.org/10.1017/S000712341800025X

Howkins, J. (2011). *Creative Ecologies: Where Thinking is a Proper Job*. Transaction Publishers.

Hughes, C. & Tight, M. (1995). The myth of the learning society. *British Journal of Educational Studies, 43*(3), 290–304. https://doi.org/10.1080/00071005.1995.9974038

Humphries, J. E. & Kosse, F. (2017). On the interpretation of non-cognitive skills – What is being measured and why it matters. *Journal of Economic Behavior & Organization, 136*, 174–185.

Illeris, K. (2018). *Learning, Development and Education From Learning Theory to Education and Practice*. Routledge.

Isen, A. M. (2001). An influence of positive affect on decision making in complex situations: Theoretical issues with practical implications. *Journal of Consumer Psychology, 11*(2), 75–85. https://doi.org/10.1207/S15327663JCP1102_01

Ivcevic, Z. & Brackett, M. (2014). Predicting school success: Comparing conscientiousness, grit, and emotion regulation ability. *Journal of Research in Personality, 52*, 29–36. https://doi.org/10.1016/j.jrp.2014.06.005

Jachimowicz, J. M., Wihler, A., Bailey, E. R., & Galinsky, A. D. (2018). Why grit requires perseverance and passion to positively predict performance. *Proceedings of the National Academy of Sciences, 115*(40), 9980–9985.

James, W. (1884). What is an emotion? *Mind Association, 9*(34), 188–205.

Jaramillo, J. A. (1996). Vygotsky's sociocultural theory and contributions to the development of constructivist curricula. *Education, 117*(1), 133.

Jarvis, P. (2007). *Globalization, Lifelong Learning and the Learning Society: Sociological Perspectives*. Routledge.

Jarvis, P. (2008). *Democracy, Lifelong Learning and the Learning Society: Active Citizenship in a Late Modern Age*. Routledge.

Jenkins, J. M., Duncan, G. J., Auger, A., Bitler, M., Domina, T., & Burchinal, M. (2018). Boosting school readiness: Should preschool teachers target skills or the whole child? *Economics of Education Review, 65*, 107–125.

Jiang, W., Xiao, Z., Liu, Y., Guo, K., Jiang, J., & Du, X. (2019). Reciprocal relations between grit and academic achievement: A longitudinal study. *Learning and Individual Differences, 71*, 13–22.

Johnson, E. J. (2015). Reprint of: Mapping the field of the whole human: Toward a form psychology. *New Ideas in Psychology, 38*, 4–24.

Johnson, S. B., Riis, J. L., & Noble, K. G. (2016). State of the art review: Poverty and the developing brain. *Pediatrics, 137*(4). https://doi.org/10.1542/peds.2015-3075

Jung, C. G. (1954). *The Development of Personality*. Routledge.

Kakouris, A. (2015). Entrepreneurship pedagogies in lifelong learning: Emergence of criticality? *Learning, Culture and Social Interaction, 6*, 87–97.

Kalin, N. M. (2016). We're all creatives now: Democratized creativity and education. *Journal of the Canadian Association for Curriculum Studies*, *13*(2), 32–44.
Kautz, T., Heckman, J. J., Diris, R., ter Weel, B., & Borghans, L. (2014). Fostering and measuring skills: Improving cognitive and non-cognitive skills to promote lifetime success (Working Paper No. 20749; Working Paper Series). National Bureau of Economic Research. https://doi.org/10.3386/w20749
Keeling, D. M. & Lehman, M. N. (2018). *Posthumanism*. Oxford Research Encyclopedia of Communication. https://doi.org/10.1093/acrefore/9780190228613.013.627
Khine, M. S. & Areepattamannil, S. (2016). *Non-Cognitive Skills and Factors in Educational Attainment*. Springer.
Klein, N. (2007). *The Shock Doctrine: The Rise of Disaster Capitalism*. Metropolitan Books.
Klein, P. D. (1997). Multiplying the problems of intelligence by eight: A critique of Gardner's theory. *Canadian Journal of Education*, *22*(4), 377–394.
Knox, A. (2011). Creativity and learning. *Journal of Adult and Continuing Education*, *17*(2), 96–111. https://doi.org/10.7227/JACE.17.2.9
Kohn, A. (2008). Why self-discipline is overrated: The (troubling) theory and practice of control from within. *Phi Delta Kappan*, *90*(3), 168–176.
Kohn, A. (2014). *The Myth of the Spoiled Child: Challenging the Conventional Wisdom about Children and Parenting*. Da Capo Press.
Kohn, A. (2015). The "Mindset" Mindset: What We Miss by Focusing on Kids' Attitudes. Alfie Kohn. www.alfiekohn.org/article/mindset/
Kyllonen, P. (2005). The case for noncognitive assessments. R&D Connections, 1–7. Retrieved August 2nd, 2020 from www.ets.org/Media/Research/pdf/RD_Connections3.pdf
Laal, M. & Salamati, P. (2012). Lifelong learning: Why do we need it? *Procedia-Social and Behavioral Sciences*, *31*, 399–403.
Lee, A. (1997). Lifelong learning: Workforce development and economic success. In M. J Hatton's (ed.) *Lifelong Learning: Policies, Practices and Programs, School of Media Studies* (pp. 303–315). Humber College of Applied Media Studies.
Lee, J. & Lee, M. (2020). Is "whole child" education obsolete? Public school principals' educational goal priorities in the era of accountability. *Educational Administration Quarterly* (first published online March 20, 2020). https://doi.org/10.1177/0013161X20909871
Lee, M. & Morris, P. (2016). Lifelong learning, income inequality and social mobility in Singapore. *International Journal of Lifelong Education*, *35*(3), 286–312.
Levin, H. M. (2015). The importance of adaptability for the 21st century. *Society*, *52*(2), 136–141. https://doi.org/10.1007/s12115-015-9874-6
Lindgren, T. (2019). The figuration of the posthuman child. *Discourse: Studies in the Cultural Politics of Education*, 1–12. https://doi.org/10.1080/01596306.2019.1576589
Linnenbrink, E. A. & Pintrich, P. R. (2000). Multiple pathways to learning and achievement: The role of goal orientation in fostering adaptive motivation,

affect, and cognition. In C. Sansone & J. M. Harackiewicz (eds.), *Intrinsic and Extrinsic Motivation* (pp. 195–227). Academic Press.

Lipman, P. (2013). *The New Political Economy of Urban Education: Neoliberalism, Race, and the Right to the City*. Taylor & Francis.

London, M. (2011). Lifelong learning: Introduction. In M. London (ed.), *The Oxford Handbook of Lifelong Learning* (pp. 3–11). Oxford University Press.

Long, A. A. (2002). *Epictetus: A Stoic and Socratic Guide to Life*. Clarendon Press.

Lopes, P. N., Mestre, J. M., Guil, R., Kremenitzer, J. P., & Salovey, P. (2012). The role of knowledge and skills for managing emotions in adaption to school: Social behavior and misconduct in the classroom. *American Educational Research Journal, 49*(4), 710–742.

Lorenzini, D. (2018). Governmentality, subjectivity, and the neoliberal form of life. *Journal for Cultural Research, 22*(2), 154–166. https://doi.org/10.1080/14797585.2018.1461357

Lubart, T. I. (1994). Creativity. In R. J. Sternberg's (ed.), *Thinking and Problem Solving* (pp.289–332). Academic Press.

Ludmer, R., Dudai, Y., & Rubin, N. (2011). Uncovering camouflage: Amygdala activation predicts long-term memory of induced perceptual insight. *Neuron, 69*(5), 1002–1014. https://doi.org/10.1016/j.neuron.2011.02.013

Lundberg, S. (2017). Non-cognitive skills as human capital. In C. R. Hulten and V. A. Ramey's (eds.), *Education, Skills, and Tecchnical Change: Implications for future US GDP Growth* (pp. 219–243). University of Chicago Press.

Lutz, C. (1988). *Unnatural Emotions: Everyday Sentiments on a Micronesian Atoll and their Challenge to Western Theory*. University of Chicago Press.

Macklem, G. L. (2007). *Practitioner's Guide to Emotion Regulation in School-Aged Children*. Springer Science & Business Media.

Marenholtz-Bülow, B. von. (1895). *Reminiscences of Friedrich Froebel*. Lee and Shepard.

Martin, J. (2004). The educational inadequacy of conceptions of self in educational psychology. *Interchange, 35*, 185–208. https://doi.org/10.1007/BF02698849

Martin, J. (2007). The selves of educational psychology: Conceptions, contexts, and critical considerations. *Educational Psychologist, 42*, 79–89. https://doi.org/10.1080/00461520701263244

Martin, J. (2015). A unified psychology of the person? *New Ideas in Psychology, 38*, 31–36.

Martin J. (2014). Psychologism, individualism and the limiting of the social context in educational psychology. In: Corcoran T. (eds.), *Psychology in Education. Bold Visions in Educational Research* (pp. 167–180). SensePublishers. https://doi.org/10.1007/978-94-6209-566-3_11

Martin, J.& McLellan, A.M. (2013). *The Education of Selves: How Psychology Transformed Students*. Oxford University Press.

Martin, R. E. & Ochsner, K. N. (2016). The neuroscience of emotion regulation development: Implications for education. *Current Opinion in Behavioral Sciences, 10*, 142–148. https://doi.org/10.1016/j.cobeha.2016.06.006

McGuigan, J. (2016). *Neoliberal Culture*. Springer.
McLaren, P. (2007). *Life in Schools. An Introduction to Critical Pedagogy in the Foundations of Education* (5th ed.). Addison Wesley Longman, Inc.
McRobbie, A. (2015). Is passionate work a neoliberal delusion? *Open Democracy: Free Thinking for the World*, April 22. www.opendemocracy.net/en/transformation/is-passionate-work-neoliberal-delusion/
Michelman, B. (2015). A lexicon for educating the whole child (and preparing the whole adult). *ASCD Learn. Teach. Lead.*, *21*(2), 1–7.
Milić, N. S., Nedimović, P., & Sturza, S. (2018). The frequency with which creativity development strategies are used in various fields. *The Journal of Elementary Education*, *11*(3), 202–214.
Mills, K. & Kim, H. (2017). Teaching problem solving: Let students get "stuck" and "unstuck." *Brookings*. www.brookings.edu/blog/education-plus-development/2017/10/31/teaching-problem-solving-let-students-get-stuck-and-unstuck/
Mohr, K. M. (2017). *The Role of Integrated Curriculum in the 21st Century School* [Ed.D., University of Missouri – Saint Louis]. http://search.proquest.com/docview/1984331853/abstract/32AE1A5CD55E4CCFPQ/1
Montessori, M. (1948). *The Discovery of the Child (M. A. Johnstone, Trans.)*. Aakar Books.
National Advisory Committee on Creative and Cultural Education (NACCCE) (1999). *All Our Futures: Creativity, Culture and Education*. Retrieved August 2nd, 2020 from http://sirkenrobinson.com/pdf/allourfutures.pdf
Nettles, M. (n.d.). *Why the "Whole Child" Matters – ETS Open Notes*. Open Notes. Retrieved April 26, 2020, from https://news.ets.org/stories/whole-child-matters/
Newberry, M., Gallant, A., & Riley, P. (2013). *Emotion and School: Understanding How the Hidden Curriculum Influences Relationships, Leadership, Teaching, and Learning*. Emerald Group Publishing.
Newton, L. D. & Newton, D. P. (2014). Creativity in 21st-century education. *Prospects*, *44*(4), 575–589. https://doi.org/10.1007/s11125-014-9322-1
Noddings, N. (2005). What does it mean to educate the whole child? *Educational Leadership*, *63*, 3–11.
Oatley, K., Parrott, W. G., Smith, C., & Watts, F. (2011). Cognition and emotion over twenty-five years. *Cognition and Emotion*, *25*(8), 1341–1348. https://doi.org/10.1080/02699931.2011.622949
Ochsner, K. N. & Gross, J. J. (2005). The cognitive control of emotion. *Trends in Cognitive Sciences*, *9*(5), 242–249. https://doi.org/10.1016/j.tics.2005.03.010
Ogata, A. F. (2013). *Designing the Creative Child: Playthings and Places in Midcentury America*. University of Minnesota Press.
Chernyshenko, O. S., Kankaraš, M., & Drasgow, F. (). *Social and emotional skills for student success and well-being: Conceptual framework for the OECD study on social and emotional skills*. https://doi.org/10.1787/db1d8e59-en
Oliver, P. (2019). *Lifelong and Continuing Education: What is a Learning Society?* Routledge.

Olson, S. L., Sameroff, A. J., Lansford, J. E., Sexton, H., Davis-Kean, P., Bates, J. E., Pettit, G. S., & Dodge, K. A. (2013). Deconstructing the externalizing spectrum: Growth patterns of overt aggression, covert aggression, oppositional behavior, impulsivity/inattention, and emotion dysregulation between school entry and early adolescence. *Development and Psychopathology*, 25(3), 817–842.

Olssen, M. (2008). Understanding the mechanisms of neoliberal control: Lifelong learning, flexibility and knowledge capitalism. In A. Fejes & K. Nicoll (eds.), *Foucault and Lifelong Learning: Governing the Subject* (pp. 34–47). Routledge.

Ooi, C. S. & Stöber, B. (2011). Creativity unbound – policies, government and the creative industries. *Culture Unbound: Journal of Current Cultural Research*, 3(2), 113–117. https://doi.org/10.3384/cu.2000.1525.113113

Organisation for Economic Co-operation and Development (OECD). (2001). Lifelong Learning for All: Policy Directions. OECD. www.oecd.org/officialdocuments/publicdisplaydocumentpdf/?cote=DEELSA/ED/CERI/CD(2000)12/PART1/REV2&docLanguage=En

Organisation for Economic Co-operation and Development (OECD). (2006). Starting Strong II: Early Childhood Education and Care. OECD. www.oecd.org/education/school/startingstrongiiearlychildhoodeducationandcare.htm#ES

Organisation for Economic Co-operation and Development (OECD). (2012). Nature of Learning: Using Research to Inspire Practice. www.oecd.org/education/ceri/50300814.pdf

Organisation for Economic Co-operation and Development (OECD). (2019). Education at a Glance. OECD. https://read.oecd-ilibrary.org/education/education-at-a-glance-2019_f8d7880d-en#page1

Park, C.-Y. (2019). *Lifelong learning and education policies to capture digital gains*. G20 Insights. www.g20-insights.org/policy_briefs/lifelong-learning-and-education-policies-to-capture-digital-gains/

Partnership for 21st Century Skills. (2009). *P21 framework definitions*. Retrieved September 20, 2010 from www.p21.org/documents/P21_Framework.pdf

Pavletich, J. (1998). Emotions, experience, and social control in the twentieth century. *Rethinking Marxism*, 10(2), 51–64.

Pearse, M. & Dunwoody, M. (2013). *Learning that Never Ends: Qualities of a Lifelong Learner*. Rowman & Littlefield.

Pekrun, R. & Stephens, E. J. (2009). Goals, emotions, and emotion regulation: Perspectives of the control-value theory. *Human Development*, 52(6), 357–365. http://dx.doi.org.proxyau.wrlc.org/10.1159/000242349

Perkins-Gough, D. (2013). The significance of grit: A conversation with Angela Lee Duckworth. *Educational Leadership*, 71, 14–21.

Peters, M. A. & Tesar, M. (2017). Philosophy and performance of neoliberal ideologies: History, politics and human subjects. In M. A. Peters & M. Tesar (eds.), *Contesting Governing Ideologies* (pp. 2–18). Routledge.

Piaget, J. & Inhelder, B. (1969). *The Psychology of the Child*. Basic Books.

Piaget, J. (1976). Piaget's theory. In B. Inhelder, H. H. Chipman, & C. Zwingmann (eds.), *Piaget and His School: A Reader in Developmental Psychology* (pp. 11–23). Springer.

Piaget, J. (2003). *The Psychology of Intelligence*. Routledge.
Pink, D. H. (2011). *Drive: The Surprising Truth about What Motivates Us*. Riverhead Books.
Pinos, V., Twigg, N. W., Parayitam, S., & Olson, B. J. (2013). Leadership in the 21st century: The effect of emotional intelligence. *Academy of Strategic Management Journal*, 12(1), 14.
Plucker, J., A. Beghetto, R., & Dow, G. (2004). Why isn't creativity more important to educational psychologists? Potentials, pitfalls, and future directions in creativity research. *Educational Psychologist*, 39, 83–96. https://doi.org/10.1207/s15326985ep3902_1
Pope, R. (2005). *Creativity: Theory, History, Practice*. Psychology Press.
Ravitch, D. (2014). Poverty matters. Diane Ravitch's Blog, March 2. http://dianeravitch.net/2014/03/02/poverty-matters/
Reichelt, M., Collischon, M., & Eberl, A. (2019). School tracking and its role in social reproduction: Reinforcing educational inheritance and the direct effects of social origin. *The British Journal of Sociology*, 70(4), 1323–1348.
Ria, L., Sève, C., Saury, J., Theureau, J., & Durand, M. (2003). Beginning teachers' situated emotions: A study of first classroom experiences. *Journal of Education for Teaching*, 29(3), 219–234. https://doi.org/10.1080/0260747032000120114
Richardson, F. C., Bishop, R. C., & Garcia-Joslin, J. (2018). Overcoming neoliberalism. *Journal of Theoretical and Philosophical Psychology*, 38(1), 15.
Robinson, K. (2005). *How creativity, education and the arts shape a modern economy*. www.ecs.org/clearinghouse/60/51/6051.pdf
Robinson, K. (2015). *Creativity is in everything, especially teaching*. http://ww2.kqed.org/mindshift/2015/04/22/sir-ken-robinson-creativity-is-in-everything-especiallyteaching.
Rose, N. (1999). *Governing the Soul: The Shaping of the Private Self*. Free Associations Books.
Rose, Nikolas & Abi-Rached, J. M. (2013). *Neuro: The New Brain Sciences and the Management of the Mind*. Princeton University Press.
Ruiz-Alfonso, Z. & León, J. (2016). The role of passion in education: A systematic review. *Educational Research Review*, 19, 173–188.
Runco, M. A. & Jaeger, G. J. (2012). The standard definition of creativity. *Creativity Research Journal*, 24(1), 92–96. https://doi.org/10.1080/10400419.2012.650092
Saltman, K. J. (2014). The austerity school. *Symplokē*, 22(1–2), 41–57.
Sandoval, M. (2018). From passionate labour to compassionate work: Cultural co-ops, do what you love and social change. *European Journal of Cultural Studies*, 21(2), 113–129. https://doi.org/10.1177/1367549417719011
Sawyer, K. (2012). Extending sociocultural theory to group creativity. *Vocations and Learning*, 5(1), 59–75. https://doi.org/10.1007/s12186-011-9066-5
Scherer, K. R., Schorr, A., & Johnstone, T. (2001). *Appraisal Processes in Emotion: Theory, Methods, Research*. Oxford University Press, Incorporated. http://ebookcentral.proquest.com/lib/aul/detail.action?docID=430304

Schleicher, A. (2018). Educating learners for their future, not our past. *ECNU Review of Education*, *1*(1), 58–75. https://doi.org/10.30926/ecnuroe2018010104

Schön, D. A. (1983). *The Reflective Practitioner: How Professionals Think in Action*. Basic Books.

Schutz, P. A. & DeCuir, J. T. (2002). Inquiry on emotions in education. *Educational Psychologist*, *37*(2), 125–134. https://doi.org/10.1207/S15326985EP3702_7

Scorza, P., Araya, R., Wuermli, A. J., & Betancourt, T. S. (2016). Towards clarity in research on "non-cognitive" skills: Linking executive functions, self-regulation, and economic development to advance life outcomes for children, adolescents and youth globally. *Human Development*, *58*(6), 313–317. https://doi.org/10.1159/000443711

Seddon, K. (2006). *Epictetus' Handbook and the Tablet of Cebes: Guides to Stoic Living*. Routledge.

Shechtman, N., DeBarger, A. H., Dornsife, C., Rosier, S., & Yarnall, L. (2013). *Promoting Grit, Tenacity, and Perseverance: Critical Factors for Success in the 21st Century* (pp. 1–107). United States Department of Education: Office of Educational Technology.

Simonton, D. K. (1975). Sociocultural context of individual creativity: A transhistorical time-series analysis. *Journal of Personality*, *32*(6), 1119–1133.

Smith, C. D. (1990). *Jung's Quest for Wholeness: A Religious and Historical Perspective*. SUNY Press.

Smith, M. K. (2000). The theory and rhetoric of the learning society. *The Encyclopedia of Informal Education*. Retrieved August 2nd, 2020 from https://infed.org/mobi/the-theory-and-rhetoric-of-the-learning-society/

Smith, T. (2014). *Does Teaching Kids To Get "Gritty" Help Them Get Ahead?* [Interview]. www.npr.org/2014/03/17/290089998/does-teaching-kids-to-get-gritty-help-them-get-ahead

Soder, R., Goodlad, J. I., & McMannon, T. J. (2002). *Developing Democratic Character in the Young*. John Wiley.

Soh, K. (2017). Fostering student creativity through teacher behaviors. *Thinking Skills and Creativity*, *23*, 58–66. https://doi.org/10.1016/j.tsc.2016.11.002

Sparks, S. D. (2015). Nation's report card to gather data on grit, mindset. *Education Week*, *34*(32), 15.

Sternberg, R. J. & Lubart, T. I. (1991). An investment theory of creativity and its development. *Human Development*, *34*(1), 1–31. https://doi.org/10.1159/000277029

Stokas, A. G. (2015). A genealogy of grit: Education in the new gilded age. *Educational Theory*, *65*(5), 513–528.

Sugarman, J. (2009). Historical ontology and psychological description. *Journal of Theoretical and Philosophical Psychology*, *29*, 5–15. https://doi.org/10.1037/a0015301

Sugarman, J. (2015). Neoliberalism and psychological ethics. *Journal of Theoretical and Philosophical Psychology*, *35*(2), 103–116. https://doi.org/10.1037/a0038960

Sugarman, J. & Thrift, E. (2017). Neoliberalism and the psychology of time. *Journal of Humanistic Psychology* (first published online). https://doi.org/10.1177/0022167817716686

Sullivan, A., Parsons, S., Green, F., Wiggins, R. D., & Ploubidis, G. (2018). The path from social origins to top jobs: Social reproduction via education. *The British Journal of Sociology*, 69(3), 776–798.

Sullivan, F. R. (2017). *Creativity, Technology, and Learning*. Routledge.

Sung, T. K. (2015). The creative economy in global competition. *Technological Forecasting and Social Change*, 96, 89–91. https://doi.org/10.1016/j.techfore.2015.04.003

Sylwester, R. (1994). How emotions affect learning. *Educational Leadership*, 52(2), 60–65.

Teo, Thomas. (2018). *Outline of Theoretical Psychology: Critical Investigations*. Springer.

Thrift, E. & Sugarman, J. (2019). What is social justice? Implications for psychology. *Journal of Theoretical and Philosophical Psychology*, 39(1), 1–17.

Tileagă, C. & Stokoe, E. (2015). *Discursive Psychology: Classic and Contemporary Issues*. Routledge.

Tough, P. (2012). *How Children Succeed: Grit, Curiosity, and the Hidden Power of Character*. Houghton Mifflin Harcourt.

Trilling, B. & Fadel, C. (2009). *21st Century Skills: Learning for Life in Our Times*. Jossey-Bass.

Trilling, Bernie, & Fadel, C. (2009). *21st Century Skills: Learning for Life in Our Times*. John Wiley, Incorporated. http://ebookcentral.proquest.com/lib/aul/detail.action?docID=468884

Tröhler, D. (2016). Educationalization of social problems and the educationalization of the modern world. In P. Smeyers & M. Depaepe (eds.), *Educational Research: The Educationalization of Social Problems. Educational Research* (Vol. 3, pp. 31–46). Springer.

Tulis, M., Steuer, G., & Dresel, M. (2016). Learning from errors: A model of individual processes. *Frontline Learning Research*, 4(2), 12–26.

Turner, J. E., Husman, J., & Schallert, D. L. (2002). The importance of students' goals in their emotional experience of academic failure: Investigating the precursors and consequences of shame. *Educational Psychologist*, 37(2), 79–89. https://doi.org/10.1207/S15326985EP3702_3

Tyng, C. M., Amin, H. U., Saad, M. N. M., & Malik, A. S. (2017). The influences of emotion on learning and memory. *Frontiers in Psychology*, 8, 1–22. https://doi.org/10.3389/fpsyg.2017.01454

Usher, E. L., Li, C. R., Butz, A. R., & Rojas, J. P. (2019). Perseverant grit and self-efficacy: Are both essential for children's academic success? *Journal of Educational Psychology*, 111(5), 877.

Vallerand, R. J., Blanchard, C., Mageau, G. A., Koestner, R., Ratelle, C., Léonard, M., Gagné, M., & Marsolais, J. (2003). Les passions de l'ame: On obsessive and harmonious passion. *Journal of Personality and Social Psychology*, 85(4), 756–767.

Vassallo, S. (2012). Critical pedagogy and neoliberalism: Concerns with teaching self-regulated learning. *Studies in Philosophy and Education, 32*, 563–580 https://doi.org/10.1007/s11217-012-9337-0

Vassallo, S. (2014). The entanglement of thinking and learning skills in neoliberal discourse. In T. Corcoran (ed.), *Psychology in Education: Critical theory~practice* (pp. 145–165). Springer.

Wang, S., Zhou, M., Chen, T., Yang, X., Chen, G., Wang, M., & Gong, Q. (2017). Grit and the brain: Spontaneous activity of the dorsomedial prefrontal cortex mediates the relationship between the trait grit and academic performance. *Social Cognitive and Affective Neuroscience, 12*(3), 452–460.

Waters, E. & Sroufe, L. A. (1983). Social competence as a developmental construct. *Developmental Review, 3*(1), 79–97. https://doi.org/10.1016/0273-2297(83)90010-2

Weare, K. (2003). *Developing the Emotionally Literate School*. SAGE Publications.

Williams, J. (2018). *Cultivating a Growth Mindset in Students*. National Professional Resources, Inc. www.nprinc.com/cultivating-a-growth-mindset-in-students/

Wilson, R. (2013). Surprise: Creativity is a skill not a gift! *Psychology Today*, June 30. www.psychologytoday.com/blog/the-main-ingredient/201306/surprise-creativity-is-skill-not-gift

Wolfe, D. A. & Bramwell, A. (2008). Innovation, creativity and governance: Social dynamics of economic performance in city-regions. *Innovation : Management, Policy & Practice; Maleny, 10*(2/3), 170–182.

World Economic Forum. (2017). The global human capital report 2017: Preparing people for the future of work. *World Economic Forum*. http://www3.weforum.org/docs/WEF_Global_Human_Capital_Report_2017.pdf

Yeager, D. S., Romero, C., Paunesku, D., Hulleman, C. S., Schneider, B., Hinojosa, C., Lee, H. Y., O'Brien, J., Flint, K., & Roberts, A. (2016). Using design thinking to improve psychological interventions: The case of the growth mindset during the transition to high school. *Journal of Educational Psychology, 108*(3), 374–391.

Yehia, S. & Gunn, C. (2018). Enriching the learning experience for civil engineering students through learner-centered teaching. *Journal of Professional Issues in Engineering Education and Practice, 144*(4), 1–6.

Zeidner, M. (1998). *Test Anxiety: The State of the Art*. Kluwer Academic Publishers.

Zembylas, M. (2006). *Teaching with Emotion: A Postmodern Enactment*. IAP.

Zembylas, M. (2005). Discursive practices, genealogies, and emotional rules: A poststructuralist view on emotion and identity in teaching. *Teaching and Teacher Education, 21*(8), 935–948. https://doi.org/10.1016/j.tate.2005.06.005

Zembylas, M. (2007). Emotional capital and education: Theoretical insights from bourdieu. *British Journal of Educational Studies, 55*(4), 443–463.

Zembylas, M. & Fendler, L. (2007). Reframing emotion in education through lenses of parrhesia and care of the self. *Studies in Philosophy and Education, 26*(4), 319–333.

Ziegler, E. & Kapur, M. (2018). The interplay of creativity, failure and learning in generating algebra problems. *Thinking Skills and Creativity, 30*, 64–75. https://doi.org/10.1016/j.tsc.2018.03.009

Index

American Enterprise Institute, 144
anxiety, 2, 10, 13, 15, 25, 64, 65, 67, 68, 70, 73, 80, 129, 136, 146, 155, 158

being versus becoming, 22–23
binary subject positions, 13–14, 153
binary thinking, 20
Brookings Institute, 144

character values, 143, *See* crisis of character
creative economy. *See* creativity
creativity, 12
    a constituitive perspective, 124
    a sociocultural perspective of, 124
    as a skill, 118
    big-C creativity, 108
    creative economy, 116
    creativity myth, 112, 122
    definition, 108–110
    democratic purpose of, 119
    democratic self, 119–121
    distributed creativity, 122
    economic instrumentalism, 117
    emergence of, 115
    features of, 113
    H-creativity, 108
    human capital, 117
    little-c creativity, 108
    natural disposition, 111
    novelty and use, 108–110
    P-creativity, 108
    sociocultural perspective of, 121–124
    teachability, 113
creativity myth. *See* creativity
crisis of character. *See* neoliberal selfhood
cycle of lack. *See* growth mindset

Darling-Hammond, Linda, 146
deficit-based thinking. *See* growth mindset
democratic self, 119–121, 150, *See* neoliberal selfhood

economic instrumentalism, 2, 7, 8, 97, 98, 117, 118, 128, 151
emotion culture. *See* emotion regulation
emotion literacy. *See* emotion regulation
emotion regulation, 10–11
    adapability, 73
    adaptability, 61, 65, 66, 70, 73–74, 75, 76, 78–80
    character, 80–81
    conceptualization, 62–65
    definition, 61, 62–65
    emotion culture, 75
    risk-taking, 80, 81, 82
    rules, 62, 75–76, 80
    stoicism, 64, 65
emotional intelligence. *See* emotion regulation
entrepreneurialism. *See* neoliberal selfhood
expressive self, 56

failure, 21–22, 25, 30–32, 42, 65, 70, 80, 113, 141
false generosity. *See* grit
Fendler, Lynn, 145
fixed mindset. *See* growth mindset
flexibility. *See* lifelong learning, whole child
fragmentation, 134, *See* whole child
French, Robert, 18–20

grit, 9–10, 158, *See* whole child
    defined, 35
    false generosity, 52
    KIPP, 47
    meritocracy, 9
    neurophysical deficiencies, 48
    passion, 9, 10, 37
growth mindset, 8–9, 17–34, 142
    assessment and measurement, 20, 32
    cycle of lack, 31
    deficit-based thinking, 24
    fixed mindset, 8, 17
    homo aegrotus, 30–31

Index

intelligence, 20–21
  lack, 30–31
  now and not yet, 22, 25, 27
  perpetual improvement, 8, 9, 27, 30
  process and product, 25–26

harmonious passion. *See* passion
historical ontology. *See* whole child
homo aegrotus. *See* growth mindset
human capital, 12, 28, 29, 50, 58, 82, 83, 107, 110, 111, 113, 116, 117, 118, 122, 124
humanism, 150

intelligence, 20–21

James, William, 63–64
justice, 3, 38, 50, 93, 98, 104, 147, 176

KIPP. *See* grit

learning society. *See* lifelong learning
lifelong learning, 11–12
  adaptability, 100–102
  child-centered, 91
  conceptualization, 85–86
  definition, 84
  democratic purpose of, 92, 94–95, 97, 98
  development, 89, 91
  flexibility, 100–102
  humanistic purpose of, 92, 95–96, 97
  learning society, 84, 89, 94
  market purpose of, 92, 93–94, 97
  OECD, 87, 88, 89
  unwilling learner, 102
  useless class, 15, 84, 93

Martin, Jack, 56, 134
meritocracy, 5, 26, *See* grit
mindset, 18–20
multiple intelligence, 20

neoliberal selfhood, 158
  consequences of, 2
  crisis of character, 13
  defined, 5–7
  democratic self, 14
  entrepreneurialism, 1, 5, 58, 65, 80, 82, 103, 107, 151, 152
  features of, 1
  responsibilization, 36, 49, 53, 78, 79, 103
  self-esteem, 2

neoliberalism
  economic logic, 4
  governance, 5, 6, 8, 15, 147
  noncognitive skills, 7–13
  responsibilization, 5
  selfhood, 6
neurophysical deficiencies. *See* grit
neuroscience, 91, 136
noncognitive skills, 3–4, 7–13, 16
novelty and use. *See* creativity
now and not yet. *See* growth mindset

obsessive passion. *See* passion
Organisation for Economic Co-operation and Development. *See* lifelong learning

passion, 158, *See* grit
  character values, 56
  conceptualization, 39
  economic productivity, 57
  entrepreneurialism, 58
  harmonious, 45–50, 52
  obsessive, 45, 46, 48, 49
  role in grit, 40–42
  schooling, 43
  success, 42
  suffering, 43
  values for selfhood, 55
perpetual improvement. *See* growth mindset
positive psychology, 19
posthumanism. *See* whole child
process and product. *See* growth mindset
psychologism. *See* whole child

relationality. *See* whole child
risk-taking, 158

social-emotional learning. *See* emotion regulation
stoicism. *See* emotion regulation
Sugarman, Jeff, 5, 7

twenty-first century
  competencies, 37, 38, 50, 62, 73, 82, 83, 87, 91, 99, 100, 106, 143
  environment, 7, 50, 84, 116, 117, 152

unwilling learner, 153. *See* lifelong learning
useless class. *See* lifelong learning

whole child, 12–13
  ASCD, 136, 137, 139, 142

whole child (cont.)
  fragmentation, 13, 134, 135
  Froebel, 132–133, 135
  grit, 139–141
  historical ontology, 130–131
  Jungian perspective, 131–132
  posthumanism, 133, 135
  psychologism, 134–135
  relationality, 133
  response to failure, 141–143
  whole child, 129

For EU product safety concerns, contact us at Calle de José Abascal, 56–1º,
28003 Madrid, Spain or eugpsr@cambridge.org.

www.ingramcontent.com/pod-product-compliance
Ingram Content Group UK Ltd.
Pitfield, Milton Keynes, MK11 3LW, UK
UKHW020256090825
461507UK00021B/996